Left Behind

Left Behind

Urban High Schools and the Failure of Market Reform

EDWARD P. ST. JOHN
VICTORIA J. MILAZZO BIGELOW
KIM CALLAHAN LIJANA
JOHANNA C. MASSÉ

Johns Hopkins University Press
Baltimore

© 2015 Johns Hopkins University Press
All rights reserved. Published 2015
Printed in the United States of America on acid-free paper

2   4   6   8   9   7   5   3   1

Johns Hopkins University Press
2715 North Charles Street
Baltimore, Maryland 21218-4363
www.press.jhu.edu

Library of Congress Cataloging-in-Publication Data

St. John, Edward P.
Left behind: urban high schools and the failure of market reform / Edward P. St. John,
Victoria J. Milazzo Bigelow, Kim Callahan Lijana, Johanna C. Massé.
    pages cm
Includes bibliographical references and index.
ISBN 978-1-4214-1787-5 (acid-free paper) — ISBN 978-1-4214-1788-2 (electronic) —
ISBN 1-4214-1787-1 (acid-free paper) — ISBN 1-4214-1788-X (electronic)   1. Urban
high schools—United States—Evaluation.   2. Charter schools—United
States—Evaluation.   3. Education, Secondary—Aims and objectives—United
States.   4. Educational change—United States.   5. College preparation programs—
United States.   I. Title.
LC5131.S64 2015
373.09173′2—dc23   2015004321

A catalog record for this book is available from the British Library.

*Special discounts are available for bulk purchases of this book. For more information,
please contact Special Sales at 410-516-6936 or specialsales@press.jhu.edu.*

Johns Hopkins University Press uses environmentally friendly book
materials, including recycled text paper that is composed of at least
30 percent post-consumer waste, whenever possible.

CONTENTS

EDWARD P. ST. JOHN is the Algo D. Henderson Collegiate Professor of Higher Education at the University of Michigan. He is concerned with education for a just society, an interest that stems from three decades of research on educational policy and practice. St. John serves as series coeditor for *Readings on Equal Education*, an annual volume focusing on initiatives seeking to reduce inequalities in K–12 and higher education. He also coedits *Core Issues in Higher Education*, topical texts for professors and graduate students with an interest in the field. He is a Fellow of the American Educational Research Association and recipient of awards from other associations for his scholarship. His recent books include *Breaking through the Access Barrier* (with Shouping Hu and Amy Fisher, 2010), *Pathways to Academic Success* (with Glenda Musoba, 2010), and *Research, Actionable Knowledge, and Social Change* (2014). St. John received an EdD in administration, planning, and social policy from the Harvard Graduate School of Education and BS and MEd degrees from the University of California, Davis.

VICTORIA J. MILAZZO BIGELOW received her PhD from the University of Michigan Center for the Study of Higher and Postsecondary Education, where she is currently a postdoctoral research fellow and evaluator for the Michigan Louis Stokes Alliance for Minority Participation. Her private consulting work includes contributions to the educational and district improvement plans for the Flint Community Schools. She is currently the arts-education planning consultant for that district. Milazzo Bigelow is a former coordinator for advanced-degree teacher certification and instructor of education and music at Marygrove College. Her research focuses on equity and access in education, particularly initiatives to address achievement gaps and support college preparation through collaborations between university stakeholders and urban schools. She is the coauthor (with Edward P. St. John) on several articles related to school-college partnerships, academic capital formation, and the transfer experience for minority STEM students.

KIM CALLAHAN LIJANA received her PhD from the University of Michigan Center for the Study of Higher and Postsecondary Education. Her research interests center on issues of educational equity, with a focus on college preparation, access, and success for students who represent the first generation in their family to go to college. Before pursuing her doctorate, Lijana worked in urban education as a high school English teacher in Washington, D.C., public schools and as a college counselor at a Washington, D.C., public charter high school. She is a coauthor (with Edward P. St. John and Glenda Musoba) of a forthcoming book from Stylus Publishing on actionable research for social justice.

JOHANNA C. MASSÉ is pursuing a joint PhD in higher education and sociology at the University of Michigan, Ann Arbor. Her primary research interests include qualitative research methodologies, educational decision making from a life-course perspective, and undergraduate social justice education. Massé holds a bachelor's degree from Brown University and a master's degree in counseling, with a focus on student development in higher education, from California State University, Long Beach. She has coauthored articles on college choice and college students' intergroup experiences.

This book would not have been possible without support and collaboration. A Ford Foundation capacity-building grant on equity in urban and higher education funded site visits to some of the innovative charter schools included as case studies in this volume as well as the production of the manuscript, and College For Every Student (CFES), a nonprofit organization, financed field work in New York City high schools. We gratefully acknowledge this assistance. The interpretations in this book are the authors' and do not represent policies or positions of supporting organizations.

Graduate students and staff at the National Center for Institutional Diversity (NCID) and the Center for the Study of Higher and Postsecondary Education also contributed to the project. Phillip J. Bowman, founding director of NCID and professor of higher education, provided organizational support. Phyllis Kreger Stillman provided editorial support throughout the project. Krystal Williams, Chris Nellum, Gilia Smith, Brian Burt, and Diane Fuselier-Thompson collaborated on site visits and in the initial review of interview data. Elizabeth Hudson shared her research on the federal Promise Neighborhood proposals. Educators and students in the case-study schools generously consented to interviews and provided documents and other resources that made this part of our study possible. Faculty colleagues at the University of Michigan provided guidance with different parts of this project: Lesley Rex, professor emerita of English and education, consulted on qualitative methods; and Dan Burns, professor of mathematics, provided guidance on math-education policy and practice.

Left Behind

Introduction

American cities are engaged in an effort to transform high schools into college preparatory institutions at the same time that market models of school choice are being promoted. While the goal of raising standards for all students is meritorious, the mechanisms used to pursue this aim have often accelerated inequalities in urban schools. Creating a new generation of high schools with competitive content niches that combine college preparation and career readiness can help extend quality education to more students, although it is clear that this remains an imperfect strategy, given the lack of public will to adequately fund and support the school-transformation process. Three decades of both market-based and standards-driven reforms have had, at best, mixed success.

Left Behind examines how policy rationales develop and affect practices in urban schools. Our analysis of policy rationales focuses on how political alliances of policymakers and researchers influenced reform agendas and eventual policy decisions. We use examples to discuss how educators in eight urban high schools navigated through the barriers and opportunities created by market policies and educational standards: four charter schools from different locales across the United States and four New York City high schools that are within a national network of schools and colleges developed by College For Every Student (CFES), a nonprofit organization that facilitates local support for low-income students in urban and rural communities.

In this introductory chapter, we present our framework for examining policy discourses and how they influence educational practice. We also introduce the schools we studied and the challenges they faced in their development to successfully compete for students in urban markets.

Policy on and Practice of Urban School Reform

Two conflicting policy trajectories—standards and markets—have converged in urban school districts, creating more-chaotic conditions for low-income families as schools compete for community resources. The standards-driven reform was framed as a national imperative related to global economic competition. This reform logic, introduced by *A Nation at Risk* (*ANAR*), a report written by a national task force,[1] has evolved through several iterations. Schools covered by urban districts have gone through successive waves of regulation implementing mandated standards. In its most recent iteration, the standards movement focuses on both college preparatory courses *and* career-oriented content, often with an emphasis on technical education in science, technology, engineering, and math (STEM) fields. The urban market strategy was promoted by John Chubb and Terry Moe's *Politics, Markets, and America's Schools* (published in 1990 by the Brookings Institution), which was a study of New York City schools. They advocated the development of markets as a strategy for improving educational outcomes in urban schools. The artifacts of this blueprint for urban school reform include charter schools and competition for students in most cities. Since charter laws exempt these new schools from the control of school districts, two types of urban schools were created—one with the freedom to innovate (the charter schools), the other (traditional public schools) with embedded constraints on their curriculum—but neither type outperformed the other on educational outcomes.[2]

After three decades of reform, there has been improvement in math preparation (as measured by required courses and national SAT scores) and college enrollment rates (as measured by the percentage and number of students attending college).[3] Although there has not been a corresponding increase in college completion rates, the total percentage of graduates in the adult population has risen as a result of the gains in access. More problematically, inequality has also increased. Minorities now actually enroll in college at higher rates than Whites, but most attend two-year colleges; they continue to be underrepresented in four-year institutions.[4] To untangle how contradictory educational policies simultaneously influenced progress and inequality, we need to consider both the cost of college *and* opportunities for employment because reform movements were rationalized, based on arguments about cross-generation uplift via educational attainment. During this same period, however, there was a decline in the middle class in the United States and an increase in poverty rates.[5]

Given the economic realities of this new age, the underlying rationales for educational reform were deceptive at a prima facie level. In addition, there has been deception that goes deeper than the incongruence between the notions of education and income that were used in these early reports, because evidence contradicting the assumptions on which they were based was consistently ignored within the alliances that promoted the reforms.

To rebuild public trust in educational policy and practice, the alliances of researchers and political operatives engaged in advocating for new agendas should have a better understanding of the links between inequalities in educational opportunity and overall progress in educational outcomes over time, as well as a realistic understanding of the ties between education, careers, and economic opportunities. We thus discuss the social justice framework and social critical perspective that have guided our inquiry into these contradictory reforms before examining how changes in policy undermine social justice in practice.

Social Justice Framework

The goal of improving social justice by expanding opportunities for college preparation has been our shared, central concern as we have engaged in analyses of policy changes in public education and finance and the strategies used by high schools as they adapted to new policies. Raising the requirements for high school graduation during the past few decades has led to numerous crucial issues related to education as a human right.

In the international literature, access to education has long been considered an indicator of national development.[6] Sadly, since the publication of *ANAR* in 1983, the United States has dropped in global rankings that are based on high school and college graduation rates, indicating a failure of U.S. educational policy compared with that of other nations, especially those in Western Europe.[7] Given state and federal efforts to provide college preparation for all high school students in the United States during this period, this is a devastating outcome. America's failure not only relates to the trajectory of public policy on and the financing of education, but it is also a consequence of changes in the political terrain of policy making in education and public finance, including taxes and the rise in both public and student debt. To build an understanding of how this happened, we reconsider the meaning of education as a human right before examining how the progressive foundations of U.S. educational policy were sacrificed for political expediency.

EDUCATION AS A HUMAN RIGHT

The advocates for school desegregation appropriately considered educational inequality as a civil rights issue.[8] Certainly, before the U.S. Supreme Court's decision in *Brown v. Board of Education*, America's schools were unequal. Correcting for hundreds of years of inequality was, however, not a simple matter. In addition to desegregation, governmental policies on K–12 and higher education promoted equal educational opportunity in the 1960s and 1970s, a period of sustained progress on all indicators of equality. Unfortunately, both K–12 and higher education policy after 1980 shifted focus, leading to greater educational inequality nationally.[9]

Using John Rawls's principles of justice as a basis for assessing the consequences of the current policy trajectory,[10] it is clear that the United States is moving rapidly toward increasing social injustice in education.[11] Research findings leading to this conclusion about policy and trends considered the following:

- overall rates of educational attainment in high school and college as indicators of progress or regress on the *basic right* to education;

- differences in the quality of K–12 schools and college completion rates across income and racial groups as indicators of *equity* in opportunity; and
- public investment in education in relation to both equity and access as an indicator of *fairness* in education.

Raising high school graduation requirements transformed the basic right to an education, now defined as college and career ready for all.[12] The new emphasis has had the support of civil rights advocates because it addresses a longstanding inequality in the curriculum available to minorities compared with Whites—a result of tracking in comprehensive schools[13] and the lack of preparatory courses in many high schools serving mostly minority students. But, as we discuss in this volume, high-quality advanced courses that engage students in learning the required content (i.e., where students actively participate in their learning) have not been available to many students, creating a new form of inequality. Without engaging advanced courses, many minority students have been denied the opportunity to complete high school, as illustrated by the growing dropout rate in most states after implementation of the new requirements.[14]

Inequality has also increased among different income groups, based on both the percentage of students who complete high school by meeting the higher standards and the percentage of prepared students who go to four-year colleges. Meaningful college access for most low-income students who fulfill the new standards has not been achieved because they have been denied access to four-year colleges due to rising costs and the declining purchasing power of need-based student aid.[15] The decline in public investment in college students—rising prices in public colleges attributable to reductions in state funding over time and decreased governmental spending on grants to help low-income students pay their college costs—has constrained cross-generation uplift and contributed to the poorer competitive position of the United States globally.[16]

END OF PROGRESSIVE REFORMS?

The past three decades represent a radical departure from the progressive century (1880s through 1980s), when both the Republican and Democratic parties at least periodically promoted economic development *and* social uplift. While there was seldom a consensus, a pattern of governmental investment in education emerged, including:

- the development of public schools in all states (starting in the 1880s) and of public universities, especially after the Land Grant Act of 1890;
- the creation of Social Security and other early social-welfare programs after the Great Depression, which provided help for low-income families, especially those with a missing parent;
- the G.I. Bill and other federal programs (e.g., the National Defense Education Act) expanding educational opportunities after World War II; and

• the Great Society programs in the 1960s (including the first federal programs pertaining to grades K–12 and higher education) and portable, need-based student grant aid in the 1970s.

Most of these programs were supported across party lines and created a momentum for economic and social progress. Yet not only did the federal government and most states fail to fund these social and educational programs at their historical levels after 1980, but the tax rates on higher income levels also declined. No major new, federally administered programs have been initiated since that time;[17] instead, market models have been used. Under these conditions, it has been difficult to maintain support for low-income populations.

In education, the major reforms since the 1980s have increasingly promoted initiatives from outside the public system (e.g., charter schools, subsidized college loans from private lenders)[18] rather than governmental programs framed in the old progressive tradition. This new approach combines the neoliberal goal of raising standards with the neoconservative emphasis on using markets and lowering taxpayer costs, but it has added to disparities by supporting a concentration of wealth in corporations, the formation of a managerial elite, and a redistribution of wealth by reducing taxes on the wealthy, an approach to public finance that is extremely different from that of Western Europe.[19]

POLITICAL ALLIANCES SUPPORTING THE NEW RATIONALES

The prevailing neoprogressive ideology has been used to build rationales for educational reform. Researchers have worked closely with policymakers to develop policy agendas informed by research, including educational research that focused narrowly on correlates between educational activities and outcomes; social research that examined differences in educational achievement across socioeconomic groups; and economic research that concentrated on levels of education, skills, employment, and earnings.

Successive policy alliances—groupings of policymakers, foundation executives, and researchers—that focus on a specific reform initiative periodically emerge. Typically, they claim there is a crisis in education and converge on a rationale that provides a solution. For example, foundations funded large experiments on private vouchers (e.g., in New York, Dayton, and other cities), and the federal government redirected Title I funds to vouchers (e.g., in Cleveland). A troubling pattern of alliances also developed, one that influenced policy through deceptive constructs. We consider the following rationalizations in subsequent chapters:

• Correlations between math courses and college success were used to argue for improvements in math education (chapter 2).[20]
• Correlations between parents' education and college success were used to argue that declines in student financial aid did not impair access for low-income families (chapter 4).[21]

- Correlations between earnings and degree levels were used to argue that if students applied for aid and took out loans, after graduation they would be able to pay off their college loans (chapter 4).[22]

These policy rationalizations are based on proofiness, a form of "fibbing with numbers."[23] Numbers can be aligned with arguments using untested assumptions about the relationships between educational attainment and economic well-being. Through successive waves of reform rationalizations, the underlying problems with the way public financing of social and educational programs influences the trajectory toward inequalities in wealth and education go without critique.

Policy alliances function at a high level in the policy discourse on public financing of education. The process is similar to insider exchanges about federal regulation of financial markets. Indeed, given the role of federal financial aid for college students, the policy alliances in education and the regulation of financial institutions actually overlap. In *A Fighting Chance*, Elizabeth Warren recalled Larry Summers's closing comments in their conversation about the underlying causes of the Great Recession:[24]

> Larry's tone was in the friendly advice category. He teed up this way: I had a choice. I could be an insider or an outsider. Outsiders can say whatever they want. But people on the inside don't listen to them. Insiders, however, get lots of access and a chance to push their ideas. People—powerful people—listen to what they have to say. But insiders also understand one unbreakable rule: *They don't criticize other insiders*. (p. 106, italics in original)

The concept of insider silence explains how senior personnel in governmental agencies, for-profit and nonprofit think tanks, and universities gain and retain the power and political position to engage in pitching ideas as part of policy rationale building. For Warren, the federal government's reaping of huge profits from student loans has been a major issue, but few other politicians or analysts even mention the problem.

In the interpersonal exchange described by Warren, Summers's comments conveyed an implied threat: back off or you'll be cut out of high-level policy conversations (or worse). Since Larry Summers was president of Harvard University when Warren was a law professor, this conversation is illustrative of the policy game within governance at major universities where grant dollars from government agencies, foundations, and corporations are crucial to their financial stability.

We now examine evidence from the content and conclusions of policy reports and books written by researchers receiving federal grants to explore the role of policy alliances in education. This political persuasion is common in government and in the governance of education and universities.

Social Critical Perspective

Social critical studies provide an alternative way of viewing the process and practice of governance in education. Most educational and policy research uses functionalist theories that assume cause-effect chains. This is problematic in educational policy and practice because there is an obvious correlation between social class and educational outcomes, regardless of the theoretical frames used to consider the links between policy and outcomes. Critical research focuses on how the mechanisms used over time by the government in the public financing of education actually relate to trends in outcomes and inequality.

Scholarship that considers both progressive and functional explanations with probing examinations of class differences is particularly useful in illuminating how self-sealing logic works within policy alliances in education and public finance. Thomas Piketty provides a compelling analysis of public finance in the United States compared with Western Europe.[25] He illustrates the ways in which a lack of taxation and limited public investment in education and social programs have increased inequality in the United States, providing a marked contrast with how European and Scandinavian nations have used these mechanisms to narrow gaps in wealth and promote education and income improvement for the majority of their populations. We return to insights from Piketty's analysis in our discussion of the market advocacy policy alliance (chapter 1).

PUBLIC INVESTMENT

It is abundantly evident that national strategies for taxation and public investment in education and social programs are linked to educational outcomes: nations that invest more have substantially better outcomes.[26] Heinz-Dieter Meyer and colleagues examined higher education finance, affirmative action, and funding for colleges and students across nations in Europe, the Americas, and Australasia.[27] They found that the privatization strategies used in Asia and the United States have increased inequality more substantially than the strategies in European nations. They also found that Brazil and South Africa have used affirmative action to significantly reduce racial inequality in recent years, while U.S. policies and court decisions have severely constrained its use, undermining one of the equalizing mechanisms employed in earlier decades.

Studies of state policies on and financing of K–12 and higher education need to drill further into the role of policy mechanisms, both because there is great variability across states and because state policies vary over time. For decades, econometric studies have documented how states' school funding improves educational outcomes[28] and their investments in need-based grants increase college access,[29] but these findings were dismissed by new ideological rationales for standards and markets after 1980.[30] With time, it has been possible for a new generation of studies to provide empirical evidence of this, as we discuss in this volume, but the problem of policy development in states is not simply a matter of providing evidence and expecting change. Occasionally there are periods when researchers have worked closely with state-level policymakers to use research on outcomes to better coordinate educational and public-finance policies (e.g., Minnesota in the 1980s, Indiana in the late 1990s and early 2000s, North Carolina in the 2000s), as documented in recent case studies,[31] but these are clearly exceptions to the normal pattern of ignoring evidence in favor of ideological arguments about standards, markets, and accountability. We chose to limit the scope of this book and not focus on public funding, but instead consider the consequences of the market model in urban settings.

SOCIAL SUPPORT

A second type of critical social scholarship has centered on the ways policy and practice perpetuate inequality.[32] In particular, the concept of cultural capital has provided compelling evidence about the ways in which educational systems and practices reproduce social class.[33] This research illustrates that cultural capital, including specialized forms of college knowledge, is built up in families and may be reinforced in schools.

More recently, Edward St. John, Shouping Hu, and Amy Fisher used a broader concept called academic capital formation (ACF)—a framework that combines mechanisms in social and human capital formation with cultural capital and uplift from Bourdieu's social critical theory—to examine how social and financial support (e.g., aid guarantees, mentoring, leadership opportunities) enable underrepresented minority students (URMs) to navigate into and through college.[34] After examining racially situated concepts in ACF along with interventions promoting college opportunities for URM students, Rachelle Winkle-Wagner identified the importance of exploring the ACF in students' experiences and in institutional actions.[35] In particular, it is vital to examine how schools organize to overcome culture-reproducing tendencies as they respond to policy mandates and the expectations of nonprofit organizations.

We used a two-level analytical method so we could examine: (1) how policymakers and researchers develop policy alliances promoting rationales while overlooking empirical evidence that runs counter to the reform they advocate (*policy* focus);[36] and (2) the ways educators in high schools navigate through governmental mandates and the expectations of nonprofit organizations funding school-based projects to provide an improved quality of education and social support for underrepresented students in urban schools (*practice* focus). Given the current policy trajectories toward standards, accountability, and markets in education and the income inequality in public finance, we are interested in identifying pragmatic approaches that advocates for social justice can use to

TABLE I.I

Systemic and Human-Action Domains of Policy Formation and Educational
Practice in Urban Educational Reform

Dimensions (*levels*)	Systemic actions	Human actions
Policy (use of research in policy decisions)	• Federal and state policies • Public financing of schools and colleges • Market incentives • Curriculum requirements • Testing and account-ability	• Development of policy rationales affecting urban school reform • Use of research in policy decisions: rationales, ideologies, and evidence • Use of accountability and evaluation information
Practice (organization / administrators and teachers)	• Organizational struc-tures: school start-ups and restructuring • Curriculum implementa-tion, market niches, and reform • Student outcomes	• Educator engagement in student assessment and curriculum change • Organizational adapta-tions through critical reflection and action inquiry • Partnerships supporting reform

contend with policy mandates and promote greater equity in educational outcomes.

Examination of Policy and Practice

Our two-level method focuses on the systemic and individually based aspects
of policy and practice (table I.I). Typically, studies at the policy level examine
how specific policies and the implementation of new mandates link to specific outcomes, and then use this information to advocate for change ("systemic
actions"). We explore how policy alliances filter out contrary empirical evidence
in the development of rationales ("human actions"). To illuminate the role of
alliances, we also consider how researchers and policy advocates write about
problems in their policy reports and publications; these provide a public record,
so it is possible to gain insight into the policy process. At the practice level,
we use case studies of schools to examine policy implementation ("systemic
actions") and adaptive change ("human actions").

This dual approach combines a critical analysis of documents with case-study
research. No attempt is made to make causative claims from the research, nor is
causality assumed. Rather than focusing on the narrow concept of "implementing" policy, we are interested in the ways in which educators adapt to policies
and respond to the interests of external funders as they make changes to address

the needs of their students. This ground-level view of education is seldom even considered by policy or educational researchers, who generally focus on narrow curriculum issues.

Typically, the policy process is framed with little attention to the ways in which systems actually work. This is a contrast with the conceptions of systemic change (i.e., planning, programming, and budgeting systems) the Johnson administration used to develop its Great Society educational programs.[37] There were many compelling critiques of these systemic approaches because they did not represent the realities of political systems.[38] By the 1980s, an issues-oriented approach had evolved in policy analysis that used logic derived from theory and ideology to advance the use of standards and markets. While the reforms of the 1960s and 1970s tried to balance social uplift and economic development, the newer directives largely overlooked equity—arguing that the older system had failed—and instead promoted radical changes in K–12 and higher education.

Whether or not we conceive of educational policy and practice as systems, there is a systemic aspect to policy and its implementation. The simplistic model typically used in educational research and policy papers in recent decades has involved identifying a problem, often framed as a crisis impairing the future of the nation or a particular state; claiming the desired policy will solve the problem (e.g., standards and markets as remedies to a wide range of problems in education); aligning research supporting the logic for the remedy of choice in reports advocating the new practice; and realigning arguments for the reform strategy if outcomes aren't consistent with the original rationalization. This approach typically avoids criticism of insiders, instead focusing on critiquing research methods, which is generally more acceptable because it argues for more research by insiders and avoids denigrating either the prior policy or the process and doesn't look at whether the newer policies were more effective than the old ones.[39] So there is a move to continually change reform rationales without considering whether the reform actually works and whether it reinforces inequality.

Our critical reviews (in the chapters on market niches, math, advanced literacy, and college knowledge) examine the effects of the myopic approaches used to rationalize reforms. The policy alliances we discuss are not groups of people intentionally seeking to hurt the poor. Progressive thinkers on both sides can typically come together on a set of issues they can support, at least for a period of time. The practice of pitching ideas can therefore be used to construct new rationales to make adaptive changes, with or without research evidence to back up those rationales.

The alignment of research conclusions with the interests of the Republican and Democratic parties is necessary to sustain a policy alliance. For example, despite more than a decade of reports by the Advisory Committee on Student Financial Assistance (ACSFA) that demonstrate a relationship between funding for Pell grants and both access and persistence in higher education,[40] it has been difficult to sustain funding for this program. Instead, research studies by the American Council on Education (ACE) claiming that students simply did not know enough about financial aid[41] and should take out more loans[42] were more persuasive because these arguments were better aligned with the interests of the lending industry, did not redirect funding from other higher education programs or research, and could gain support from both conservative and liberal legislators.

The ACE policy reports were influential—and, if having an influence is the aim of applied-policy researchers, this is noteworthy—but other research and policy decisions (e.g., the ACSFA position) had only a modest impact on the trajectory of educational policy.[43] Liberals tend to support any funding for education that they can squeeze out of the political process, while conservatives tend to favor policy that reinforces the wealthy managerial elite (e.g., the banking industry) over the interests of low-income students. The result is that lending prevails over need-based aid in the political sphere.

While these relationships have at least been examined in student-aid policy at the college level, they have not received much attention at the K–12 educational level. The reform of high schools has been high on the agenda for both Republicans and Democrats, along with the argument that a new, highly skilled workforce is needed for economic competitiveness in the twenty-first century. *ANAR* set the stage for raising standards, which both conservative and liberal analysts bought into. The fact that raising these standards supposedly did not cost money ensured the support of both political parties, including the conservatives among them. This argument also aligned with long-standing traditions in social research that used attainment theories to explain inequality, and those in educational research that advocated for new methods of teaching. Over time, the rationales marshaled to argue for higher standards—and for using testing and accountability to punish educators, schools, and educational systems that did not measure up—have transformed and morphed, but the basic concepts have remained largely unaltered.

It is important to note that the structure of the educational system in the United States differs substantially from that of other nations. Both Sino and Western European countries—the nation-states thought to be the biggest competitors in the global economy—maintain dual educational options (technical and academic) for high school and college students, while the standards movement in the United States is using a narrower concept of college readiness that includes advanced-content courses for all students. Because of these restrictions, the U.S. system pushes more students who cannot meet the standards out of the system at a time when most other national systems maintain more flexibility.

This is not about lowering standards—a notion promoted by *ANAR*, as Diane Ravitch notes[44]—but rather is an argument about options and opportunities, a logic that was once part of the American educational tradition.

PRACTICE

In urban areas, the rapid evolution of competitive market systems has substantially complicated the efforts of high school educators to meet the new standards. The latest effort to define a road map for reform—the Common Core State Standards (CCSS)—consolidates the new vision for education and provides avenues for schools to link career readiness with college preparation, but this does not lessen the challenge of having all students reach these standards.

Educators struggle to find ways to meet the new standards, and many urban high schools do not have an opportunity to garner the external support needed to achieve competitiveness. In examining the strategies used by these high schools, we had the opportunity to learn about adaptive change as the institutions responded to policy mandates. We limited our study to the few locally noteworthy schools to which we could gain access, so in that respect our sample is unrepresentative, and it is not possible to generalize our findings to all urban high schools. Instead, we were interested in discovering patterns of adaptive change that might inform urban educators about how to craft their own strategies. By comparing and analyzing the school-change processes in this small sample of schools, we also hope to provide information to policymakers and researchers who pitch ideas within the policy alliances, as well as to educators within urban high schools laboring to create learning environments that support more students.

PRAGMATIC STEPS FORWARD

We hold no illusions that this or any other critical analysis of policy will somehow change the trajectories toward standards or markets in urban education. Instead, we focus on steps social justice advocates might take as they seek to improve learning opportunities for underrepresented students within market systems. A pragmatic frame should be used when looking at governmental programs and schools as individuals conduct, evaluate, and try to put into practice the findings from educational research, or as schools and colleges seek to improve educational opportunities. We encourage educators, researchers, policy analysts, and administrators to emphasize social justice in schools and in policy to bring a better balance to policy development and educational practice, using this as a means of reducing gaps in outcomes through an uplift of URM students.

We recognize there are many barriers to narrowing gaps in high school achievement. Making arguments about new directions in policy is beyond the scope of this book. Instead of advocating for radical policy changes,[45] we focus on illuminating the roles of policy alliances and the potential for adaptive change to encourage more thoughtful, reflective, and responsible professional action in both schools and governmental agencies that promote change in education. We argue for a critical social consciousness, which can bring greater kindness, care, and support into reform mechanisms.

Critical Challenges Facing Urban High Schools

There was a global redistribution of employment opportunities after the end of the Cold War, followed by a redistribution of wealth in developed countries.[46] These trends accelerated the isolation of minorities and low-income families in urban schools, a pattern set in motion by the U.S. Supreme Court–ordered desegregation of public schools.[47] The reality of educational opportunity has become that those who can afford it—either through higher property taxes in suburbs or by paying tuition for elite private schools—have better access to higher-quality college preparatory education than poor and working-class families living in neighborhoods in American cities with large concentrations of poverty.[48] Market mechanisms have done little to reduce these inequalities in most American cities.

After providing an overview of the selected schools, we then discuss the four critical challenges that have been created, at least in part, by policy changes over the past three decades and are faced by these urban high schools. We also introduce the crucial role community support can have—an overarching issue that emerged in our study of the selected high schools.

Case-Study Schools

Initially, we thought it was important to consider how different public charter schools adapted to state requirements for graduation as they sought to improve college preparation for the underrepresented students they served (phase I). Our focus evolved as we had the opportunity to visit NYC public district schools recognized for developing student-support programs (phase II). The comparison of these two types of schools provides insight into the school-transformation processes now underway and points to strategies that can be used in reform efforts.

Schools selected for this study were recommended to us as locally noteworthy high schools by colleagues in universities, foundations, and nonprofit organizations.[49] The schools had garnered supplemental resources from foundations and nonprofit organizations to develop competitive strategies or market niches to attract students. The eight schools served mostly minority and low-income students. Their competitive positioning within district school-choice schemes played a substantial role within the change processes in these schools.

DEVELOPMENT OF COMPETITIVE MARKET NICHES

During the first phase, we visited four public charter high schools: two in the Midwest, one in the Atlantic region, and one in a western state. In the interviews, we asked about the original curriculum, challenges that emerged, and how the school adapted to meet those challenges, including the development of competitive market niches, math education, and advanced literacy. We also asked how they provided college knowledge content to inform students about college choice, the selection of a major, and navigation through college, hopefully enhancing both their college and career success.

The public charters had the same graduation requirements as the district schools in their states, but they had greater flexibility to make adaptive changes in their curricula and had partner organizations that provided grants and other resources to facilitate change; in contrast, the NYC public schools had curriculum constraints imposed by their school district. This finding surprised us, not only because the NYC schools were distinctive, but also because the city had been in a competitive market environment longer than most other cities. All eight schools had developed successful competitive strategies, which we refer to as market niches (see table I.2). The strategies schools used to develop and market themselves to students were tightly linked to the market niches they developed, a topic that was central to the analyses in the study.

The charter schools not only had greater flexibility to adapt their curricula to create market niches (e.g., the integration of career content into the curriculum), but they could also align the curriculum for social support of their students as they navigated through high school and planned for college. The NYC schools used social support organized through their partnership with CFES to strengthen the niches they had developed. Support provided by CFES enabled students and teachers to build relationships with community organizations and college partners, thus providing alternative means to compete within the urban market.

TESTING SCHEMES IN URBAN MARKETS

While student achievement on tests was not a criterion for selection in our case studies, most of these schools were competitive on the tests used in their school districts and states. To illustrate how academic competitiveness evolved within the schools, we use math scores (table I.3) from the states for the charter schools (part A) and from the city for the NYC schools (part B). We argue that the meaning of test scores is constructed within the market niches schools use to recruit students.

The math achievement by the charter schools was competitive in their local market. Two of the charter schools were exemplary: all the Beta High School students passed the state proficiency exams in math, although this school was in a city that did not report scores in recent years, and almost all of the students at Alpha High School passed. These high scores were sufficient to ensure the

TABLE I.2

Locally Distinctive High Schools Included in Our Two-Phase Study of Adaptive Change in Urban High Schools

School	Focus of study	School type	Interviews with
PHASE I: PUBLIC CHARTER HIGH SCHOOLS			
Alpha High School (eastern state)	curriculum and change processes (college knowledge)	charter, social justice specialization	teachers, administrators, founder
Beta High School (midwestern state)	curriculum and change processes (math)	university-based charter, college prep specialization	teachers, administrators
Kappa High School (midwestern state)	curriculum and change processes (market niches)	charter, technical specialization	teachers, administrators
Sigma High School (western state)	curriculum and change processes (literacy)	community college–based charter, college prep specialization	teachers, administrators
PHASE II: NYC DISTRICT HIGH SCHOOLS			
Acme Collegiate Academy	college preparation, school-college partnership	small independent high school academy carved out of a large comprehensive high school campus, CFES	students, teachers, administrators, mentors
Onye Nkuzi High School	college preparation, K–12 partnerships (internships)	small high school, urban, teaching specialization, CFES	students, teachers, administrators, mentors
Remus High School	college preparation and school-college partnerships	medium-sized comprehensive high school with four internal academies (medical, engineering, humanities, academic prep), CFES	students, teachers, administrators, mentors
21st Century Technological Academy	college preparation	small independent high school academy carved out of a large comprehensive high school campus, urban, mathematics and science specialization, CFES	students, teachers, administrators, mentors

competitive position of both schools in their cities. The other two charters were in the midst of a period of decline: 79% of Sigma's students were proficient in math in 2008–9, but only 64% in 2013–14; 61% of Kappa's students failed to pass the test in 2008–9, and this remained almost the same (60%) in 2012–13. Although these scores may be troubling from a state perspective, Sigma was one of the best options for immigrant students in its city, while Kappa's proficiency

TABLE I.3
Indicators of Math Achievement for Locally Distinctive High Schools

PART A: STATE PROFICIENCY FOR CHARTER SCHOOLS

School	Pre-2011	Post-2011
Alpha	state math test, 2009–10 advanced: 5.75% proficient: 65.52% basic: 27.59% below basic: 1.15%	state math test, 2013 advanced: 9.7% proficient: 77.7% basic: not available below basic: not available
Beta	state math test, 2009–10 proficient or above 10th grade = 100% 11th grade = 100%	state math test:, 2012–13 proficient or above 10th grade = 100% 11th grade = 100%
Kappa	state math test, 2008–9 proficient or above: 5% partially proficient: 36.6% not proficient: 60.6%	state math test, 2012–13 proficient: <10% partially proficient: 34% not proficient: 60%
Sigma	state math test, 2008–9 proficient or above: 79%	state math test, 2013–14 proficient or above: 64%

PART B MATH ACHIEVEMENT IN NYC SCHOOLS

School	Math achievement on state math test, 2009–10, state scores math B (geom. II / alg. II / trig.): n = 39,309; 61% passed integrated algebra: n = 275,747; 72% passed geometry: n = 161,494; 73% passed algebra II / trigonometry: n = 84,947; 65% passed	Math achievement on state math test, 2012–13, state scores math B: N/A integrated algebra: n = 232,360; 74% passed geometry: n = 162,346; 74% passed algebra II / trigonometry: n = 116,469; 66% passed
Acme Collegiate Academy	math B: n = 24; 21% passed integrated algebra: n = 92; 59% passed geometry: n = 95; 86% passed trigonometry: n = 81; 68% passed	math B: N/A integrated algebra: n = 235; 85% passed geometry: n = 139; 74% passed trigonometry: n = 109; 54% passed
Onye Nkuzi High School	math B: n = 9; 33% passed integrated algebra: n = 271; 67% passed geometry: n = 42; 71% passed algebra II / trigonometry: n = 42; 31% passed	math B: N/A integrated algebra: n = 220; 60% passed geometry: n = 107; 52% passed trigonometry: n = 61; 20% passed
Remus High School	math B: n = 38; passed 39% integrated algebra: n = 477; 71% passed geometry: n = 328; 55% passed algebra II / trigonometry: n = 164; 34% passed	math B: N/A integrated algebra: n = 390; 55% passed geometry: n = 367; 45% passed algebra II / trigonometry: n = 170; 44% passed
21st Century Technological Academy	math B: n = 5; 80% passed integrated algebra: n = 107; 85% passed geometry: n = 139; 71% passed algebra II / trigonometry: n = 81; 68% passed	math B: N/A integrated algebra: n = 235; 85% passed geometry: n = 139; 74% passed algebra II / trigonometry: n = 109; 54% passed

rates were actually higher than most of the charters and district schools in the city from which it drew most of its students.

NYC uses multiple methods of measuring student achievement, including a complex system of peer and citywide school comparisons that factor in historical data. They also use a 1 through 4 proficiency scale; this scale changed, however, over the period of our study. The most stable scale for comparing math achievement across time is the Regents' Exam (RE) score. The RE scores for two of the NYC schools, Acme Collegiate Academy and 21st Century Technological Academy, were competitive with those of schools throughout the state. Acme student scores in integrated algebra improved vastly over the period of our study, but dropped in upper-level math. In fact, all of the schools except Remus showed lower scores in upper-level math; this may be related to all four NYC schools experiencing a change in principals during the study. State scores remained stable during this period.

Comparative test scores are, at best, only one indicator of school success that parents and students consider when choosing a school, but the competitive rankings on scores were an indirect factor influencing practices in all eight schools. Our case-study analysis addresses how the schools dealt with selection schemes and student capacity to complete rigorous courses, as well as other components related to achievement. There has long been a relationship in public education between rates of attrition within cohorts (e.g., retaining them in grade level, referring them to special education, and encouraging dropouts or transfers) and competitive rankings. For example, the NYC admission system considered prior student achievement and other factors, creating marketing incentives among the competing schools to entice high-achieving students to include them in their list of preferred schools. Charter schools informally sorted students, encouraging them to enroll if their educational goals were aligned with those of the school. These selection and attrition mechanisms were an integral part of the competitive positioning in the schools we studied.

Critical Challenges Facing Urban High Schools

The radical changes in public policy for both K–12 and higher education have placed great pressure on urban high schools, but the introduction of market systems during the same time period brought two contradictory forces into urban education: one of the policy thrusts (standards) was addressed through central control of the curriculum, while the other (markets) forced local adaptive change as a means of competing for students and resources.

CHALLENGE 1: MARKET COMPETITION

Chapter 1 examines policies promoting school choice in urban communities and ways in which high schools have adapted to market systems that may necessitate resource acquisition beyond public funding. Some urban high schools have been able to attract additional support from within their communities as a supplement to public funding. These ancillary resources from foundations and community organizations have often been necessary to develop strategies for competing with suburban schools, as well as with private schools and publically funded charter schools.

Charter schools are exempted from the regulatory curriculum controls imposed by public school districts, while district schools face constraints that limit their ability to adapt, creating an unequal and unfair competitive-market system. For example, it was easier for the charter schools to integrate career content into college prep courses when they chose technical content themes; with their curriculum constraints, the NYC schools had to use co-curricular support services to enhance their school themes. Charters, however, have not always achieved better student outcomes than public schools, despite their greater academic freedom, but, like some public high schools, they have been able to compete for students because they often appeal to the specialized interests of different groups within urban communities that can provide supplemental funding.[50]

The development of career-oriented market niches can change the relationship between high school preparation (especially the new STEM high schools) and the first two years of college, which traditionally focus on the liberal arts. Yet two of the schools we visited decided to concentrate explicitly on preparation in the liberal arts: a NYC school adopted liberal arts as a second theme to improve its competitive position in the district school-choice scheme; and Beta, a charter high school, was founded with this theme.

CHALLENGE 2: ADVANCED MATH AND STEM PREPARATION

As globalization of the labor force progressed in the 1990s, educational-reform advocates used the idea of changing labor markets to argue for raising educational standards. Rationalizations for STEM preparation are an integral part of the new concept of being college and career ready, but chapter 2 addresses the notion that advanced math (e.g., requirements for completion of algebra II in Michigan and Indiana) is necessary may have been misguided.

Upgrading the high school curriculum was rationalized by the idea that other nations threatened the economic viability of the United States. One argument was that the United States would have to retool its educational system to provide highly skilled labor to lead in the design of products as manufacturing continued to shift to lower-cost labor markets.[51] This argument overlooked the fact that China and India have surplus graduates in science and engineering, altering the employment opportunities for these graduates and those from the United States and other nations. A closely related argument was that all students would need superior skills in math and science to find jobs in the new labor market.[52]

There was a fundamental difference between these two rationales: the argument for advanced education for a design strategy aligns with the advanced math education required for entry into a four-year college,[53] while the argument for a technical work force promoted a 9–14 concept of education and was used to frame the workforce arguments by Jobs for the Future.[54]

Interestingly, most nations moving forward in science do not require advanced math for all students. For example, the current college preparatory curriculum in China includes geometry but not algebra II. Further, with the government's central control of educational policy, China has rapidly increased the number of college graduates in STEM fields, but these students have not had the freedom to choose their field as students do in the United States.[55] Along with China, South Korea is making rapid progress toward collegiate education in science, engineering, technology, and math, but both have vocational as well as college preparatory high schools,[56] and testing is used to assess students for specific high schools, rather than to evaluate high schools. Technical education does not necessarily require competency in geometry, algebra II, or calculus, but for those students who need it, these nations provide excellent and engaging math education in high school.[57]

While urban areas once had separate vocational, regular, and college preparation high schools, suburban and rural communities developed comprehensive high schools with all three options. Since the history of tracking within schools resulted in segregation, with more minority students in vocational programs and more Whites in the college preparatory alternative,[58] the concept of multiple pathways fell out of favor in the United States, and the nation developed the concept of being college and career ready as the new standard for all high school graduates. The argument that all students should be prepared in advanced math (e.g., algebra and more-advanced courses) became dominant among educational analysts, who reported correlations between college outcome and high school math preparation.[59]

The relationship between high school preparation and the first two years of college has changed in multiple ways, reducing the saliency of arguments for a liberal arts curriculum in the initial two collegiate years as a means of informing students about educational pathways, increasing incentives to align and integrate community college and high school courses, and forcing a college major be considered by middle school students as they chose their high school, many of which have content themes.

Not only did STEM become a rallying notion for market competition among advocates of high school reform, but math educators in urban schools were left to figure out how best to teach advanced math concepts to students who had not been prepared for this curriculum. We discovered (through a review of the U.S. literature on advanced math education) that the "best and brightest" students were channeled into abstract advanced math courses, but little attention was given to how average students could best learn advanced math. As a result, the requirement that all students complete advanced math became a serious barrier to high school graduation for many students.

Chapter 3 examines the challenges posed by the CCSS and market niches for literacy education in urban schools. Advanced literacy education was transformed by the coupling of market competition with the partial resolution of long-standing arguments about the best methods for teaching literacy. The ways schools develop advanced literacy education vary in relation to their content themes. For example, in schools that have a STEM focus, there is a need for specialized texts related to STEM education (e.g., health, engineering, etc.), while schools that retain a concentration on the liberal arts use more traditional approaches to literature.

For many years there had been conflict between meaning-oriented approaches to teaching reading and writing that focused on engagement, and phonemic methods (decoding) that emphasized sound-letter relationships and comprehension. A renewed effort to build consensus recognized that both meaning and decoding were important. The CCSS initiative promotes a balance between the two approaches, integrating literacy across the curriculum. The NYC school district placed constraints on its English curriculum, thus limiting the flexibility of its schools, while the public charters we studied had the freedom to develop their own curriculum, which made it easier to integrate technical topics into literacy education.

Challenges related to diverse social contexts, which can marginalize critical literacy, have been overlooked. Critical literacy advocates have argued that literacy education should be culturally situated: students from underrepresented backgrounds would need access to literature across the curriculum, and language-minority students would need a curriculum that addressed their unique and culturally situated learning needs. Educators in the schools we studied found that it was difficult to address cultural differences in knowledge acquisition, an artifact of both the linkage between career content and other courses and the constraints on the curriculum.

The development of thematic curricula had further consequences for advanced literacy education because the nature of advanced literacy—in the symbols and interpretive methods used—varies across collegiate fields. The strategy of providing a foundation in the liberal arts during the first two years of college gave students the opportunity to find the subjects in which they were most interested and choose a major based on an exploration of various disciplines. Pushing specialized content knowledge to the high school level alters the ways in which advanced literacy skills are introduced and taught, especially since the symbols and methods of interpretation vary across fields, creating multiple versions of advanced literacy. Using these specialized symbols and meanings in high school can engage students because they can more easily see their application, but it also alters the older pathways between high school and college.

These developments—the integration of new literacy standards across the curriculum, coupled with the thematic redesign of the curriculum in many schools—have serious consequences for the alignment of high school and college curricula. We found that the competitive nature of the educational market and the pressure to specialize content complicated literacy education in high schools. For example, in our interviews with students in NYC public schools, we learned they reflected on the constraints of their particular curriculum in relation to what they were learning about content pathways (majors and fields in colleges). Historically, engineering and nursing were among the few fields that had specialized content for entering students. While the college-ready aspect of the new curriculum seems to support the traditional emphasis on liberal arts education, the career-ready aspect leads to an increasing specialization of content that has historically been part of upper-division courses in college.

The changing nature of literacy curricula in high school, along with the struggle to adapt these curricula for the CCSS, make it necessary to learn more about and address the core standards. We raise new issues, based on insights that emerged from our analysis of policies, trends, and our case studies. Many of the problems we discovered are far from resolved. The restructuring of urban high schools has introduced market forces that can actually limit college pathways and the types of colleges and majors students can choose. While the literature on the CCSS initiative espouses the intent of college ready, the standards are implemented in diverse ways—a result of partnerships between high schools and colleges, the market niches of schools, and the culture of the students they serve. Urban high schools appear to be on a trajectory away from, rather than toward, effective literacy education.

CHALLENGE 4: COLLEGE KNOWLEDGE

Chapter 4 examines how the movement toward universal college preparation and career readiness has pushed content related to college majors and career paths more deeply into the high school curriculum. The CCSS recognizes aspects of this challenge by linking career technical content, the social sciences, math, and literacy, but this can undermine the older liberal arts concept of college preparation and the flexibility of the first two years of undergraduate education.

In the conversion to college and career pathways, the range of content and the quality of instruction in advanced courses has been radically altered by decisions about competitive niches in high schools. Some high schools are aligned with community colleges to offer collegiate courses to their students, but the market forces that influence educators in urban high schools may result in courses that meet technical requirements without actually preparing students for college. Students now need information on college pathways in middle school, if not earlier, because in urban educational markets their eventual college choice can be constrained by the content type, as well as the quality, of the high school they enter.

The concept of college *and* career ready assumes students know about career and college pathways, an aspect that is not included in the CCSS. Many schools find that the career-ready imperative requires this dual content to be offered, which exacerbates inequalities within urban educational systems: students from families with a history of college education grow up with more of this information than do students whose parents have no prior college experience. Families from a working-class background are at an extreme disadvantage in the new market system because of their limited exposure to this prior knowledge.

Most of the schools we visited had developed content knowledge related to education and career pathways within their high school curriculum. This was a fascinating—and probably necessary—adaptation to the supposedly common curriculum. The ways schools created specialized content niches constrained the types of educational and career pathways emphasized within them, which was evident in their marketing strategies to middle school students and their families.

All of the schools we studied found ways of integrating college and career knowledge. While the public charter schools had more flexibility in aligning their curricula with specialized content related to career and college pathways, the four NYC schools we visited were part of a national network of schools and colleges. On occasion, these schools had to modify their strategies to address contradictions created by clashes between their thematic approaches and the aim of preparing students; students' expectations also had an influence on the adaptation of organizational and curriculum strategies within most of our case-study schools.

Community Resources

Not only do urban high schools face a complex set of locally situated challenges if they are to build curricula that provide the college and career readiness needed for their students, but they often cannot afford to address these challenges without support from community organizations. While we do not include a chapter on this topic, external resources were crucial in these high schools as they addressed the four challenges we examined.

The capacity to attract community resources—especially partnerships with colleges, nonprofit organizations, and corporations—played a crucial role in improvements in both the NYC schools and the charters. The specialized charter schools we studied had funding support for curriculum innovation from local universities, foundations, and corporations; the NYC high schools adapted to market competition through partnerships they developed with nonprofit organizations, including CFES.

Building community support for college preparation has become a major theme among foundations that fund college-access programs.[60] The case studies in this book illustrate the importance of community support. Because of their flexibility, the four charter high schools could work with community partners in reforming both academic and social support for an educational uplift of urban school students (table I.4). The four NYC high schools faced curriculum constraints that impeded a school-based adaptation of the curriculum to strengthen the career connectivity of their college preparatory courses; the organizing support provided by CFES partially compensated for this, however, by enabling adaptive change.

Given the crucial role community-based organizations played in the academic and support strategies used in our case-study schools, a fundamental rethinking of urban school reform is needed. A few changes with an explicit focus on social uplift have survived the new waves of school reform. For example, the Harlem Children's Zone (HCZ), which began in 1971, has focused on expanding opportunities for low-income students by adding after-school programs, truancy-prevention services, and antiviolence training for teenagers.[61] The HCZ has become a model for providing social support for students and families as they adjust to a new economy with fewer working-class employment opportunities. But, as we document in our critical analyses of policy development, most governmental programs have a narrower focus: regulating educators and addressing specific topics thought to be related to college success.

Transforming Urban High Schools

It is important to explore how community-based reforms are infused into urban markets where students often attend schools outside their neighborhoods. As we reflected on our case studies, we realized that our comparison of charter and public district schools provides insight into the development of *new urban schools* as distinctive schools with strong cultures, a college preparatory curriculum, and strategies to compete for students. While we used the comparison of charter and NYC district schools to illuminate the challenges facing high schools in urban markets, we realize that each school must find its own pathway. There is not a one-size-fits-all formula for change in either charter or district schools. High schools are facing difficult challenges created by contradictory policies, especially the inherent conflict between markets and district-constrained cur-

TABLE I.4

Examples of Community Resources Used in Academic and Social Support in Our Case-Study Schools

School	Academic support	Social support
Alpha	• foundation-sponsored social justice charter theme, with supplemented educational costs	• foundation-sponsored scholarship guarantee, counselor, and internship programs
Beta	• sponsored by university's School of Education (liberal arts model) • tried out 9–14 model for advanced math education	• strong emphasis on support of "Dream" students • integration into a community college setting
Kappa	• corporate foundation–supported development of technical program • joint advanced courses with local university	• students had opportunities for internships and career focus through a corporate foundation
Sigma	• community college–sponsored charter, with provided facility • foundation-supported transition to full 9–14 model	• social support provided by high school educators working in partnership with community college faculty and staff
Acme Collegiate Academy	• thematic small school • NYC educational policies constrained curriculum adaptation for themes	CFES organizing strategy for • pathways (college networks) • mentoring (social networks) • leadership through service (community engagement)
Onye Nkuzi High School	• thematic small school • NYC educational policies constrained curriculum adaptation for themes	CFES organizing strategy for • pathways (college networks) • mentoring (social networks) • leadership through service (community engagement)
Remus High School	• opportunities to complete university courses for themed programs • located adjacent to partner university • NYC educational policies constrained curriculum adaptation for themes	CFES organizing strategy for • pathways (college networks) • mentoring (social networks) • leadership through service (community engagement)
21st Century Technological Academy	• thematic small school • NYC educational policies constrained curriculum adaptation for theme	CFES organizing strategy for • pathways (college networks) • mentoring (social networks) • leadership through service (community engagement)

ricula. The process of transformation is not complete; it will be an ongoing challenge for high schools in urban educational markets.

The school-standards alliance has dominated national educational policy in recent decades, often narrowly defining change within schools as a curriculum problem, while market strategies create unequal competitive markets for urban schools (with district schools facing more constraints than charter schools). The

CCSS, college and career ready, and other pipeline notions pushed curriculum mandates onto schools, but they provided little or no direct support for the change process. The schools that became distinctive as they made their way through this complex terrain benefited from community resources. Chapter 5 (the conclusion) identifies possible next steps in high school reform to provide academic preparation for underrepresented students in urban communities, suggesting a contextualized theory for the transformation of schools as social institutions.

The contradictory nature of the two policy trajectories (standards and markets) complicates the change process within schools. The ones we visited found new ways to involve their communities in redesigning and improving high schools. New graduation requirements restrict the courses that can be offered in all types of schools. Market incentives make it possible for charter schools to innovate in how they deliver these courses, while mandated standards and an aligned curriculum constrain adaptive changes in district schools, especially for math education. Given the financial constraints on urban high schools, improvement in the quality of urban education appears to be dependent on additional funding from foundations *and* increased connectivity to community organizations. Our book provides a new perspective on high schools as institutions engaged in a larger goal of social transformation in urban communities.

While the new urban high schools can promote educational uplift by expanding opportunities for low- and middle-income students in urban communities, it is unlikely that market competition can solve the inequality problem. Small schools that successfully compete for students exclude some of the most-challenged students through (1) admission schemes that sort students, (2) test results that track students within schools, (3) the retention of students in grade level, (4) the failure of some admitted students to complete requirements, (5) transferals to other schools by students who seek easier pathways through high school, or (6) even dropouts. The class-reproduction process is still evident in both public charter and district schools within urban market systems.[62] Nevertheless, the new generation of urban high schools remains an important part of the educational reform process.

CHAPTER ONE

Market Niches

Urban schools are adapting to market conditions by devising academic strategies that enable them to attract students and external funding. Chubb and Moe's *Politics, Markets, and America's Schools* advocated a market model of school reform in New York City. Their report had a substantial influence as NYC entered a period of experimentation with privately funded vouchers for low-income students and a gradual move to a market model in the public system. The charter school movement also accelerated in urban areas after this report, and there were large-scale experiments with private vouchers to test this concept.

In addition to documenting how policy alliances promoted market systems, in this chapter we examine challenges encountered by urban high schools. Advocacy by policy alliances has created successive waves of market-based policy reforms and, more recently, the testing of new market mechanisms within city schools. Both charter and district schools in urban public systems have had to navigate through these policy changes. We start with a critical analysis of market rationales and the mechanisms used to organize research to inform policy logics promoting markets. Next, we analyze our case studies, with a focus on a connected curriculum and competitive niches.

Policy Rationales for Urban Markets

While a systems approach was used to develop the Great Society programs when federal educational initiatives emerged in the 1960s and 1970s,[1] the 1980s brought a shift to an advocacy approach to policy research and development,[2] which was adopted by both liberal and conservative reformers. Starting in the mid-1980s, the Reagan administration required policy researchers to emphasize market models in research that would support governmental policy initiatives, which focused on student loans in higher education and market models in K–12 education. A similar rationale was used in the 1990s to test new strategies that linked vouchers and charter schools as a market mechanism to promote urban educational reform. While these policies were ostensibly empirically grounded, they overlooked evidence that contradicted their arguments.

Policy alliances were built through research and policy networks. Researchers responded to requests for proposals and engaged in other grant-seeking behaviors to finance their investigations. Funding officers in educational agencies and foundations often promoted changing existing systems in ways consonant with their own interests and political agendas. Researchers may claim neutrality, but policy studies conducted in response to advocacy agendas are hardly neutral, especially when reports are vetted by political operatives to ensure that the proper rationales are advocated.

We first examine the emergence of market mechanisms in K–12 education during desegregation, and then discuss vouchers, charter schools, and the underlying logics of the various market-reform strategies developed and tested by alliances of researchers, policymakers, and foundations.

Situating Market Policies Historically

There has been a succession of reforms promoting school choice in urban schools: starting with magnet schools as a mechanism for desegregation; followed by school-wide reform models as part of the shift from targeted supplemental education; and, recently, market strategies, voucher trials, and charter schools that have created a context for the new market policies.

DESEGREGATION AND SCHOOL CHOICE

To understand the role student choice plays within urban school systems, it is important to reconsider how early choice schemes were created: as remedies for segregation. The first wave of desegregation was for legislated (de jure) racial separation in southern states. Before school desegregation, there had been few private schools in the South, but private Christian schools flourished during desegregation as Whites fled public schools.[3] In the North, segregated urban neighborhoods had fueled de facto segregation of neighborhood schools, a problem addressed in the second wave of desegregation cases. Identified originally in what is known as the Coleman report,[4] the concentration of low-income and disadvantaged populations in cities became a common pattern.[5] Innovations undertaken during the desegregation period have had a lasting impact.

The primary legacy of desegregation was the competition between urban and suburban K–12 systems for upper-middle-class students. As new school districts developed in communities surrounding cities, the rising middle class residing there brought new tax revenues and a will to provide top-quality education for their children, while cities were in a state of decline. The competition between urban and suburban districts has influenced the emergence of market models (including niche schools and charters) for K–12 education as cities have tried to attract the upper middle class back from the suburbs.

A second legacy is the breakdown of school-district boundaries within urban public school systems. Redrawing district boundaries and busing students to different schools were early remedies for both de jure and de facto segregation.

School desegregation altered the relationships between communities and their schools, which were stronger in cities before *Brown v. Board of Education*, although there was also great inequality within schools. There was an effort to equalize opportunity through Title I of the Elementary and Secondary Education Act of 1965, the primary federal reform program in education that played a major role in equalizing students' reading abilities in schools.[6] After 1985, a widening achievement gap, along with changes in Title I, ushered in market models. It is important to consider how both market mechanisms and accountability requirements altered this program.

In response to court-mandated desegregation, magnet schools were widely adopted in northern urban school districts as a choice-based remedy that focused on the quality of education.[7] Some successful magnet schools have persisted and evolved, becoming integral to the new urban markets. For example, Lusher School was a magnet elementary school in New Orleans that grew into a K–9 school after taking over an abandoned high school building in 1990. After Hurricane Katrina, the school was adopted by Tulane University and became a K–12 school providing education for the children of faculty and staff of the universities in the city; its opening signaled the return of an educational system to New Orleans.[8] Lusher School illustrates the evolving role of market mechanisms as an integral aspect of urban renewal.

HIGH SCHOOL REFORM MODELS

The Elementary and Secondary Education Act of 1965 promoted equal opportunity through Title I, supplementing educational opportunities for students who were thought to be disadvantaged. Funding was initially distributed to districts and schools with high poverty rates. After the pullout strategies used in Title I fell into disfavor in the 1980s, the federal government began to experiment with alternatives. A series of school-wide options were tried that exempted schools from district regulations.[9] A period of innovation followed, with schools having the option to work with private vendors that marketed new reform models, especially after the passage of the Obey-Porter legislation in 1997, which promoted comprehensive school reform (CSR). A number of new high school models evolved. Schools had to write proposals for funding, with an emphasis on research that investigated the model chosen for their school; the fortunate received large grants to implement these reform models. While CSR models continue to be used, research has not confirmed their having a positive impact on student outcomes.[10] Two programs help illustrate the ways CSR designs influenced the evolution of the school-based models studied in this book:

- America's Choice emphasized doubling up in math courses, along with creating small schools within schools. Doubling up meant students who came into schools with less math preparation would take two periods of math, usually starting in the 9th grade;[11] the methods used to teach this math, however, did not necessarily change. This practice was used by many of the schools studied in this book. Small schools within larger schools provided opportunities to try out different specialization (niche) schools, an approach that has been widely adapted in other reform models.

· The Talent Development High School with Career Academies model breaks large high schools into smaller schools, each having separate teachers and administrators and a different theme (e.g., STEM education, arts and humanities, etc.).[12]

Variants of these school-reform models continue in American education, and the small-schools concept has been adapted in the new urban school markets. For example, the Bill & Melinda Gates Foundation, which has made a substantial investment in high school reforms that are based on many of the lessons learned from reform strategies initiated through Title I and Comprehensive School Reform, contributed more than $1 billion toward small high schools in 2000, believing that reducing the size of schools (frequently through creating multiple schools on the campuses of large urban schools) would improve student outcomes. There were documented examples of successful schools under CSR,[13] but the evaluation research found that the reforms had little impact.[14] Nonetheless, the Gates Foundation still advocates for small high schools and early college programs that bring community college courses into high schools.[15]

Choice schemes in urban education altered the tracking system that had previously been used to sort students. Specialized pathways give qualified students more options, but they make the choice of which high school to attend a critical issue. Parents and students must think about content and career specializations when they choose a high school, which occurs much earlier in their educational path than with the traditional comprehensive high school model. It is difficult for some families, especially those with little or no college experience, to make informed choices. Nevertheless, the new niche schools provide opportunities to gain specialized content knowledge for those savvy enough to take advantage of them.

It is also difficult for students who change their minds about these early choices to switch schools, at least in NYC. When students decide their career-themed school is not a good fit, it may not be easy for them to transfer into one that might work better for them. A transfer student who doesn't meet screening requirements for a desirable school or who finds that no seats are available is likely to be placed in whichever school has openings.

Testing Alternative Market Strategies

Two market strategies (vouchers and charters) attracted substantial public and philanthropic funding in the late 1990s and early 2000s. While research did not demonstrate that either strategy had better outcomes, charters have persisted while voucher schemes have declined. An examination of the evolving alliances supporting these strategies helps further illustrate the complexity of urban school markets.

In voucher schemes, money should go to students rather than schools. Historically, extreme conservatives considered vouchers to be a better way to fund education. The argument had been initiated by Milton Friedman in *Capitalism and Freedom*,[16] and it was bolstered through studies of tax rates and the benefits of public education.[17] The voucher argument influenced the Nixon administration's study of higher education[18] and the creation of Pell grants.[19] During the Reagan administration, the idea of vouchers was suggested to researchers conducting federally funded studies of returns on federal student-aid programs.[20] The concept of vouchers entered the mainstream of policy scholarship on K–12 education after Chubb and Moe's report for the Brookings Institution.[21]

In Milwaukee and Cleveland, public funding for voucher schemes was tried as an adaptation to the allocations through Title I. Research showed that the achievement of voucher students was not significantly different from similar students in traditional schools,[22] and that frequently the vouchers did not cover the entire cost of enrolling in private schools.[23] There was also evidence in Cleveland that slots in private schools were not open to many urban school students.

Private foundations funded voucher schemes in a few other American cities, including randomized experiments in New York City and Washington, D.C., with scholarships for low-income students. The primary researcher for these programs was Paul Peterson, an advocate of vouchers, whose research reports a modest effect for vouchers on student achievement, along with a more substantial impact on parental satisfaction.[24] Since recipients of the vouchers were randomly selected, his results meet contemporary causal standards.

While vouchers were promoted by the federal government and by foundations, charters—a market-based school-funding model—evolved as a catalyst for change in urban school systems. In charter schools, government funding follows students, introducing market forces through competition with district-governed urban school systems. Relieved from many of the accountability requirements imposed on public district schools, charter schools essentially tested the theory that market forces would improve educational outcomes through innovation and efficiency.

States experimented with charters while neoconservatives promoted vouchers. Minnesota, a state known for innovation in education, passed the first charter school law in 1991; California was second in 1992.[25] Other states rapidly followed in creating charter schools. The research on the performance of charter schools now clearly indicates they do not significantly affect achievement outcomes,[26] but advocates of charter schools have remained undeterred by this evidence, instead encouraging others to learn from the successful schools,[27] an approach we adopt here to examine the intersections between urban school policies and adaptive change within schools.

The Underlying Logics of Market Rationales

We have illuminated the progression of rationales that have moved public school systems toward market models. The overarching policy logics of innovation, choice, and efficiency run across these waves of reform (table 1.1). The concepts of choice and innovation have been integral to policy rationales that aligned liberals—-and many educational researchers—with policy advocacy groups promoting market mechanisms coupled with higher standards. Conservatives also championed market rationales, thinking there would be efficiency gains leading to reduced funding needed for education and public services, which were often linked within the rationales for reform.

IDEOLOGICAL CRITIQUE OF LIBERAL EDUCATION

Whether the idea that neoliberals actually intended to undermine the liberal rationales for reform depends on one's view of educational reform in the 1960s and 1970s. Ravitch, a national leader in the standards movement, provides insight into its intent:[28]

> *A Nation at Risk* [*ANAR*] was a response to the radical school reforms of the late 1960s and early 1970s. Whoever remembers that era fondly is sure to dislike *ANAR*; conversely, whoever was skeptical toward the freewheeling forms of those years is likely to admire *ANAR*. No one who lived in that time will forget the proliferation of experiments and movements in the nation's schools. Reformers differed mainly in terms of how radical their proposals were. The reforms of the era were proffered with the best of intentions; some stemmed from a desire to advance racial equity in the classroom and to broaden the curriculum to respect the cultural diversity of the population. (p. 23)

Placing *A Nation at Risk* in the context of the long-term battles about educational innovation and improvement and the efforts to contend with and respect diversity illustrates the role of ideology in education. Many innovations were developed as remedies to racial inequality in education (e.g., magnet schools); *ANAR*, however, advocated standards across the curriculum, along with raising graduation requirements.[29] This approach overlooked the concepts of care and uplift in the African American tradition,[30] and instead aligned with the White tradition of education.

While high-stakes testing per se was not emphasized in *ANAR*, adding testing to the standards movement became the primary means for evaluating public schools and constraining innovations thought to be too radical by political conser-

TABLE 1.1
Policy Logics Used in Market Rationales

Policy logics (*reform rationales*)	Innovation (explicit)	Choice (explicit)	Efficiency (implicit and deceptive)
Magnet schools	Focused on elevating schools of choice as a desegregation mechanism	Used choice as an alternative to busing for desegregation	Reduced social conflict by altering images of racially defined schools; low-cost desegregation strategy
Comprehensive reforms	Focused on shifting from compensatory education to school-wide reform	Tested small schools within schools as a model of choice and reform	Redirected specialized funding promoting equal opportunity and uplift
Vouchers	Funded students who could chose schools within a market system that included religious schools	Provided low-income families with financial support to attend private schools and/or purchase instructional services	Redirected federal funds (Title I) for school-based programs to subsidies to private vendors and/or vouchers for private schools; used philanthropic support to test theory
Charters	Focused on family choice of schools; developed as independent public schools with their own local boards and leaders	Provided an alternative to public schools; threat of loss of students would stimulate innovation in public schools	Redirected public funding from district schools; added to dysfunction by increasing ratios of administrative compared with educational costs
Career-connected	Focused on educational links to the labor market	Linked career content to advanced college prep curriculum	Used markets to stimulate change; reduced per-student funding

vatives. Ironically, magnet schools, created as a means of achieving desegregation through quality education, were among the radical reforms critiqued by advocates of *ANAR*. Since U.S. rankings on international educational metrics have dropped since *ANAR* and the equity gaps in educational achievement have increased, neither goal of this scheme has been met. The decline in U.S. educational rankings continues to be a theme of the reform movement,[31] but there is little evidence of a correlation between the implementation of current policies and this outcome.

SELF-SEALING REFORM LOGICS

Self-sealing logic denies evidence that does not confirm one's own position.[32] In her introduction to *The Death and Life of the Great American School System:*

How Testing and Choice Are Undermining Education, Ravitch asks and answers an important question:[33]

> What should we think of someone who never admits error, never entertains doubt but adheres unflinchingly to the same ideal all of his life, regardless of new evidence? Doubt and skepticism are signs of rationality. When we are too certain of our opinions, we run the risk of ignoring any evidence that conflicts with our views. It is doubt that shows we are still thinking, still willing to reexamine hardened beliefs when confronted with new facts and new evidence. (p. 3)

Student test scores became the generally accepted indicators of achievement in the standards movement. The high-stakes aspect of the mechanism involved penalizing the schools and the teachers of students with low scores. But the proponents of this model seldom, if ever, examined the ways in which the policies they advocated actually influenced student outcomes.[34] As a result, low-income students and their teachers became the victims of this reform movement.

The market model ushered in by Chubb and Moe's critique of New York City schools[35] included an emphasis on innovation, despite *ANAR*'s intent of wiping out initiatives from prior decades when K–12 outcomes were improving. The *ANAR* model had widespread conservative support, including extensive funding from private donors and foundations for vouchers and charters. The conservative Fordham Foundation, however, found the innovation argument to be of sufficient importance to fund studies of school effects,[36] which found that the alignment of standards and testing undermined innovation in the public schools. This further illustrates the constraints on change within public systems created by contemporary educational policy influenced by *ANAR*.[37]

While there has not been confirmatory evidence that market models result in improved educational outcomes, market logics and mechanisms are deeply entrenched. Of the two choice schemes—charters and vouchers—charters eventually prevailed and are now advocated as a model for governmental agencies and foundations supporting high school reform over the next two decades.[38] Because the focus of many charters is on finding a market niche, it is crucial to consider how this concept fits with the more dominant reform strategy of using standards to align the curriculum with tests.

Qualitative research that digs beneath the surface of these reforms has been limited, but findings illustrate some of the problems with market assumptions. The Fordham Foundation funded a qualitative study of the implementation process in an urban area using private vouchers, interviewing educational leaders, school administrators, teachers, and parents. The following were some of its observations:

- The senior system administrators in the private and public systems adapted to the introduction of the voucher scheme. The public school system introduced choice zones; many of the elite private schools espoused openness if students qualified, but few of them followed through; the suburban districts refused to take students from the city despite a state law that permitted state funds to follow students across districts; the Catholic schools had already implemented tuition reductions, so they were saturated with low-income students; and the Lutheran and Christian school systems opened their doors and benefited from the vouchers.[39]

· The school-leadership article from the study also examined adaptations within Catholic and public schools. Increasing the number of low-income students in Catholic schools changed their learning environment and necessitated a wider range of services, while public schools struggled to implement the market niches promoted through the district's choice scheme because of the constraints imposed by state testing.[40]

· The study publication focusing on parents found that, as a result of having choices, they were more satisfied with both public *and* private schools.[41]

These findings illustrate the complexities introduced into educational systems as a result of choice schemes. Perhaps the most compelling evidence of innovation—one touted by market advocates—was in public schools, where attempts to develop school-based market niches created changes in school missions and, to a lesser extent, in the curriculum. This adaptive change process is our focus in the analysis of our case studies.

Reframing the Market Challenge

In the past few years, the logic of the college and career ready concept has accelerated adaptive market-based changes in urban schools, including the development of content niches in both charter and district schools. Specifically, the argument for college preparatory content in math, literacy, and science provides an incentive for schools to integrate advanced content in math and literacy with a career-oriented focus, an approach now encouraged by the CCSS. The development of competitive strategies to meet standards for college preparation reinforces the niche-building process; there is not an equal playing field for this competitive game, however, because public schools are more constrained than private and charter schools, even in NYC, where the market model has the longest history in a public system.

Income inequity and educational reforms are intertwined. Despite three decades of standards-driven reform with modest gains in educational outcomes, equality is a more distant goal than it was in the 1970s; in fact, equity declined in the 1980s and 1990s. As with income inequality,[42] there was greater equity in educational outcomes in the 1970s than in subsequent decades.[43] In his analyses of income inequality in the twenty-first century, Piketty provides the following critique of the economic-productivity rationale for educational reform:[44]

> The most striking failure of the theory of marginal productivity and the race between education and technology is no doubt its inability to adequately explain the explosion of very high incomes from labor observed in the United States since 1980. According to this theory, one should be able to explain this change as the result of skills-based technological change. Some U.S. economists buy this argument, which holds that top labor incomes have risen more rapidly than the average wages simply because unique skills and new technology have made these workers much more productive than the average. There is a certain tautological quality to this explanation (after all, one can "explain" distortion of the wage hierarchy as the result of some supposed technological change). It also has other major weaknesses, which to my mind make it an unconvincing argument. (p. 314)

We concur with this interpretation because our review of standards and market logics reveals similar tautological thought. There is a consistent pattern of a selective filtering of research to rationalize faulty market policies in educational reform and public financing of K–12 and higher education.

Our stance is that educational leadership should recognize these problems and think through how to contend with them, because this deeply entrenched policy trajectory is unlikely to change any time soon. Currently, one of the fundamental challenges in urban high schools is how to develop competitive content niches to compete for students, but there are risks to this approach. Development of a competitive posture in school can undermine equity, especially if only test scores are used to screen students into the highest-quality schools; lower-achieving students may end up in less-competitive schools or may drop out. These patterns are evident in both public and private urban schools that attain sufficient distinction to make them popular choices among middle school students.

We now examine how schools—both new charter schools and restructured NYC district schools—navigated toward distinction in urban markets. We do not advocate the niche approach, but we recognize that adaptive change is necessary in the market. We focus on finding ways to improve equity *and* quality in educational outcomes. Developing competitive niches may be a necessity in contemporary urban educational markets, and we hope our critical analyses using case studies will help illuminate methods of improving equity within the constraints of this system.

How Schools Developed Market Niches

Competition in markets could be fundamentally different from the trends of prior generations of publically controlled educational reforms. Before the transformation in the policy trajectory that occurred in the late 1970s and early 1980s, public schools had to contend with state requirements and compete for federal grants, policy mechanisms that encouraged isomorphism.[45] While central control continues within public systems—and is especially strong when states determine the curriculum (i.e., approval of textbooks)—comprehensive public schools in urban areas must compete with newly developing charters with content-based themes. Even though public controls restrict curriculum choices, public schools face pressure to develop competitive niches in choice-based school systems like New York City's.

The concept of competitive market niches provides an alternative lens for examining the ways both public and charter high schools are adapting to the new competitive conditions in urban settings where students and their parents are confronted by multiple school choices. No longer is it taken for granted that students will enroll in neighborhood high schools. Instead, in many cities it is expected that high schools will provide college preparation plus a specialization or competitive niche, and students will choose a high school based on their interests.[46] A niche is the content or process around which schools specialize so they can compete for students, for the money following students, and for other funding attracted through grants. The capacity of administrators and teachers to write proposals and network in political and philanthropic social circles is a crucial part of academic capital now, since reforms frequently require more resources than can be provided by public tax dollars alone.

By focusing on adaptive niche building as a first step in our study of public district and charter high schools, we illuminate the ways in which schools seek to distinguish themselves from other schools that also must comply with the new standards. First, we examine patterns in four NYC public high schools, explicitly considering how they used community-resource networks provided through CFES as part of their competitive positioning. The core practices in the CFES program made it easier to make adaptive changes that improved their competitive position despite the curriculum constraints examined in the next two chapters. Second, we explain how the public charter schools used their academic freedom to develop competitive niches as part of their core curriculum, a process that is simply not possible in district schools. Finally, we use a case study of the development of a market niche at Kappa High School to illustrate the process of refining curriculum to meet higher standards while maintaining a career orientation across the curriculum.

Market Niches in Locally Distinctive NYC Schools

The contexts and atmospheres within NYC high schools changed as a consequence of implementing a formal citywide school-choice program in 2002. The Bill & Melinda Gates Foundation, the federal government, and other funding

TABLE 1.2
Adaptation of Market Niches by Selected NYC District High Schools

Original approach	Emergent challenges	Adaptations
Acme Collegiate Academy: a small school founded as part of the breakdown of a large school on a large campus	The school emphasized college preparation in competing for students; the district's curriculum constrained the development of advanced courses	The CFES program provided opportunities to build a strong culture and develop college connections
Onye Nkuzi High School: the school initially focused on teaching and social programs; located in an affluent neighborhood, it attracted predominately female (approximately 80%) students from several different boroughs	Due to social-class differences between the students and the community, the school had a tense relationship with its neighbors and had to relocate; many students directed to the school had no interest in teaching; teachers questioned how their programs would address academic challenges related to college preparation	The principal didn't want to marginalize the students who weren't interested in becoming teachers, so he developed a second academy equal to the teaching academy; this is different from Remus, where the students not in one of the academic-profession academies are essentially warehoused
Remus High School: located on a university campus, the school was designed to mirror the university structure with multiple small academies—medical, engineering, and humanities	The school became a default choice for a segment of the population who were assigned to it, rather than a "destination" school; school counselors report the transition to academies has been challenging	The school aligned CFES selection with the Engineering Academy, providing a means of increasing competitiveness; students participate in marketing visits to middle schools as part of their service learning
21st Century Technological Academy: initially part of a large school, the Academy became a small school on a large campus	The new school specialized in technology, with an explicit emphasis on math and science, to develop a distinctive niche	The school used networking with a college through CFES to develop strategies for integrating math and science into the curriculum

organizations have encouraged "small schools" in New York City by breaking up larger schools into smaller independent schools, often housed within a larger school complex. Neighborhood schools are decreasing in size as more students attend schools of choice. In their high school applications, middle school students rank 12 high schools they would like to attend. Some schools are not schools of choice, instead functioning as neighborhood schools for students who do not qualify for the merit portion of the choice scheme. Table 1.2 summarizes how our four case-study schools within this category adapted.

The introduction of the market system corresponded with adaptive changes in all four of the case-study schools. *Onye Nkuzi High School* started out with a focus on teaching and social interventions. The school attracted students from across the boroughs, partly because it was in a safe, upper-middle-class neighborhood, but the infusion of low-income minority students into this neighborhood led to conflict between the school and its local community. Illustrative of the power of the upper class in NYC, the school then moved to a new building in a lower-socioeconomic-status neighborhood. The collaboration with college networks through CFES introduced administrators and teachers to the liberal arts model of choosing a major and, to improve their competitiveness in the school-choice process, the school developed liberal arts as a second specialization.

Remus High School had been a medium-sized comprehensive high school and adapted to compete in the market system by developing content-oriented "academies" (engineering, medical, and the humanities) for which students were selected based on test scores and other criteria, as well as one academy with no admissions standard. To improve its competitive position in the new market model, Remus administrators decided to align their selection of students for CFES with the engineering academy, a tactic that would increase the competitiveness of the program and draw in more of the superior students. Since Remus was created in partnership with a local university campus, they could offer specialized elective courses at the university for students who scored 80 or above in subject-matter courses (English, math, science, social studies).

21st Century Technological Academy and *Acme Collegiate Academy* were both located in a closed high school building. Both schools provided the district's mandated curriculum and made modest changes compatible with their competitive themes. The restructuring of a large school into smaller autonomous schools illustrates how the strategies tested in America's Choice were easily adapted by schools in urban districts.

Critique of the NYC School-Choice Scheme

One of the underlying problems in urban schools has been that in the old scheme, only relatively few of them were oriented toward college preparation; the great majority of high schools had a general and/or vocational curriculum, and students could track into elite schools only through high grades, test scores, and recommendations from counselors. The older system was severely criticized because of its emphasis on tracking.[47] The new NYC market system uses student achievement, along with parental preference, in a hierarchical choice scheme that distributes some students to their choice schools and limits others to local schools that may not have made substantial progress toward the new standards; tests are used to compare and reward schools within the accountability scheme. This process essentially raises the pressures on low-income families by increasing the stakes of the testing systems used in the allocation of school slots. Students may lack the preparation to get through the filtering screen and into their schools of choice; they thus suffer from being directed into lower-quality schools, mimicking the former tracking system.

Inequalities in neighborhoods, the concentration of poverty, a lack of professional role models, and myriad other social and economic factors still influence inequalities in preparation prior to a student's "choice" of school. In reality, only public schools that were either excellent to start with or able to adapt in ways that improved their competiveness have been able to attract stellar students. The NYC schools we visited were enmeshed in this competitive market, trying to rise within the choice scheme used to distribute students.

Comparison of Selected Public Charters

The four public charter high schools had distinctive missions that developed as they became established in their communities. All four served low-income, mostly underrepresented minority populations from the inner city, and each one faced challenges as they developed their competitive strategies (table 1.3).

Alpha High School was founded by law students who believed high school students could be empowered by using legal principles as teaching tools. Alpha was located in an inner-city, low-income neighborhood that had largely been overlooked by urban renewal. The school's dual-content themes of law and college preparation were dependent in part on partnerships with local law firms and community organizations. Alpha found that it had to adapt its initial curriculum and after-school programming to provide an experience that was aligned with its two-pronged mission. The law theme attracted the city's network of lawyers, who supported the school with monetary and in-kind donations that have been invaluable in providing students with college preparatory education and law enrichment.

Beta High School was founded as a partnership with the School of Education in a private university and focused on advancing college preparatory pedagogies for inner-city children. The school enjoyed substantial support from philanthropists, including the Bill & Melinda Gates Foundation, which contributed to efforts to develop a new school model for college preparatory education.

Sigma High School, formed as a partnership with a community college in a southwestern city, provided a mechanism for completing high school and gaining college credit for immigrant students who might not otherwise have had these opportunities. Grant funding helped the school as it adjusted to state policies that made it difficult to maintain the school's mission.

Kappa High School was sponsored by a corporate foundation as it developed a focus on college preparation with a career orientation that emphasized business, engineering/technology, and health care. Founded as a charter school in a suburb adjacent to a major U.S. city, it attracted students from the inner city. Kappa adjusted to an upgrade in state graduation requirements by maintaining a focus on all of its students receiving college credits in a rigorous high school program.

Each of these schools had substantial external support from philanthropists, local colleges, and community groups. This funding helped fuel a strong ethos

TABLE 1.3
Adaptation of Market Niches by Selected Public Charter Schools

Original approach	Emergent challenges	Adaptations
Alpha High School: a law-themed emphasis helped meet the school's mission of preparing "students to succeed in college and to actively engage in our democratic society"; partnership with a local non-profit provided wraparound services	Partnership with the local organization was for only two years and limited in scope; no infrastructure for managing a wide array of programs and local partnerships with law firms	Full-time director of programs hired to oversee all extracurricular activities, including those related to the law; additional law emphasis: 9th grade law day; 11th grade law firm tutoring; 12th grade street law
Beta High School: initially founded as an early college high school; established through a partnership between a local private university and the public school system	A failed school levy caused massive staff cuts in the public school system; some students who entered were seriously deficient; the school needed more time to prepare students for college	School restructured into a charter high school; added a junior high school to serve students in grades 7–12; continued to adapt the curriculum to promote access to elite colleges
Kappa High School: charter school formed as its own school district and focused on a college preparatory curriculum (business, engineering/technology, and health care tracks), integrating the last two years of high school with the first two years of college; originally 11th and 12th grades only; started out on an abandoned university campus; initially was not concerned with state standards or its corporate partner's curriculum	Disciplinary issues hindered learning; students entering below grade level in math and English indicated a need to expose students to concepts earlier; original facility became an impediment to learning; partner-university environment problematic for both college and high school students	Integrated corporate partner's curriculum; moved to a new campus; more grades added; new STEM track under development, geared toward increasing students' exposure to science; national/state recognition for successful private/public partnership (93%–95% graduation rate); curriculum based on state standards and partner's focus; placement aligned with students' test scores, not on last grade successfully completed
Sigma High School: started as an alternative school, a key feature of the school was flexibility; the curriculum was self-paced, with the only requirement being that students complete 20 hours/week; the school was open from 8AM to 8PM for further flexibility	School attendance was an issue; lacked a system to monitor student progress toward graduation; didn't meet federal and state regulations (No Child Left Behind and Exceptional Student Service Department).	School restructured into an early college high school; entire staff had to reapply for their jobs; devised new student-recruitment methods; increased curricula integration (high school and community college); community college credits now a high school graduation requirement

and sense of community as the schools became distinctive, with well-defined niches in local educational markets. It probably would not have been possible for them to develop their specialized missions without this external support. In contrast, district schools have constrained funding, a restricted use of funds, and a more limited capacity to attract foundation grants for their curriculum, which puts them in a poorer competitive position.

Locally Distinctive Charters

The four public charter schools we visited in cities across the country were rigorous and rose to the challenge of preparing most of their students for college. Students in several of the charters and one of the public district schools (Remus) could obtain some college credits as part of their high school experience. Public charter schools, however, also faced the challenges of serving students with basic educational needs. Three had high departure rates, with students going on to less-rigorous schools or dropping out. The exception, Kappa High School, required its students to repeat 8th or even 7th grade if they weren't ready for the challenges of 9th grade when they applied, yet Kappa was also the school with the least-competitive test scores before it restructured its academic programs to meet the new state standards.

Complex issues related to the missions and ethos of schools underlie the competitive aspects of school-niche development. Since the United States started on the path to excellence, urban public schools have been confronted with whether to hold students back so they could increase test scores.[48] Now the new career-oriented charter schools are faced with a parallel tradeoff: having rigorous courses that drive out some students versus finding ways to keep all students.

Case Study: Kappa High School

Kappa is a charter school authorized by a specialized private university (SPU), consistent with state charter law, with between 320 and 330 full-time students in grades 9 through 12. The school focuses on a college preparatory curriculum. Initially, it was located on a refurbished Catholic school campus. After raising $13.5 million, the school relocated to its current site (a converted college campus). Students are able to dually enroll in classes in high school and the SPU collegiate programs; these classes are taught at the high school. Teachers have to be approved as adjunct faculty at the SPU, and their class syllabi for 11th and 12th grade classes must be approved by the appropriate department chair at the SPU. Kappa teachers present the high school curriculum along with college-level material. There are two distinctive elements at Kappa:

- Career Focus is a work-readiness curriculum that centers on English, math, observation, business writing, reading, listening, looking for information,

and applied technology. This helps students identify potential career pathways. About 95% of Kappa students receive a National Career Writing
Certificate, which is a portable work credential.

· When the school relocated to the current campus, the administration
began to work with the world headquarters of the sponsoring corpora-
tion. This relationship ultimately influenced the introduction of the corporate sponsor program (CSP) into the curriculum, an inquiry-based,
modular-designed program for teaching and learning aligned with both
state curriculum standards and the components of the Partnership for 21st
Century Skills framework.[49] The underlying rationale is that real-world
applicability is made possible through community, business, and school
collaborations.

The CSP started as a stand-alone class, where 15 modules were taught in
sequence over two and one-half years. After the state implemented new comprehensive graduation standards, Kappa moved toward incorporating the project-
based aspects of the CSP into different classes, becoming the first school to
do so. In order to meet state and college standards for dual enrollment while
incorporating CSP materials, Kappa had to extend the length of many of its
courses beyond one semester. The CSP is currently evolving into what is referred
to as "next-generation learning": instead of concentrating on teaching specific
projects, the focus is on using the CSP model as a resource for the philosophy of
teaching. The pressure to graduate students ready for college STEM courses was
not the only reason Kappa made curriculum changes. It turned out that most of
the high school students had to retake the dual-enrollment courses when they
went to college because they had not been allotted enough time to learn college-
level material, so the school decided to slow the process down.

Kappa was attracted to the CSP model because of its interdisciplinary technology concentration and its focus on presentation and communication skills.
Students choose among three different pathways at the school—business,
engineering/technology, or health care—each of which is supported by the CSP
curriculum. Kappa's CSP will often pilot new materials at the school and ask
for the staff's input. Material from the CSP is incorporated into the college
courses offered at the school, and Kappa has implemented a curriculum that
complements the CSP at the lower grade levels. The school administration has
proposed to the corporate sponsor that Kappa become the national institute for
the CSP, so other institutions could lease space and additional resources and
Kappa could offer distance-learning courses to other CSP schools.

Kappa carefully considers a student's academic exposure in its admissions process, including students who matriculate from lower-grade-level CSP schools on
their campus. If a student applies for admission to the 9th grade but the admin-

istration does not believe he or she will be able to keep pace with the other students, that student can be admitted but will have to start at a lower grade in Kappa's middle school. Sometimes parents object to this approach, but the school insists that this is best for the students. An administrator indicated that when they find students who are not academically prepared,

> we tell the . . . parents that it's . . . not because we want to do that, it's because we do not think they'll be successful unless they have the skills in order to start in the 9th grade. I mean, what's the use of starting them there if we know that even with all the things we have in place, they're not going to be able really to get up to that point and then they're just going to keep getting behind and behind? Most of the time, parents are okay if you say, "Maybe they should go back to 8th grade." They're okay with that. When you say two grades, especially if they're coming into 9th grade, they do not want to go back to 7th grade. They're not so sure. So, what they do is they might try a different school.

Kappa's graduation rate is between 93% and 95% for each 9th grade cohort. Most of the graduates are accepted by a college. The school is often recognized for its academic achievement and was named one of the best U.S. high schools by a national news magazine. The corporate sponsor also received an award from the governor for being part of the best public/private partnership in the state. Kappa has been asked to represent the CSP schools nationally.

KAPPA'S DEVELOPMENT

Kappa was founded using grant money from the state's educational and career-development agencies. Initially, the school enrolled students in the 11th and 12th grades. A number of students who enrolled at Kappa were below grade level in math, writing, and reading. Accordingly, the school administration decided to include additional grade levels in order to better prepare students for college-level work in high school. The school expanded to include 9th and 10th grades and eventually worked with the SPU to found an affiliated middle school on the same campus that focuses on strengthening each aspect of the pipeline so students have a chance to prepare for the high school.

Kappa has undergone a number of curriculum changes since its inception. Initially, the curriculum centered primarily around ACT Career Focus pathways, which at that time was a priority for the state's governor, who had developed other Career Focus centers. In the beginning, the school was not concerned with the state's educational standards, which were not rigorous. Local school districts could determine what was needed for graduation, and Kappa functioned as an independent school district. At the time, many students across the state were graduating without the skills necessary to be productive in the labor force or in higher education. A Kappa administrator noted: "All these school districts are turning out feel-good degrees. . . . They didn't care what skills you mastered. They had a diploma for everybody and everybody graduated. And so, what we did is, we ended up with one of the poorest educational systems in the state."

The high school has refined its grading policies as it adjusts to the credit partnerships with the SPU. College teachers working in high school classrooms did not always understand the challenges. When Kappa first started to offer college courses, many students were getting Ds; because the school did not want the classes to negatively impact students' college transcripts, a policy was adopted that students earn a grade of A, B, C, or "no credit."

The school has implemented a number of programs to expand opportunities for teacher input about changes and improvements necessary within the school. The administration established professional learning communities, which are teacher-guided professional development programs that focus on student motivation, best practices, technology, student/parent engagement, and skill development, using data analysis to inform content. Kappa has also invested in other instruments and collaborative efforts to improve their teachers' professional development, and school administrators often consult with the teachers to get feedback about the effectiveness of new initiatives. The school administration feels this approach helps the teachers take ownership:

> Rather than having three people . . . telling us what we should do as a school, to improve the school, it's the entire school coming together and saying, "This is how we really think that we should change" and everybody buying in and having everybody work together. So, we'll see how it goes, but everybody's been very, very happy about these changes so far.

RECONSTRUCTED ACADEMIC PROGRAM

When Kappa was at its original locale, the school environment was not conducive to learning, and Kappa administrators observed that students had difficulty adjusting to the school. At the school's new location, students appear to feel a sense of pride and ownership. One school representative offered the following insight about the original site: "That school is . . . a dark, dungeon-y kind of a school. We did our best to keep it clean and keep it beautiful, but the kids just didn't feel like this is their home." Later, this administrator noted: "There's just a big difference, a big shift. And watching the students and observing how well they're learning and knowing that they feel like 'This is where I am meant to be.' . . . A lot of times, they come from homes that are not so great, come here, they feel safe. . . . You just see them feeling at home."

Within the new learning environment, Kappa has developed a distinctive curriculum that links college preparation with a career focus. Key features of the curriculum and support programs include:

- *Science, Technology, Engineering, and Mathematics (STEM) Program.* Kappa implemented a new STEM program designed to increase the students' exposure to science. To facilitate this process, Kappa constructed five state-of-the-art, college-level labs for students in high school, as well as at lower grade levels. Elementary school teachers are required to teach one hour of math every day. Teachers with STEM expertise were hired to supplement grade school teachers.
- *Reach Program.* This program requires students to sign an agreement to be civically and academically responsible. The school promotes responsible behavior through posters that highlight respect, enthusiasm, achievement, citizenship, and hard work. The program was inspired by the Amistad Academy in New Haven, Connecticut.
- *Support Programs.* Students at Kappa are served three meals a day; Kappa sponsors their students' participation in week-long summer camps at the SPU; various colleges visit Kappa each year to recruit students; and students have access to study-abroad opportunities in conjunction with the CSP.
- *After-School Clubs and Sports.* Kappa offers a number of extracurricular clubs, including National Honor Society, Eco-Club, Newspaper Club, Chess Club, Debate Club, Dance Club, and Business Professionals of America. Kappa also offers some team sports: a boys' basketball team in both the middle and high schools; a girls' volleyball team in the middle school; and girls' softball in high school.
- *Academic Support.* Students who are in need of extra academic assistance can attend after-school tutoring programs. Kappa offers seminar classes to students in grades 7 through 9 to reinforce academic progress in their regular math and English courses. The school also has an ACT preparatory course.
- *Coordinated Learning Experiences.* Students at Kappa participate in a number of field trips throughout their matriculation, including trips to universities, museums, and businesses related to the career options of health, business, and engineering/technology.
- *Dual Enrollment.* Students can earn college credit through the SPU and other local universities.

FACING NEW CHALLENGES

Kappa continues to develop its programs and support services. Teachers and administrators are attuned to the students' attitudes and experiences as they make efforts to refine strategies; administrators are also receptive to teachers' concerns. The following, however, are a few of the challenges facing the school leaders as they look ahead.

First, both teachers and students have some difficulties adjusting to the philosophy of teaching that is part of the CSP. A school administrator offered the following insights about their teachers' initial response to the CSP:

> When you're teaching CSP, it's pretty open ended. What you're doing is you're giving the responsibility to the student, pretty much taking that away from the teacher. And, the teacher's only leading them. And . . . so, some teachers did find a little bit of a problem with that, I would say, but, as they saw, maybe, the benefits of it, and as they went through it maybe a couple times and they were more experienced with the way it is presented, they became more and more comfortable. So, right now, no one really questions it. They're pretty much all on board and . . . and, they do it.

Instead of the traditional teaching model—where the teacher presents a problem, provides an example, and uses a standard grading scale—students have to use their creativity to develop a solution to different problems, and the answers they craft may be different from those of their classmates. School officials recognize that this type of teaching and learning can initially be frustrating, especially for incoming 9th grade students.

Second, Kappa redesigned some aspects of professional development for its teachers. Teachers currently participate in various development opportunities but do not share the things they have learned with the larger community at the school. Kappa plans to implement a professional development structure where teachers instruct their colleagues about the things they learn and explain how those techniques can have a positive impact on students. While describing why the school was considering this approach, a Kappa administrator offered the following:

> The best way they're going to learn is from peer to peer, teacher to teacher . . . remediation . . . learning and teaching . . . I'm kind of struggling with spending all this money and then not having them be able to come back and really share. We just do not have the time in the calendar to have them do the teacher work days and giving them the adequate amount of time, all the time to really re-teach that teacher. So, really, we're going to have to do pullout programs or readjust the schedule next year or something along those lines to really give them professional development that will be sustainable.

Third, some teachers do not feel comfortable confiding concerns that emerge at the school to administrators, although administrators try to assure teachers that their input is important and teamwork is necessary for student success. A school administrator made the following comment: "We are just here as a community to develop and learn together . . . and really, if you have any concerns, please let me know. . . . I'm not gonna say anything. I'm more here to help you than to hurt you, to harm you, or anything. I only can grow as much as they'll let us all grow it together. So, I'm really guiding the ship in terms of really working together."

In sum, the challenges were severe at the time of our site visit in 2010, when few students were proficient in math (table 1.3). The curriculum restructuring at Kappa had not improved its math preparation by 2012–13. The school had still not achieved competitive status on math achievement tests, a critical indicator for a technology high school of this type, particularly for a school receiving substantial private investment.

Competitive Forces in Urban High Schools

Looking across these schools, it is evident that it takes investment to build distinctive schools, and the NYC schools did not enjoy the same levels of external funding from philanthropists. While CFES urban schools were successful in their support of student development, many faced challenges in the competitive environment created by the No Child Left Behind Act of 2001, coupled with changing state educational standards. All of the schools were striving for excellence, which created strong cultures in support of going to college. Themed schools provide avenues to careers, and in urban areas there is potential for a diverse array of niche-oriented schools to give families choices about the educational pathways for their children.

The idea that college is associated with higher earnings has been pervasive in selling the college preparation concept. Within any generation there will be differentials in earnings attributable to variations in degree attainment, but under current conditions educational uplift may be required in the working class and middle class, just to maintain their economic status. This means that there are mixed messages for students and families. Many working-class students struggle to complete a rigorous education, one not available to their parents, while parents contend with new expectations for their children as they face challenges to continue earning wages and supporting their families in local economies with fewer traditional jobs. Distinctive schools bolster students who want to achieve a higher education and strive for uplift.

Conclusions

The past three decades of reform have promoted a new vision for market-based urban schools. After generations of market reforms, public charter and district high schools within urban settings like New York City, Chicago, Detroit, and New Orleans now compete for students. There are underlying tensions: most schools that make progress have substantial external support from foundations or government grants; school-choice systems create new winners and losers among schools in competitive urban markets, thus increasing economic and social stratification and developing a de facto replication of some of the dysfunctional earlier tracking schemes; the base per-student funding often is not sufficient for schools to support mandated reforms without external support; and the overall rate of improvement is slow, as large numbers of students who start 9th grade still do not graduate from high school in many locations.

The competitive niches developed by these high schools were, for the most part, inherently aligned with grouping of college majors (e.g., STEM, engineering, liberal arts, teaching), but they further complicated the adaptive change processes in these schools. The content links between high school niches and prospective collegiate content raise issues for the development of an undergraduate college curriculum, which in the past had assumed students had a basic foundation of knowledge, but this issue has not been considered in either K–12 or higher education research on college preparation or college access.

Market mechanisms related to public-fund distribution (dollars following students) are the driving force behind the competitive niches in high schools: public schools use their competitive niches to attract students through the school-choice scheme. For the schools we studied, rising within the choice hierarchy seemed a more potent force driving niche development than competition per se. In addition, fund distribution within the public system had more influence on public schools than did their loss of students to public charters and private schools, at least in NYC. Since decisions about the life and death of public high schools are still largely driven by political factors—and the use of high-stakes tests—public high schools have an array of financial and policy constraints that public charters simply do not have to contend with as they develop their market niches.

It is evident that the district schools face competitive disadvantages. Not only do they lose public per-student funding for students who go to charters, but, because of their curriculum constraints, they are less attractive to foundations that want to fund a specific curriculum reform. In addition, market-based school reforms complicate the educational landscape middle school students and their parents face as they make school choices. Middle school students and families often have limited support when choosing a high school. Students who decide to attend a specialized-niche high school may be shaping their major, college choice, and career opportunities at the age of 13 without understanding the future implications. The principle behind markets is that the best schools will thrive, while others will have to restructure to attract students or close.

In the new system, the best schools attract the best students as well as the additional resources necessary to deliver a top-tier education. Unfortunately, there are currently not enough resources (tax dollars, donations, foundation grants, etc.) in the system to allow all students to get a high-quality education.

Math Problems

During the past three decades, all the states in the U.S. have raised their math standards, most have increased the level of math required for high school graduation, and the CCSS continues to promote further rigor. Recently, arguments for more stringent math requirements have become intertwined with advocacy for providing year-round and technical education for all students, an extension of the skills-based workforce narrative. Whether or not contentions about an undersupply of STEM-educated workers hold up, providing engaging education in advanced math remains a challenge in many high schools. This chapter examines how rationalizations about requiring advanced math courses have evolved and analyzes the ways the locally distinctive urban high schools adapted to these requirements.

Policy Rationales for Advanced Math

The evolving policy rationales for raising math requirements provide a remarkable illustration of the political uses of faulty logic and a misapplication of statistics to make policy claims. To tell this story, we review how research was misinterpreted to rationalize a new policy, the consequences of overlooking the role of funding in college access, and the ongoing debate over statistical errors in the math studies. We also examine the relationship between policy decisions and related outcomes, along with the ways these math rationales were grounded in the underlying policy logics of neoliberalism.

Situating the Math Rationales

Soon after *A Nation at Risk* was published,[1] policy researchers at Pelavin Associates were asked to examine why, starting in 1980, there was a gap between college enrollment rates for underrepresented minorities (Hispanics and African Americans) compared with Whites and Asian Americans.[2] We discuss this pivotal study and its legacy before discussing the career and technical education rationale for math reform.

The college enrollment gap that started in 1980 corresponded with a decline in need-based grants.[3] At the time, it was well known in the policy-research community that student aid was correlated with enrollment and persistence by low-income students.[4] Political operatives in the Reagan and the first Bush administrations would not include student aid in officially released policy reports on the topic of access.

The U.S. Department of Education (USDE) commissioned a minority enrollment study, but the agency would not release reports prepared for the study that focused on the effect declines in federal student aid had on enrollment or the impact of financial disparity between high-income and low-income groups.[5] Several researchers quit Pelavin Associates because they wouldn't make unproven claims about the reasons for the enrollment gap. The eventual report used the correlation between the completion of algebra in middle school and positive college outcomes as the explanation for the enrollment gap.[6] Had the report used comparisons of student cohorts entering college in 1972, 1980, and 1982 that had been provided to them by researchers who originally worked on the study,[7] these serious problems probably would have been avoided.

THE REPORT LEGACY

Subsequent researchers continued this trend as they developed statistical models for analyzing college enrollment.[8] Their regression models omitted financial aid as a variable influencing enrollment and persistence,[9] but the alliances of research and policymakers persisted with arguments that math education was the cause of the widening gap in enrollment after 1980. This conclusion was illogical, because math scores had not suddenly declined for underrepresented minorities in the early 1980s, nor had they improved for Whites. Income and student aid were realistically the only feasible explanations.

The policy alliances in Washington, D.C., were silent about the deception until the Advisory Committee on Student Financial Assistance (ACSFA) addressed the link between the enrollment gap and the decline in student aid in *Access Denied*.[10] Unfortunately, the ACSFA report did little to influence the rhetoric about the gap being attributable to math education.[11] In 2003, the ACSFA commissioned Donald Heller and William Becker to review some of the studies by the National Center for Education Statistics (NCES).[12] One of the major errors they found was omitted-variable bias (i.e., leaving student aid out of the equation). After two decades of exclusion, the ability to pay reemerged as a necessary part of policy studies, alongside academic preparation. Despite these findings, reports on access released by the USDE continued to focus on math and college preparation as the primary means of expanding access.

Eventually, a task force under the George W. Bush administration developed *A Test of Leadership*,[13] a report that emphasized both preparation and financial aid. This was not a perfect document, but it at least acknowledged some of the persistent modeling errors that had plagued research on the factors that affect educational attainment. The ACSFA has continued this line of research, most recently with *Inequality Matters*;[14] student aid is only now reemerging as a central issue in the access debates.

Advocacy for coupling a career and technical education (CTE) option with advanced math in small schools has a long history. Katherine M. Barghaus, Eric T. Bradlow, Jennifer McMaken, and Samuel H. Rikoon argue for multiple pathways in curricula:[15] "Multiple pathways refers to a strategy where students simultaneously enroll in traditional academic coursework along with one or more electives concentrated on the acquisition of career and technical skills" (p. 47). These authors offer the following logic for using statistical analyses for the construction of a new proposal for educational reform:

> The underlying logic of recommending public pathways in high school is that advanced academic knowledge is of limited utility if students are unable to connect the material learned in the traditional courses to the practical working world. Explicit instruction in both core skills derived from academic study and also generic skills helps students integrate their knowledge in the manner that will be required in the workforce. Hoachlander sees the implementation of multiple pathways in American high schools as a method of ensuring that academic coursework retains its rigor without losing its relevance to the real world contexts students find themselves in upon graduation. (p. 47)

The CTE logic traces back to research by Gary Hoachlander, a longtime advocate of integrating advanced math education with vocational education.[16] His research firm in Berkeley, California, has conducted studies of vocational education since the 1980s, and his work has enjoyed extensive support from the NCES and other educational agencies and organizations. His is also the firm that completed many of the NCES reports, using the correlation between math courses and educational attainment to advance the academic-preparation rationale.[17] Hoachlander, like Sol Pelavin, has been a long-time advocate for advancing math education, but the former has based his arguments on linkages.

To sum up, by the late 1980s the U.S. Department of Education had begun to promote an academic-preparation agenda as an access strategy. It was evident at the time that the increasing enrollment gap corresponded with declining college affordability, but research on the impact of grant aid was never officially disseminated. The released reports aligned with the agenda of emphasizing academic preparation, even as student loans made their way into the officially sanctioned discourse. Private firms were intertwined in this trajectory of policy research. Eventually, some of this ideological reporting of statistics underwent valid external review,[18] but the political insiders in the successive presidential

TABLE 2.1

State Policy Indicators for Selected Years, 1990–2010

	1990	1995	2000	2005	2010	2013
Policy-related variables						
States with established content standards in math	7	46	50	50	50	50
Require three or more math courses for graduation	11	12	21	28	31	42
Require at least algebra I or above	0	2	12	22	26	34
Exam required for high school diploma	15[a,b]	12	14	19	28	30
Percentage of schools participating in AP[c]	45%[a]	51%	58%	62%	67%	60%
SAT test variables						
Percentage of students taking SAT[d]	42%[a]	41%	44%	49%	47%	50%
SAT critical reading mean	500	504	505	508	500	496
SAT math mean	501	506	514	520	515	514
SAT critical writing mean[e]	—	—	—	—	491	488
SAT combined	1001	1010	1019	1028	1506	1498

Sources: St. John, Daun-Barnett, & Moronski-Chapman 2013, with updates from *2013 college-bound seniors: Total group profile report*, http://media.collegeboard.com/digitalServices/pdf/research/2013/TotalGroup-2013.pdf; "Detail on mathematics graduation requirements from public high schools by state [June 5, 2013]," www.centerforpubliceducation.org/Main-Menu/Policies/Understanding-the-Common-Core/Out-of-Sync-Many-Common-Core-states-have-yet-to-define-a-Common-Core-worthy-diploma/Detail-on-mathematics-graduation-requirements-from-public-high-schools-by-state.pdf.
[a]Based on numbers reported in 1991.
[b]This number is higher than anticipated but cannot be externally validated.
[c]Reflects the median percentage for AP and the median dollars per FTE for K–12 expenditures.
[d]These numbers are the national figures reported by the Educational Testing Service.
[e]Writing section implemented in March 2005.

administrations continued to overlook the role of financial aid in providing an opportunity for low-income, college-prepared students to enroll in four-year colleges.

Reform Rationales Continue Math Deceptions

The policy rhetoric that rationalizes higher math standards continues in CCSS. We provide a brief review of the evidence about outcomes before summarizing how CCSS math standards perpetuate the common logics of pipelines and educational uplift that underlie the math rationale.

ACTUAL OUTCOMES

By the middle 2000s, most states had switched to K–12 policies that were based on the flawed research, but there was no change in college enrollment rates, especially in four-year colleges.[19] The new policies had unintended consequences, including: (1) the new math and testing requirements caused serious problems in schools that had not previously offered advanced math courses;[20] and (2) multilevel statistical models using national databases revealed that, although scores on the SAT improved when the new policies were implemented, there was also a decrease in high school graduation rates.[21] In addition, although higher percentages of African Americans graduating from high school were prepared for college, many of them were from low-income families for whom college cost too much, even with maximum grant aid.

Trends in the adoption of higher math requirements and related outcomes are evident in states' policies on high school graduation requirements (table 2.1). Only 7 states had established state-level content standards for math in 1990, but all 50 had done so by 2000, illustrating the influence of math researchers.[22] The number of states requiring at least three math courses rose from 11 in 1990 to 42 in 2013. Typically, multiple new policies were being implemented simultaneously without coordination or consideration of the changes required within schools to implement the new policies.

THE "NEW" MATH STANDARDS

The recommendations from the CCSS do not substantially alter the requirements, but they do advocate a new approach to teaching;[23] for example, they suggest offering algebra in 8th grade (p. 15). The report provides the following talking points for reform advocates about college and career ready math:

1. *Improved math achievement.* Juniors and seniors who take higher-level mathematics make larger gains during the last two years of high school.
2. *College success.* Enrollment in high-level mathematics is the best predictor of college success. According to research by Achieve, students' enrollment in advanced mathematics actually doubles their chances of graduating from college by reducing remedial rates.
3. *Career success.* Technology has driven up the complexity of virtually every career. The advanced mathematics skills required by electricians, plumbers, and heating and air conditioning [workers] now match what is necessary to do well in college.
4. *Level playing field.* Advanced mathematics promotes equity in college access and success as well as in economic opportunity. Taking advanced mathematics has greater influence on whether students graduate from college than any other factor—including family background. For those students who go straight to college, taking advanced mathematics in high school boosts completion rates by 36 to 59 percent among low-income students and from 49 to 59 percent among Latino students. (p. 16)

These statements, taken directly from promotional material for the CCSS math standards, forward the illogic and the misleading statistics in the report to make an access argument that ignores the role of finances. Specifically, this contention neglects other correlations that link more directly to college enrollment by low-income students: (1) financing for schools, the most critical link to educational improvement in urban schools; and (2) need-based financial aid, a necessity for access to and success in four-year colleges for students from low-income families. If a more balanced approach is not used in policy rhetoric, the claims about math reform will continue to be a false promise for many low-income students.

These arguments distract the attention of policymakers and the public away from policies that could make a difference in degree-completion rates. Many analysts in the informal alliance of policy insiders (including those preparing the report by Achieve and collaborators) continue to uncritically accept these rationales about standards and the more-sophisticated number spinning in reports on earnings.[24] Given the role of public finance in inequalities in education and income, the perpetuation of this flawed policy rationale is astounding. While Anthony P. Carnevale, Nicole Smith, and Jeff Strohl extol the economic virtues of degrees in STEM disciplines, they never even mention how school funding and student aid are related to academic success and degree completion. With a growing number of college-prepared, low-income students being squeezed out of four-year colleges because they can't afford them, it is troubling that the policy reports continue to be so unbalanced.

Policy Logics Underlying Math Rationales

The neoliberal policy logics of innovation, choice, and efficiency aligned well with the rationales that emerged for promoting math education (table 2.2). In the early 2000s, arguments were made for aligning high school and community college education, a strategy promoted through national meetings with researchers, policy analysts, activists, foundation representatives, and policymakers.[25] Like the current push for the production of degrees in STEM fields, the initiative was rationalized on Carnevale's analyses of degrees and employment.[26] As discussed in chapter 1, this rationale was also seriously flawed.

The 9–14 rationales carried forward the same logic about math but reasoned that community colleges could teach these courses. This strategy was widely adopted and improved community college enrollment rates, but it also contributed to declining retention rates in those same colleges. Often the college credits were financed through the K–12 funding scheme, providing free college credit for high school students. After they graduated from high school, many students discovered they could not afford full-time enrollment in the two-year college. Often students alternate working and attending college, extending their time-to-degree beyond the three-year threshold for reporting on degree completion in community colleges. There are also problems with the transferability of com-

TABLE 2.2

Policy Logics Used in Math Rationales

Policy logics (*reform rationales*)	Innovation (explicit)	Choice (explicit)	Efficiency (implicit and deceptive)
Academic access	Focused on math as the reason for increased inequality in access, ignoring student financial aid	Used improved education for all as a means of dismantling vocational education; postponed career education to the postsecondary level	Shifted the focus of higher education reform to K–12 education; distracted access advocates from considering the implications of cuts in need-based grants and a shift to loans
9–14 education	Focused on the realignment of high schools and community colleges, using community colleges to provide advanced math education in high schools	Integrated collegiate math into the high school curriculum via alignment of college credits with high school courses; bridge to contemporary CTE rationales	Substantially increased community college enrollment in many urban areas, but contributed to the decline in degree-completion rates; community college math often did not easily transfer as advanced STEM courses into four-year colleges
Career and technical education (CTE)	Focused on linking math education and CTE as a means of promoting STEM career pathways	Used urban school markets to promote CTE; linked to advanced math courses; aligned with urban school choice	Cutbacks in school funding rationalized by school choice; rationalized high tuition / high loans, based on expected earnings in STEM professions
STEM career pathways	Focused on the goal of preparing STEM workers for a global workforce	Encouraged urban students to take steps to prepare for STEM fields by taking CTE courses, limiting options in small high schools	Failure to fund need-based grants contributed to a decline in minority degree-completion rates, despite improved math preparation based on test scores
Career-connected	Focused on educational links to the labor markets	Linked career content to advanced college prep curriculum	Used markets to stimulate change; reduced funding through policy deception

munity college courses to STEM programs in four-year colleges (see the Beta High School case-study section below), contributing to the growing number of students requiring remedial education.

The rationale for realigning career education with advanced math courses is fraught with irony, coming at a time when many of the general and technical pathways within traditional comprehensive high schools have been eliminated as part of implementing the new, higher-level graduation requirements, and the smaller size of the new high schools limits the number of vocational options they can offer. Technical and academic skills in a vocational content need to be reintegrated into the curriculum.

Math education is central to the global discourse on the science and engineering workforce. The math rationales were aligned with neoliberal arguments about efficiency, choice, and innovation, along with arguments for STEM education. These rationales have become a global force, with the unintended consequences of undermining fairness in access and increasing economic stratification in higher education internationally.[27]

Engaging Students in Learning Advanced Mathematics

We now turn to a new aspect of the math challenge: the systematic failure to teach math courses in ways that engage all of the students required to take them. Part of the problem is that for generations in cities like Detroit, most high schools offering vocational and regular diplomas did not have advanced math courses; college preparatory curricula were available at only a few select high schools in most cities. As new reforms have been implemented, many urban school children are the first generation in their family to take advanced math and thus may have difficulty getting help with their math homework. Further complicating the situation, many math teachers who did not teach advanced math in the past have not received any additional support or training. Our analyses focus on the ways schools adapted to the new state-mandated requirements. Based on our case studies, we argue that engaging math instruction is crucial as standards and requirements rise.

Underlying Problems with Math-Education Policy

It is important to acknowledge that the higher-level requirements were originally proposed as an instrument for increasing college access and success, and they continue to be rationalized on this basis. Improving the percentage of students who complete advanced math—and maintaining or increasing the graduation rates in states that require it—means we must focus on math teaching. We summarize the research on improving and updating math education to further explore the underlying reasons for the differences between math achievement and college success, two related matters that are not necessarily causally linked.

RESEARCH ON MATH EDUCATION

Research has emphasized raising standards as a means of reducing inequality. How and when algebra should be taught was a hot topic as the new math requirements evolved.[28] There was research indicating that instructional reform in urban middle schools could help students narrow the mathematics performance gap.[29] By 2000, all states had adopted standards aligned with the National Council of Teachers of Mathematics' (NCTM) principles and guidelines.

There is little doubt that math education in algebra and geometry, which must be mastered before moving on to more advanced algebraic equations, remained a critical issue during the first decade of the new century. Authors of the NCTM standards argued that teachers should pay attention to the standards in their classroom teaching.[30] Yet, as these standards were adopted, research did not show a clear relationship between the standards and learning outcomes.[31] In their review, Karen Graham and Francis Fennell concluded that improvements in teacher education and professional development were crucial.[32] In a similar vein, Jo Boaler argued that research into inequality in math preparation must go beyond the curriculum and pay attention to the methods used in classrooms.[33] Raising math standards and improving teaching are different mechanisms for improving students' math achievement. The integration of culturally and contextually situated pedagogies into math education remains in the domain of adaptive instruction and thus is difficult to promote through centrally mandated policies. It is essential to engage math educators in the process of reflecting on how their students learn math and how to adapt to meet their pupils' learning needs, an issue we examine in our case studies.

Now that advanced math is commonly required for high school graduation, engaged math learning by urban students becomes even more important.[34] Robert Moses's Algebra Project is one of the most noteworthy successes.[35] His approach is centered on arguments about civil rights and focuses on teaching algorithmic thinking in ways related to the life experiences of middle school students. Moses and others have participated in an initiative—using methods derived from the Algebra Project—in Ypsilanti, Michigan (in collaboration with the University of Michigan), but to date this intervention has not been the subject of research studies, nor is there evidence of improvement in school outcomes.

ENGAGING MATH EDUCATION

Trends in International Mathematics and Science Studies (TIMSS), an international survey of student achievement, has become an important resource because it provides an opportunity to examine the relationship between methods and outcomes across nations. In their review of previous research on TIMSS, Joseph Furner and Sally Robinson concluded that preparing teachers in the use of interactive methods was important, including having them show students how geometric patterns relate to algebraic equations.[36] In comparative studies, content activities designed to help students discover and retain mathematical concepts emerged as important elements, along with contextual factors.[37]

In the 2007 TIMSS study, Singapore, Korea, and Japan came out on top in 8th grade math, while the United States was average in algebra (ranked eighth) and below average in geometry (ranked fourteenth).[38] Math strategies that were positively associated with high test scores in Japan included using basic math (addition, subtraction, etc.) without a calculator and teaching procedures for complex problem solving. Cooperative learning had a negative association with scores in both the United States and Japan.[39] Cross-national comparisons stressed the importance of teaching methods and teacher preparation.[40] The TIMSS research reinforces the use of manipulation and the discovery of formulaic concepts as a part of math teaching in advanced subjects.

The international studies supported the idea that the United States needed to alter its methods of teaching algebra and geometry. The realization that experimentation was necessary to increase the percentage of students who would be successful in advanced math came at the same time as states were requiring more students to take these courses. One of the problems facing many educators who attempt to innovate in math is that they can run into problems with testing. There were numerous innovations in math education in the 2000s, but researchers have only recently begun to examine outcomes regarding student success. In a qualitative study of early college high schools (ECHS), Kennedy Ongaga found that caring relationships with teachers in schools and a rigorous, challenging curriculum were important factors for student success.[41] At the same time, Ongaga expressed concern that foundation funding for the ECHS strategy could be lost at the very time research was beginning to show what worked within these schools. We argue that the exploration of what practices are successful in schools is a crucial step in research on math education.

RESEARCH ON THE IMPACT OF MATH POLICY CHANGES

The systematic study of the impact of large-scale interventions on student learning has proven difficult because of the complexities in tracking student cases across grade levels and educational systems. For example, when students move from public middle schools to public charter schools, most cities do not track them.

One city that has made progress in this area is Chicago, where, for more than a decade, universities have collaborated with schools on data systems. High school dropout rates did not increase when Chicago implemented its requirement for algebra in 9th grade, but indicators from data analyses raised questions about the policy, including increased course failure and no improvement in high school graduation and college-going rates.[42] Math researchers from DePaul University, the University of Chicago, and the University of Illinois–Chicago have had some recent success with using data that tracks large numbers of students to study the efficacy of experiments that focus on preparing urban students for algebra,[43] but they are still seeking funding for large-scale experiments in the city and have not ventured into the advanced subjects of geometry and algebra II now required for students in many states. Expanding access to these subjects—in classrooms with skilled advanced-math teachers—remains the crucial issue, and it is especially problematic for students with no family history of this type of rigorous college preparatory math curriculum. Sadly, access to high-quality advanced math remains an elusive goal, especially in urban schools.

While there is international research on math practices related to math outcomes, there is not much research on the impact of math-reform methods in urban systems. There is a serious need for studies tracking students across urban schools into college, especially ones that evaluate and contribute to the refinement of intervention methods in advanced math education. Unfortunately, there is very little information on how new standards have been implemented and on the impact of these changes.

THE PROSPECT OF ENGAGED MATH INSTRUCTION

If advanced math is a requirement for graduation, math education should be delivered in ways that are engaging for most students. Another way to look at the problem is that historically, only a minority of students had access to and success in advanced math courses in high school, making it difficult to assess whether the ways advanced math has been taught made it accessible to most students and whether math teachers were adequately prepared to teach the subject matter. The problems in aligning the content and pedagogy of advanced math courses merit more attention.

There has long been a debate about math content and pedagogy. Historically, the debates focused on the sequencing of content,[44] but more recently, researchers have found that to reach greater equity in math acquisition, it is necessary to pay attention to differences in the ways students learn advanced math in their classrooms.[45] Achieving greater equity in learning advanced math is crucial, especially as current standards demand higher levels of math. If students are required to pass a subject to graduate, they should have a fair opportunity to learn it.

Math Reform in the NYC Public High Schools

All four of the NYC high schools we studied scored higher on math achievement than the city average.[46] In the NYC public schools, however, the district chooses the math curriculum as well as the math sequence, and these predetermined choices can cause problems for some themed high schools.

ANALYSIS OF OUR INTERVIEWS

For the NYC schools with STEM themes, the state's math requirements were not well aligned with the district-mandated curriculum. Many students in these schools were not ready for integrated algebra; offering remedial math ate up the budget that could have been used to offer pre-calculus and calculus, and only a few students were ready for those courses. This was particularly true at Onye Nkuzi and Remus High Schools. The core curriculum simply did not always work as intended. One teacher raised this issue when comparing the NYC schools to schools nationally: "New York State did this [reorganized the advanced math sequence when] . . . everybody else in the country was still doing algebra, [geometry,] trigonometry. So they said 'It's still algebra and trigonometry and geometry, but a combo' and they just moved the units around. And it was difficult and it didn't work."

The principal at Remus, a medium-sized comprehensive high school with multiple themes (including engineering), developed an approach to working through challenges arising from the misalignment of school strategy and a predetermined curriculum: "Our math folks meet together once a week, our English folks meet together, our science, and here we're, we're talking about instruction and assessment and the curriculum on a weekly basis, and what does that look like."

Finding and taking the time for this type of intentional, participatory, and engaging process of change can be difficult, but Remus's administration considered it to be central to the school's success. Of the four NYC schools we studied, Remus was best able to offer the requisite, challenging advanced math curriculum for students in the engineering and medical programs, although they worked with a university partner because the high school's budget was too constrained to offer these courses on their own. Remus also confronted the challenge of developing remedial math courses for students in the general curriculum, and their average math score was in the middle range for NYC high schools (table I.3).

COMPARISON OF CHANGE PROCESSES IN NYC PUBLIC DISTRICT HIGH SCHOOLS

NYC requires six semester credits in yearlong courses in algebra I, geometry, and algebra II. To graduate with a Regents' Diploma, students have to pass the state exam in one of these courses; to complete an advanced Regents' Diploma, students have to pass the state exams in all three subjects. The alignment of these courses, the curriculum, and the statewide Regents' Exams limits adaptive change (table 2.3). In addition, at Remus and Onye Nkuzi, student readiness for algebra I was a problem, and both schools had to increase their remedial math programs. We conclude that the process of shifting to a college preparatory model for all schools was not well conceived: requirements were raised, but the on-the-ground reality of educational challenges was not considered. Adminis-

TABLE 2.3
Mathematics Challenges in Selected NYC Public District High Schools

NYC requirements	Emergent challenges	Adaptations
Acme Collegiate Academy: to graduate, student has to complete six semester credits in math (using the CCSS) and pass exams for each year	Students enter unprepared for 9th grade algebra; students are expected to complete four years of math, including algebra II and pre-calculus	Students receive extensive tutoring
Onye Nkuzi High School: same as above	The school admits students of all academic levels and interests through a district lottery; many students assigned to the school enter several grades behind in mathematics	The school offers double blocks of 9th grade integrated algebra, which includes a review of pre-algebra as well as a survey of algebra; algebra and geometry classes are frequently taught with double class time
Remus High School: same as above	A number of students enter unprepared for high school mathematics; the school offers remediation through pre-calculus; due to budget constraints, this limits the upper-level mathematics offerings	Partnership with the adjacent university enables dual enrollment in advanced mathematics courses for the school's engineering and medical academy students
21st Century Technological Academy: same as above	Students enter with more ability than preparation; students are required to complete four years of math through calculus	Students are immersed in an advanced curriculum; the school provides after-school tutoring to support the students

trators scrambled by shifting the amount of time students spend in math courses and school resources to meet the challenges that emerged.

Comparison of Public Charter High Schools

The four locally distinctive charter high schools we studied also experienced problems with math education, finding it difficult to meet the standards in their states. They offered algebra, geometry, algebra II, and one or more advanced course to at least some students. The average scores in math in three of the four charters exceeded their state averages.

The charter laws in the different states define how schools accept students, whether by a lottery or other means. Alpha, Beta, and Sigma High Schools did not consider scores for admission, but instead developed a supplemental curriculum for high-need students within the school when they found part of their attrition was due to the rigor of the math requirements. Kappa High School, which used test scores for admission, developed a junior high school program:

students whose math was not up to the level expected for 9th grade attended the junior high school program for a year or two; those requiring more than a year of extra work often chose not to attend.

Sigma High School's mathematics program was standards based and college preparatory. Alpha High School had both honors and regular sections. The 9th grade students took algebra I for 90 minutes every day, while all of the students' other classes met for 90 minutes every other day. At one time, the school offered pre-algebra, but the students who might earlier have placed into pre-algebra now take a math-resource class during 9th and/or 10th grade to support their math-skills development.

All four of the public charter schools had undergone changes in their approaches to advanced math instruction and the curriculum after challenges emerged from their original math models. Alpha, Beta, and Sigma addressed the obstacles through change strategies that involved teachers in a review of the challenges and in testing of new strategies (table 2.4). At Alpha and Beta, the math educators and school leadership devised new approaches, based on their own assessment of the causes for the challenge (see the Beta case study below). At Sigma, math educators in both the high school and middle school were involved in planning for the realigned 9–14 model. In contrast, Kappa leadership slowed down the math sequence, teaching one-semester college-level courses over two semesters. Kappa also required entering students with low scores to repeat a grade of middle school—a remediation strategy—before allowing them to enter 9th grade. Interestingly, and perhaps not surprisingly, Kappa was the one school in the study that did not have math test scores that were higher than their state's average. Perhaps the engagement of math educators in the revision of curriculum is linked to finding better ways to accelerate math learning, an intermediate hypothesis we explore further in the conclusion to this chapter.

Case Study: Beta High School

Beta High School was founded (with extensive external support) as a public charter high school on the campus of a private university within a large midwestern city. The majority of Beta's students were Black, but there were also White and Hispanic students from the city. With support from a major national foundation, the school was designed to test new strategies for instruction in math and other areas of the curriculum. It is not unusual for students who enter Beta in the 9th grade to profess aspirations for careers in math-related fields, such as engineering. The challenge is in finding creative ways to make up for lost time, in order to bring students' math proficiency to the level necessary for them to graduate from high school and be successful in a college engineering program. According to Beta's director of curriculum, students entering in the 9th grade score from 4th to 9th grade math-proficiency levels on exams that

TABLE 2.4
Adaptive Changes in Math Education in Public Charter High Schools

Original approach	Emergent challenges	Adaptations
Alpha High School: integrated math sequence comprised of concepts from algebra I, geometry, and algebra II across four years of high school; remediation courses taught after school by volunteers	Students entered 9th grade needing remediation to be successful in algebra I; course sequence did not offer calculus; math educators in the school engaged in redesign of the math curriculum	Encourage all incoming students to participate in a five-week summer prep program; remediation addressed during the school day, as double-block scheduling for 9th graders and academic workshops for 10th graders; calculus offered as a pilot program in SY 2010–11 for students with high math skills
Beta High School: initially students took math courses offered by the community college	Students placed below grade level, with significant basic-skills deficiencies; scored below the ACT benchmark; students were not prepared for STEM programs; math educators and school leaders collaborated to develop a new approach	Developed an on-campus program so students could be better prepared for STEM fields at four-year colleges; curriculum sequence is inquiry-based 9th grade math, geometrical optics and algebra, algebra II, pre-calculus, and calculus (offered to advanced students); development of 7th and 8th grade pipeline
Kappa High School: all students were required to successfully complete three units of mathematics (algebra I, geometry, algebra II); in-house assessments; dual-enrollment courses were taught on college campuses; students transferred in at any time; traditional pedagogy, with the exception of the dual-enrollment courses; students were expected to be college ready by junior year	Many students entered 9th grade one to three years behind in math skills; assessments not linked to ACT, Work Keys, or other standardized assessments; students transferring after 9th grade experienced culture shock; pedagogy not based on developing twenty-first-century skills; many students not college ready by 11th grade; students were not testing into college math; school leadership slowed down the math sequence	Math curriculum mapped by teachers to ACT math readiness, state merit-curriculum standards, and Work Keys; algebra I the lowest-level math course offered at the high school; remediation offered through Title I programs (after school); algebra II the college gateway course, with dual enrollment for both high school and college credit; taught at the high school by teacher hired as adjunct faculty by the college; mapped to college syllabus and state curriculum standards; probability, statistics, and pre-calculus added as fourth-unit options
Sigma High School: initially the school had a self-directed, unstructured curriculum that consisted of packets of workbooks; the goal was for students to take Mathematics of Finance at the community college; students were expected to test into college-level math during their junior year on completion of the high school math curriculum	Students matriculated below grade level, with significant basic-skills deficiencies; many students had difficulty testing into college-level math; math educators redesigned the math program	Teachers designed a standards-based curriculum; direct instruction linked to a student-learning-outcomes assessment plan; students required to complete four units of math to graduate (algebra I, geometry, algebra II, and advanced math); developed creative ways to introduce additional math courses; curriculum aligned to prepare students to take college algebra as seniors

measure academic performance, and they lack critical-thinking skills. As one math teacher put it: "They're at grade level because they've memorized their formulas. They know how to spit problems back out, but getting them to think about anything is really complicated."

The state requires math proficiency through algebra II for high school graduation, which is a high standard. Students entering 9th grade lacking basic skills face significant challenges in meeting this requirement, as measured by passing state exams and scoring well on the ACT. For Beta, the challenges are meeting annual yearly progress levels, obtaining sufficient funding, and fulfilling its mission as a college preparatory school. Given its emphasis on engineering, engaging students in meaningful ways and working towards filling proficiency gaps in math has been a focus for its teachers. Toward this end, Beta has taken the following steps:

- Added a junior high school and pushed the 9th grade basic-skills course into the 7th and 8th grades.
- Aligned the math curriculum with the state's curriculum benchmarks and standards for math and ACT objectives.
- Offered a summer math academy and identified sources of tuition assistance to fund it.
- Focused on algebra II.
- Used graphing calculators and other technology.
- Provided focused study sessions.
- Collaborated with two local universities to create an inquiry-based 9th grade math course in which students plan and build 3-D model homes. The course is interdisciplinary and introduces many of the math standards tested on the state exam.
- Collaborated with the Engineering Department at a local university to engage students in a national research laboratory to develop an inquiry-based course that teaches the principles of algebra and geometry through the field of optics, using many laboratory activities.
- Added pre-calculus and calculus courses to introduce students to additional mathematical language.
- Sent the lead math teacher to professional development conferences.
- Encouraged math teachers to begin an informal mentoring program.

The math curriculum is currently lockstep. Students are placed into courses based on their test results. A Beta math teacher commented that some students do not make a serious effort to do well on the test and are placed below their actual proficiency level. A new preparatory course was added as an option in the 9th grade for students not ready for advanced courses,[47] a cleverly disguised review of 7th and 8th grade math. Drawing from multiple fields, including engineering and accounting, students review proportions, ratios, linear equations, and other basic concepts while constructing a three-dimensional model house. In 10th grade, geometrical optics and algebra provides another opportunity for students to enact math concepts in an engaging, experiential format through the study of optics.

Algebra II and pre-calculus are taught in a traditional lecture format to expose students to the type of teaching they will experience in college, but at a slower pace. The first year these courses were offered in this format, students floundered. The Beta teachers have now integrated group problem solving into the courses, with more favorable results. Although the state only requires proficiency in algebra II, Beta teachers feel that their students are better served by being exposed to pre-calculus prior to entering college. Few students have taken calculus. All students in the program have passed the math portion of the state tests; ACT test results are still below state levels but are steadily improving.

The Beta faculty has made adaptations to the math sequence over the years. They described the original math curriculum as "patchy" and "existential." A teacher noted: "We ran into a problem, and actually when I taught high school math here . . . our curriculum was kind of all over the place because we were a newer school. . . . We started a 9th grade academy that kind of was supposed to help catch them up, kind of get everybody on the same page for the high school classes, more people would be eligible for the upper classes, especially math, pre-calculus, or calculus"

Teachers found that the original curriculum lacked the rigor necessary to prepare students for exams or for four-year college programs in engineering and other STEM fields. Many students took core classes at the local community college, but this practice did not work for advanced math: "The community college courses were not as rigorous as what we would do here. . . . So they were not as well prepared and so a lot of those kids changed their major from engineering . . . or they downgraded from engineering to engineering technology, which is not as rigorous." Taking advantage of community college courses in math had become a barrier to college success for Beta graduates.

After a significant number of the original math faculty had left the school, the first-year academy concept was established, including organizing the school into thematic clusters. Teachers hypothesized that making math enjoyable while aligning the courses with the indicators would improve outcomes.

The addition of a junior high school evolved after representatives from Beta visited successful schools throughout the country and felt that having a junior high school had been a factor in their success. Beta's teachers opted to move the current 9th grade course to the 7th and 8th grades. The principal noted: "I see a lot of creativity. We're teaching the math associated with building a house in 7th and 8th grade and we, we still have to do it one more year in 9th grade, but we will move all of that. We just started 7th grade last year so this is the first year we've had 7th and 8th." Teachers were able to move courses around and develop a new curriculum whenever they thought it was necessary.

At Beta, 100% of their students taking the state test passed on their first try in 2010, 2011, and 2012; in 2013, 96.2% passed on their first try and the rest passed in 11th grade. Additionally, 10th and 11th graders were tested for the first time using the ACT End-of-Course Assessments and algebra I subtests, with Beta students performing above the high school pool average in each category. Nonetheless, reports indicate that, on average, Beta students are performing just below the ACT benchmark in math and below the state average; some students still place into developmental math courses, such as algebra, in college. The creation of the 7th and 8th grade pipeline should decrease the range of challenges for Beta's math teachers and result in an improvement in standardized-test achievements. The most recent scores indicate Beta students continue to perform at higher-than-average levels in math (table I.3)

As Beta tried to improve its math scores and close proficiency gaps, questions arose about teacher assessment, mentoring, and professional development. Prior to 2011, teacher evaluations in the state were conducted every few years, based on observations by the principal; teachers were rated "satisfactory" or "unsatisfactory." Evaluations were generally not used in promotion and termination decisions. Since 2011, evaluations occur every year (except for the top teachers). Half of the evaluation is based on observation, but the other half is based on the heinous "value-added" measure, which incorporates student test scores. The evaluations are now used to determine promotion and termination decisions.[48]

Although team building and informal mentoring relationships appear to be encouraged, no formal mentoring program has been established. Professional development was encouraged, but there appears to be no mechanism to support it.

Lessons Learned from the Cases

Urban public charter high schools, like their public district counterparts in NYC, faced challenges when implementing new curriculum models and requirements. When math educators in charter schools focused on finding better methods to encourage student learning in advanced math subjects, they solved emergent challenges—a pattern evident in Alpha, Beta, and Sigma High Schools. Math educators expressed frustration with the curriculum when their responses to the challenges facing student success in math were constrained by their district's curriculum—a pattern apparent in NYC schools and Kappa High School. The NYC public schools found ways through the problem, as evidenced by their students' math scores.

A crucial step seems to be the engagement of math educators in the process of solving pedagogical challenges. Historically, urban school systems have had only a few high schools that offered advanced math; students were tested before they could enter, and the curriculum and student courses were aligned in ways that resulted in higher-than-average math achievement. In Kappa High School, teachers were hired on one-year contracts, which made it more risky to voice discontent to central administrators. The resolution at Kappa—slowing down the curriculum—did not improve test scores.

Three of the public charter schools admit most of their students through a lottery. Students do not have to have any particular achievement level to gain entry, so these schools differ in a basic and fundamental way from the older college prep high schools. Clearly, the math teachers in Beta High School were dedicated to solving the learning challenges facing their students, as was the case at the other innovative high schools we visited. Adaptations were made when intended procedures did not work. Beta High School, like Kappa and Sigma,[49] ran into difficulties because the community college courses their students were taking lacked the rigor needed for advanced math in a four-year college and did not prepare students for STEM programs.

It appears that the four public charter high schools we studied were doing a better job of providing opportunities for advanced math than the NYC public high schools. There were relatively high dropout rates at Alpha, Beta, and Kappa, however, and it was assumed that these dropouts went on to other high schools in their cities.[50] It is difficult to measure the comparative success of different types of high schools without data systems that can track students after their departure (either by dropout or transfer) to determine their eventual outcome.

Serious challenges face urban high schools when implementing new math standards. When teachers were engaged in decisions about how to adapt instruction for advanced math courses to serve a larger percentage of their school population, their schools had a more measurable success. Historically, insufficient attention has been given to math pedagogy because of a preoccupation with finding appropriate sequences of content;[51] a new challenge is to find ways to teach this content successfully to the majority of students. Both Alpha and Beta High Schools had teachers who experimented with new approaches and eventually took responsibility for teaching advanced math courses. At Beta, the collaboration with the engineering program at a local university helped strengthen the math offerings.

Conclusion

The global, neoliberal educational reform rationales focus on STEM education as a means of workforce uplift and on math education as a crucial link between high school and college success. In this section, we discuss policy rationales, the urban context, and the practice of math reform.

The Policy Promoting Math Reform

The rationale for math reform in the United States has been based on analyses of trends and correlations. To restate the contemporary rationale used to promote CCSS math standards: (1) there is a gap between the number of STEM graduates and jobs for these graduates; (2) there is a correlation between high school math courses and college completion rates in STEM fields; and (3) the notion of raising requirements and standards was advanced politically by arguing that correlation means causality, and that changes in requirements and standards will raise college graduation rates.

The core rationalization used by advocates of math reform is based on statistical correlations between math courses and college completion, an argument dependent on proofiness for a quarter century. This rationalization is perpetuated by researchers who used the same untested assumptions time after time, but these assumptions have proven false. Specifically, all states have raised standards and increased graduation requirements in math, based on these arguments. The evidence on test scores supports the core claim of reform advocates that these policy changes improve achievement, as measured by tests (we used the SAT, but similar patterns were evident from analyses of the ACT), but the policy changes did not result in narrowing the gap in college graduation rates between minority and majority students, which had been part of the rationalization argument.

In light of our analyses of changes in funding and markets in chapter 1, it is evident that implementation of high tuition/high loans policies corresponds with the recently widening gap in college completion rates. Given the improvement in math achievement for students entering four-year colleges—as indicated by the growing numbers of students taking entrance exams and their increased average scores—and the expanding gap in college completion, it is obviously false to continue to argue that raising standards and requirements further will reduce this gap, at least if there are not concurrent changes in public funding for schools and need-based grants. In other words, *corrections in the way public finance is used to promote fairness in the higher education market must occur before math improvements can have an impact on reducing gaps in degree completion between minority and majority students in STEM and other fields.*

The urban market model has been promoted, in part, through linking career and advanced math contents as a means of creating distinctive market niches in urban high schools. The arguments for this are: (1) linking career content with math content will engage urban students and provide career pathways; (2) using this approach and dividing big schools into smaller, thematic schools will overcome the historical limitations of tracking, and (3) taking this approach will improve urban economies. Each of these notions merits scrutiny, given recent trends in policy and outcomes.

The argument that the new CTE logic about math education will overcome discrimination is an overreach. While tracking was a problem relative to racial segregation within schools, the CTE argument simply does not fit many urban public school systems that service mostly poor and underrepresented minority students. Many middle-class families migrated to the suburbs in cities like Detroit because of the flow of jobs, the quality of the schools, and a deterioration of social life (due to the concentration of urban poverty). In the cities and schools we visited, most of the students were underrepresented minorities from low-income families. Racial aspects of tracking are not as salient in these newly reconfigured schools. Whether the new schools will attract more middle-class students into the urban public district and charter schools remains uncertain. Many cities like New York, New Orleans, Chicago, and Detroit are making this transition. The reform issues in urban education are far removed from the history of school segregation and the use of tracking to separate out groups of students within large schools, which remain a historical tragedy in our nation, but these reforms still run the risk of perpetuating educational inequalities.

Small schools with thematic content provide a potential mechanism for reform. Our case studies of selected schools reveal that it has not been easy for high schools to adapt to the new requirements or develop niche-related content, but the schools we visited appeared relatively successful at building an understanding of the challenges and organizing their responses in ways that made it possible to address these difficulties through adaptive change. We found that the math-education literature provided a perspective on engaged learning of advanced mathematical reasoning, and that the engagement of math educators in the school-based reform process was essential. Interestingly, and sadly, the centralization of curriculum policy in a traditional urban school system can constrain the opportunity for educators to engage in adaptive changes in the curriculum.

The Practice of Math Reform in Urban Schools

The reform of math education in urban high schools is situated within the transition to markets and a choice of high schools. The shift to market strategies has been imperfect, as we noted in chapter 1. While most charters use randomization to select students when there is an excess demand, the NYC public school system continued to consider achievement tests and other factors in the assignment of students. In addition, the freedom of math educators to engage in reform was curtailed by a centralization of decisions about the math curriculum.

The four public charter schools we visited did not have the constraints on curriculum faced by the NYC district schools, so there was greater freedom to address challenges when they emerged. Even in these schools, however, the strategies used by their leaders were important (e.g., involving teachers in finding solutions). The central control mechanisms employed in charter schools merit attention, as prior research on successful public charter schools has argued,[52] but these mechanisms are not independent of leadership strategies.

At Kappa High School, for example, it was evident that central control was part of its site-based leadership strategy. The CTE component was at the heart of its curriculum design, but the college criteria for math dominated instruction rather than fostering an integration of career and technical content with math education. Kappa's attempt at a solution—slowing down math education by shifting the length of some courses from one semester to two—did not seem to solve the problem. In contrast, it was evident that Beta High School emphasized learning together—as a school community—what does or does not work, and why. Its leaders decided to rethink the use of community college courses and more deeply engage math educators within the school in devising ways to accelerate math learning. While we cannot generalize from a single case (or even from the analysis of all eight case studies described in tables 2.2 and 2.3), it appears that engaged learning is central to student success in math.

In some schools, the core problem with math education seems to be related to the ways in which math educators engage in improving math learning in relation to their overall mission and strategy, as well as to the content niche of the school. At Beta, for example, its liberal arts college prep focus provided the incentive to accelerate the school's math curriculum rather than have students attend community college math courses, since the transition of Beta's graduates to four-year colleges was a core part of its original mission. In another example, Sigma more closely coupled math education in the high school with the community college. It is important to remember, however, that Sigma had a distinctive mission: to uplift immigrant children into collegiate access and encourage the completion of two-year degrees.[53]

The idea that educators should focus on engaged learning emerged as a theme in the math-education literature; this requires more emphasis on professional development. Certainly it was part of the lessons learned about reforms in math education in the schools we visited. For example, the principal at Remus used an inquiry-based approach to working with math educators, which encouraged thinking about context and gave teachers an opportunity to adapt in a system with a history of local, centralized control of the curriculum. Engaging educators in reflecting on pedagogies that work for their students is an important element of reform, a form of professional action related to the academic freedom of educators to teach.

CHAPTER THREE

Advanced Literacies

Market competition among urban public schools substantially alters the context for advanced literacy education, as does the emphasis on career readiness. In the late twentieth century, the college preparatory curriculum in English was oriented toward preparing students for the liberal arts; advanced placement was a mechanism for giving students college credit, but not all students had access to this advanced curriculum. The new standards now push all schools to a deeper integration of advanced literacy into content across the curriculum, a step aligned with college literacy requirements, but they also further complicate challenges in urban high schools.

While the CCSS standards for advanced literacy partially recognize the need to connect literacy instruction with career content, they are not fully sensitive to socially situated literacy challenges. There is also a wide gap between critical literacy, defined as the ability to read and write at a college level,[1] and the knowledge and skills tested by college entrance exams and state tests. The two concepts are obviously correlated—students with high scores in English on the SAT are more likely to complete college—but the tests measure only a portion of college readiness. In particular, language education related to the development of social skills and self-understanding are left out of cognitive exams, even though noncognitive variables and strengths-based indicators may be better gauges of the potential for college success.[2] A broader conception of advanced literacy should consider the range of content in thematic schools, the links between content specializations and college entrance requirements, and the social (i.e., socialization) processes that encourage and support the development of these advanced skills.

Literacy standards are too frequently disconnected from the broader set of challenges facing urban high schools. Two crucial topics are often overlooked in the policy debates about college preparation: integrating advanced language education into the specialized content of niche schools and programs (an altered form of advanced literacy); and pedagogies appropriate for the life contexts of students as they acquire advanced skills in reading and writing for college (critical literacy). The literature on literacy education provides some insight into ways in which schools can address these challenge. We examine how this puzzling situation developed, along with strategies schools used to provide an advanced literacy curriculum in thematic urban high schools serving low-income, under-represented students.

Policy: Conflicting Rationales

The rationales for literacy reform are more varied than arguments about math reform because there are multiple paradigms in literacy education. The dominant reforms targeted at advancing literacy include:

- raising high school standards to meet college entry requirements, construed narrowly as test scores and broadly as the ability to interpret, understand, and present arguments in written form on topics across the curriculum;
- improving critical, culturally relevant literacy by using texts that engage students as they learn the skills of decoding, writing, and argumentation; and
- increasing content-connected literacy, a framework that takes on new meaning when we consider the marketization of urban schools as part of the context for literacy reform.

These problems are intertwined and must be examined from the viewpoints of both K–12 and higher education to untangle them. First, we examine the K–12 policy puzzle as such. Second, we develop a college vantage to build a better understanding of the multiple links between college content and specialized high school content. Finally, with this background, we propose a K–20 framework for examining literacy challenges. Our discussion of the collegiate vantage and the K–20 framework consider numeracy in addition to literacy because the required knowledge in both literacy and numeracy vary across collegiate disciplines.

The K–12 Policy Puzzle

In many respects, the lack of visible signs of progress on high school literacy outcomes is puzzling. There was a substantial investment in early-reading reform in the late 1990s, and then an increase in English requirements for graduation in the early 2000s. This was followed by a rise in early-reading outcomes for elementary schools (as measured by the National Assessment of Educational Progress), which may be attributable to the increased investment in early-reading programs. Surprisingly, there was no improvement in high school outcomes. To untangle this problem, we examine evidence of the widening gap in early-reading skills and the lack of progress in policy outcomes before introducing our literacy-skills framework to provide a plausible explanation for this lack of improvement.

WIDENING OF THE GAP IN BASIC READING SKILLS

There has been overall progress on early reading, as measured by average scores. Between 1999 and 2009, the National Assessment of Educational Progress (NAEP) reading scores for 9-year-olds rose substantially, but reading gaps among different demographic groups were significantly lower in the 1970s, when targeted interventions were widely used, than in the 1980s and 1990s, when school-wide strategies were emphasized, or in the more recent decade of improvement (1999 and 2009), when early reading was the focus.[3] Thus, although there was an improvement over the period during which school-wide methods were emphasized, the earlier strategy of supplemental education for high-need students in low-income schools appears to have worked better to address inequalities.

There have been many attempts to define a concept and a strategy for literacy education. In the 1990s, there was a federal push to improve early reading based largely on the theory of phonics, a letter-sound approach to reading that looked promising, according to some empirical evidence.[4] The Reading Excellence Act of 1998 provided funding for states to undertake "research-based" reform. That same year, the *Preventing Reading Difficulties in Young Children* report focused attention on reading as a national priority.[5]

One root of the problem has been the limited attention paid to cultural diversity in literacy education, a pattern evident for decades.[6] John Baugh, for example, documents the importance of recognizing the role of language within speech communities.[7] The widely accepted, research-based phonics approach to reading instruction overlooks differences in literacy acquisition across cultural groups with different patterns of speech.[8] The variations in speech and language across communities—social, racial, and disciplinary[9]—are central to the role of interventions and the construction of a core curriculum in language education. The movement toward nationally standardized tests and curriculum can undermine efforts to develop approaches that address the linguistic needs of minority groups with limited English.

HIGH SCHOOL LITERACY OUTCOMES

Even though educational requirements in English (i.e., the number of required courses for graduation) rose in parallel with the requirements in math, there is little or no evidence of an impact on educational outcomes. The trends in student achievement on SAT verbal scores do not show the improvement evident in SAT math scores (table 2.1). The logic of increasing the number of courses in English does not appear as sound as the logic for increasing math requirements. For math, there was a skills sequence that could be emphasized, but there was not a similar, commonly agreed-upon method for advanced literacy.

After three decades of standards-driven literacy reform, it is evident there has been limited progress in high school literacy education. As previously indicated, there was improvement in NAEP scores for 9-year-olds between 1999 and 2009, but the scores for 13- and 17-year-olds remained unchanged.[10] It is time to ask whether the policies that were implemented, instead of leading to improvements, were part of the reason for a lack of any visible sign of progress. The mandated strategies in K–8 literacy education possibly actually undermined the capacity of high schools to make progress, a prospect we explore using a skills-based framework.

LITERACY SKILLS

To better understand the complicated policy matters related to literacy education, it is important to consider the diverse skills that underlie the development of reading abilities (as measured on standardized tests), along with the advanced literacy skills needed for college readiness. Literacy development in K–8 schools is appropriately viewed as a sequential process of skill development. We use the following definitions for the underlying skills:[11]

- *Emergent literacy*: Reading readiness as an appreciation of literature that creates an enthusiasm for reading.
- *Decoding A*: Context-free decoding focusing on letter-sound relationships independent of literature.
- *Decoding B*: Meaning-oriented decoding focusing on letter-sound relationships in the context of literature and one's daily life.
- *Comprehension*: The ability to understand a text based on discerning the meaning of written words in context.
- *Composition*: The ability to write stories that communicate ideas, experiences, and themes.
- *Critical literacy*: The ability to read and analyze texts across the curriculum, as well as think about their meaning in relation to one's own experiences.

Reading education implicitly assumes that these skills are sequential. Emergent literacy is fostered in preschool and kindergarten, while the K–3 curriculum focuses on the development of decoding and comprehension skills. After the addition of a writing component to college admissions tests, composition is now also taught in most elementary programs. Pullout programs (like Reading Recovery) are frequently used to provide supplemental support for students who are not ready or slow to learn the basics. Comprehension becomes important in upper elementary school, and it is expected that students will be able to use reading comprehension and composition skills across the curriculum by the end of middle school, so they are ready for the college preparatory curriculum in high school.

The two different methods of teaching decoding skills—the research-based approach that emphasizes the phonemic strategy (decoding A) and the context-oriented learning of sounds, words, and meanings (decoding B)—provide a way to untangle the problems with K–12 literacy interventions. The Indiana reading studies—the origin of the outline of skills identified above—found that elementary schools using the direct-instruction approach had significantly higher test scores but also more retentions in grade level (i.e., failure of grade) and special-education referrals.[12] This approach increased scores, but also added to the number of underprepared students. In contrast, reading programs that emphasized critical methods improved the percentage of grade promotion. Schools in which both direct approaches and critical methods were used improved both scores and promotion across grades.

While the Indiana studies had little influence on the polarized debates outside the state, they did point to an alternative—finding an appropriate balance in reading interventions—and that state improved reading scores *and* reduced the gap.[13] The Indiana concept of balance in the curriculum acknowledged empirical research,[14] but it also drilled into and measured the actual features of instruction at the classroom level:[15] the findings from surveys of teachers corresponded with school-level outcomes. Thus, for a period of time in one state, a balance in reading education was found that promoted both equity and achievement.

ADVANCED LITERACY SKILLS FOR COLLEGE READINESS

When students enter high school without basic literacy skills, they are severely challenged in completing the advanced competencies in the CCSS. The push to integrate specialized content that is tied to market niches into the high school curriculum limits the time educators have to focus on basic reading skills. In fact, when high schools develop themes across the curriculum, students need to loop back through a process of learning new symbolic codes. To accelerate learning, it is essential to recognize when students have basic problems with decoding and comprehension because, when problems exist, they will need to simultaneously learn these skills along with the new forms of coding and symbols related to their theme. If students and their parents make good school choices (i.e., the school theme is well aligned with the student's interests), it may be easier to engage them in the dual challenge of learning specialized content across the curriculum while developing decoding and comprehension skills.

While there is little disagreement that students need to be able to graduate from high school and enter college with advanced literacy skills (defined as the ability to understand content across the college curriculum), the notion of a single standard for college-ready skills in reading and writing may be too narrow. College subject matter is diverse in content, with, at one extreme, an emphasis on interpreting meaning (English, history, and other humanities subjects) and, at the other extreme, decoding numeric and scientific symbols (STEM fields).[16] Different disciplines use various kinds of symbols and methods of argumentation, requiring divergent types of decoding and interpretive skills. Historically, college has emphasized general education in the liberal arts during the first two years, but the professions frequently have had different entry requirements. Indeed, there was a longstanding debate about general education versus "useful arts."[17] Attempts to integrate preparatory standards for liberal arts and advanced technical fields have long been fraught with discord in higher education.[18]

LIMITATIONS OF CCSS LITERACY STANDARDS

The new standards do little to resolve these underlying problems related to college preparation in urban high school markets. When the range of expectations included in the CCSS for advanced literacy are considered, they appear to be the result of a political compromise rather than an attempt to respond to the diversity in preparatory standards required by specialized fields in higher education. While the math standards push the STEM ideology, the literacy standards still seem to be based on general education.

The CCSS standards for reading and writing encompass several rationales regarding literacy.[19] They emphasize both comprehension (higher standards and more engaging texts) and advanced literacy (content-connected learning). These standards promote a broad range of advanced skills: independence (including "command of standard English"), strong content knowledge in a broad range of subjects, responsiveness to varied demands, valuing the use of evidence (including historical and scientific evidence) in the interpretation process, and the strategic use of technology. This advanced skill set is logically aligned with the intent of the liberal education traditionally offered during the first two years of college.

If the goal of the literacy standards is to prepare students for general liberal arts education within a centrally controlled public school system, along with a cursory understanding of the technical content of one or more fields, then the new standards may provide a sound framework. These standards are not easily reconciled with the specializations developing in urban high schools engaged in competitive markets, however, especially in schools that lack the flexibility to adapt their curriculum.

The CCSS standards do depict the literacy preparation in urban elementary schools. Many students enter urban high schools with basic learning needs (i.e., challenges with decoding and comprehension) that make it difficult to jump directly into a college preparatory curriculum, as illustrated by our case studies for Kappa High School (chapter 1) and Beta High School (chapter 2). Thus, in addition to providing content connected to the school theme as well as career content, educators must deal with the development of basic literacy skills. The older approach used in Title I provided mechanisms for supplemental education for students who needed it, but too often school-wide strategies that focus on college preparation leave only limited opportunities for addressing these basic-skills issues.

LINGERING LITERACY CHALLENGES IN URBAN HIGH SCHOOLS

The alignment of comprehensive standards with the diverse cultural contexts of urban schools remains a serious problem. The more compelling issues include (1) a direct link between policy and classroom methods, which may have a negative effect on challenged readers;[20] (2) narrow definitions of language and reading education that make it difficult for students whose cultural contexts and native languages do not fit this pattern;[21] and (3) marginalization of groups through deficit thinking related to the achievement gap.[22] The new standards include an emphasis on cultural diversity, but they may limit the capacity of schools to use culturally relevant approaches to help students build their literacy skills. For example, in a language-minority area within a large city (e.g., a sizeable Mexican American population) it may be appropriate to use students' language and culture as part of the foundation for advanced literacy instruction (see the Sigma case study below).

Another problem is that centrally determined, standardized approaches to advanced literacy often conflict with the marketization of urban schools, as is evident in our NYC case studies. Although career-connected content across the curriculum may interest parents when they choose a high school and can motivate students to pursue a college degree and uplift across generations, this transition is dependent on high-level literacy skills.

A Collegiate Vantage on Advanced Literacy and Numeracy

The K–12 literacy challenge has been defined too narrowly relative to the types of literacy skills needed in college. The combination of two factors—college preparation for all *and* high schools with themes that run across the curriculum—creates a new context for thinking about both literacy and numeracy. To untangle this aspect of the problem facing high schools engaged in college preparation, it helps to examine the problem from a collegiate viewpoint.

Arguments for the reform of high school education have been dominated by claims of the need for an expanded STEM workforce. Increasingly, alliances between researchers and policymakers rely on a new self-sealing logic: learning about science helps promote literacy, and vice versa. Arguments for integrating literacy into math and science education appear to have had an influence on the CCSS literacy standards.[23] The basis of this argument—that special advanced literacy skills are needed for advanced math—is reasonable, but the challenge is not limited to STEM fields, even though at times STEM rationales dominate over historical arguments about the liberal arts within educational policy debates.

Multiple Collegiate Literacies and Numeracies

The ways of knowing—developing and using content, conducting analyses, interpreting evidence, and applying logic—vary substantially across academic fields in higher education. A number of frameworks have been developed to examine differences in students' learning experiences in college; for example, Holland's career typology has been widely used.[24] While it may be possible to use this framework to examine math and literacy skills, it was based on working backward from professions to fields of study; it can, however, help identify how students' interests and reasoning relate to their choice of a major.

The means of structuring organizational problems and concepts of justice differ across fields in ways that parallel the use of coded language and mathematical evidence. Therefore, we start by considering the ways of framing justice. In *College Organization and Professional Development: Integrating Moral Reasoning and Reflective Practice*, St. John developed a method for viewing collegiate fields and professional ways of knowing in relation to social justice, providing a critical lens for examining professional pathways (table 3.1).[25] For example, some fields emphasize the meaning of justice, while others focus on the measurement of justice. The meaning of justice in action—including the ways justice and care are understood—varies across professions, as do other forms of professional responsibility. The orientation toward justice can be differentiated into four frames:[26]

- *interpretive*, which focuses primarily on the meaning, experience, and understanding of justice and injustice;
- *critical*, which focuses on injustice as a problem;
- *social*, which focuses primarily on social interactions, which may include caring for others; and
- *technical-scientific*, which focuses primarily on technical and scientific subjects and can have an explicit emphasis on environmental preservation.

The themes used by the high schools we visited are noted as examples in the bottom row of table 3.1. This alignment of themes and professions is potentially problematic because the choice of a major (and a career) is usually reserved for college students, and in many colleges students are expected to explore the liberal arts curriculum for two years before choosing a major. Therefore, emphasizing careers as themes in high school complicates assumptions about the standardization of curriculum content. Linked courses may make it necessary to offer basic content with different examples that use linguistic and numeric forms congruent with specific fields.

TABLE 3.1
Typology of Basic and Applied Professions: Interpretive, Critical, Social, and Technical-Scientific Perspectives on Justice

Orientation toward justice	Interpretive (justice as interpretation and experience)	Critical (justice as advocacy)	Social (justice as social interaction and/or caring for others)	Technical-Scientific (justice as analytical, technical, and scientific expertise)
Applied professions	• journalist • legal (human rights) • musician • artist	• lawyer • politician • advocate • preacher • service personnel	• school teacher • counselor • nurse • manager • analyst	• engineer (most specializations) • management • chemist • medical doctor
Basic fields of study	• languages • literature • history • arts and music • philosophy • religion	• political science • law • policy studies • seminary • cultural studies	• social sciences (e.g., sociology, anthropology, political science) • psychology • education • economics	• basic sciences (e.g., chemistry, physics, biology) • information science • environmental sciences
High school examples	• liberal arts (Beta HS) • early college high schools (Sigma HS) • NYC curriculum	• social justice (Alpha HS) • leadership through service (CFES in NYC district schools)	• teaching (Onye Nkuzi HS)	• STEM (Kappa HS; NYC: 21st Century, Acme, Remus's engineering and medical academies)

Subject matter varies substantially across academic fields, along with orientations toward justice, care, and other issues, similar to the concept of organizational frames. Whether a professional field is basic or applied depends on the use of evidence in action: applied fields emphasize using evidence in practice, while basic fields often focus on the rigors of proof. The roles of advanced literacy and numeracy also vary across the professions. Interpretive frames are used in fields largely dependent on the interpretation of text, skills that link directly to reading for understanding and argumentation (i.e., advanced forms of comprehension). In contrast, the content knowledge of scientific/technical fields is more substantially dependent on numeracy and reading for scientific content. Science and literacy are like a continuum between the two ways of knowing—literacy (based on some empirical understanding) and numeracy (based on some linguistic decoding of complex texts and symbols)—which provides an alternative way of thinking about literacy and content fields. Using an orientation toward justice as a starting point, we can readily see that each way of knowing holds certain assumptions about justice. These four frames provide a basis for rethinking the linkages between basic and advanced literacy concepts and teaching practices aligned with thematic approaches to academic preparation for collegiate-level literacy, and they form a reasonable standard for high schools.

K–20 Advanced Literacy and Numeracy Framework

In the past, when the pathway to college was traveled by a limited number of students, it wasn't necessary to promote collegiate skills for all. Students who had advanced literacy in high school were more likely to be tracked into a college preparatory curriculum, while students who lacked this set of skills were more likely to end up with either a general or a technical diploma. Since there is now a tighter alignment between K–12 and college curricula, it is important to reconsider the components of literacy, both as they are expected to develop in grades K–12 and how they are applied in higher education. Using a skills-based approach provides a framework for illuminating challenges emerging from the new emphasis on college prep for all students in urban education markets.

To illustrate the complexities introduced into college preparatory education by taking a thematic approach, we present the four frames as a way of conceptualizing how college content in academic disciplines links to content-based preparation in advanced literacy and numeracy in high school (table 3.2). In practice, this means of differentiating frames relates more to ways of interpreting them in action than to classifications of their content. They were developed originally by Lee Bolman and Terrence Deal as a basis for interpreting how different points of view can be used to study problems,[27] but they can also be used as a heuristic device for showing how different types of careers align with college

TABLE 3.2
Preparation for Interpretive, Critical, Social, and Technical-Scientific Expertise and Orientations

Dimensions of preparation	Interpretive (literacy primary, numeracy secondary)	Critical (balances literacy and numeracy)	Social (balances numeracy and literacy)	Technical-Scientific (numeracy primary, literacy secondary)
Readiness	• reading and writing • argumentation • preliminary content	• reading and writing • argumentation • interpretive uses of data	• reading and writing • use of empirical evidence • statistics[a]	• reading and writing • preparation for science content • advanced math (calculus)[b]
Decoding	• understanding arguments in texts and other media	• understanding rationales of a field (e.g., legal reasoning)	• understanding theoretical claims and the related use of evidence	• understanding algorithmic expression • understanding science content
Comprehension	• capacity to interpret text, discern themes, and compare texts	• capacity to think critically about texts in social and political contexts	• capacity to apply theory to social problem solving and social discourse	• capacity to use experiments as methods of proof
Writing	• writing themes and using arguments from literature	• composing arguments and counterarguments (e.g., debate)	• analyzing social problems and contexts using theory	• explaining abstract and technical concepts
Critical thinking	• understanding symbols and contexts for meaning	• understanding the role of action in transforming social problems	• ability to relate to and empathize with others, based on social contexts	• ability to envision technical solutions to physical and/or biological problems

[a]For undergraduate education in the social sciences, math through algebra II is appropriate. A variety of statistical and measurement methods are used across the social sciences. For graduate education in the social sciences, including the field of education, calculus may be important for some programs.
[b]Advanced math preparation is necessary for college-level sciences, including preparation for a medical education.

content and school themes. Our discussion of the frames relates specifically to the problem of curriculum alignment between high schools and colleges.

The *interpretive* frame is aligned with the humanities, that is, with the types of reading and interpretation historically used in literature, history, and other classical liberal arts disciplines. Traditional approaches to advanced education in the field of English, including but not limited to advanced placement and international baccalaureate courses, seem to work well and are compatible with this frame, although there are competing theories of literacy education, especially for educationally challenged and ethnically diverse students. Advanced literacy education was once reserved for students who might specialize in these fields, and SAT II exams measure students' preparedness to study in these fields, as they do for the sciences. There are compelling arguments that the interpretive literacy skills from the humanities tradition have been left out of technocratic high school reform.[28]

The *critical* frame is aligned with strategies applied to culturally situated interpretations and advocacy for fairness and justice. As an approach to advanced literacy, this logic has been used to encourage and teach college-level writing.[29] When schools choose to adopt critical frames, as was the case at Alpha High School (chapter 4), they can seek to prepare students for law and other professions that emphasize social critical and contextualized understandings of social contexts. The critical frame can also be logically situated in a social justice construct that uses numeracy and literacy strategies that empower students and their families. In classrooms and schools that focus on empowerment, it is appropriate to emphasize remedies to social inequality, the stance we take in our introductory chapter. Unfortunately, the corporate view of markets and education currently dominates to such a degree that older concepts of the social good, once a common tenet of American education, can be left out, depending on the curriculum choices made by schools and districts.

The *social frame* aligns with social studies in grades K–12 and the social and political sciences in college; applied fields, like education and social work, are also included in this approach. At the collegiate level, the social sciences use statistical analyses that employ different mathematical terms than the sciences. With the evolution of quasi-experimental methods in social science research, a strong case can be made to include advanced math as part of a student's preparation, although the methods of stating and testing concepts differ from those of the hard sciences. Onye Nkuzi High School started out focusing on teaching as a theme, but they added an emphasis on liberal arts when a critical mass of educational-option students enrolled who weren't necessarily interested in teaching (chapter 4). The shift to a liberal arts theme at Onye Nkuzi includes preparation in the statistical methods used in the fields of education and the social sciences, but it also implicitly includes an emphasis on preparation for

STEM fields. Our Beta High School case study (chapter 2) illustrates how a liberal arts–focused school adapted math education to prepare students for the full range of college subjects, from interpretive disciplines through STEM fields. The *technical/scientific frame* represents the STEM rationale that has been dominant in educational reform (chapter 2), and the emphasis on advanced math illustrates this orientation. Historically, U.S. high schools taught different types of math that were aligned with a range of technical jobs. STEM careers include technical work—plumbing, carpentry, emergency medical services—that historically did not require advanced math but benefited from math competency; business math was an option in technical and vocational tracks in most schools. When states started to require algebra II for graduation, however, and some schools had to double up on math so students could pass the course, business math was usually eliminated.

The CCSS gives schools the freedom to integrate an emphasis on a technical curriculum into English courses and pedagogies for improving reading and writing into technology courses. Students who live in poverty may also benefit from a curriculum that includes an emphasis on interpretive, critical, and social ways of understanding. For example, given the low math achievement at Kappa (table I.3), one can legitimately ask whether its emphasis on STEM courses is appropriate for many of its students.

These four conceptual ways of understanding literacy were not important when the liberal arts model was used as a basis for college preparation and when only some students planned to go to college. Our Beta High School case study (chapter 2) illustrates that liberal arts–oriented high schools may require more rigorous coursework in math, especially when their mission focuses on preparation for four-year college programs. There is also a lingering general-diploma model, however, that is now oriented toward community college education. This approach is illustrated by our Sigma High School case study in this chapter.

The typology of academic fields provides an alternative way of thinking about academic preparation for college, especially if schools adopt thematic content that is aligned with professions. There may not be one single threshold of preparation for literacy or math, as is assumed by contemporary political rationales; instead, different types of academic fields have varying kinds of preparation needs. Colleges still depend on ACT and SAT scores as the primary indictor for college preparedness in literacy skills, although other assessment instruments are used in many higher education systems to determine a need for remedial courses in English. The 9–14 model, illustrated by our Sigma case study, may ease the transition to college, at least for students going to community colleges.

The extent to which graduation standards in math or literacy address college preparedness for a specific field or profession will depend to some extent on the knowledge requirements of that field. Whether the implementation of such standards meets the needs of scientific and technical fields (and, to some extent, even those in the social sciences) depends in part on the ways critical literacy is framed and taught and on whether there is some integration into the forms of numeracy used in those fields.

Contemporary efforts to define a single minimum threshold for college preparedness in literacy and numeracy may not fit the content structures of academic disciplines or the preparedness needed for them. Our reconstructed concept of the threshold of preparation (table 3.3) provides a way to gauge how students may adapt as they go along: students who have difficulties with the math preparation for science often change their focus to other, less mathematically rigorous fields of study; at the college level, they may transfer to less-demanding colleges or to colleges that provide more supplemental instruction in math.[30] The notion of a threshold of preparedness is embedded in college curricula, since many colleges offer remedial and transition courses in math and English.

The primary difference between this construction and the CCSS in literacy is that the former identifies advanced literacy skills within a specialized area, rather than emphasizing broad approaches that may be more superficial. This concept is more compatible with the small-schools design of contemporary urban high schools, which limits content options and emphasizes specialization. The new urban schools need the flexibility of going in-depth within their specialized content, unless their emphasis is on liberal arts preparation. As our Beta case study (chapter 2) illustrates, small high schools that emphasize liberal arts as their central theme may need to accelerate advanced math education to prepare their students for fields such as engineering.

Students attending high schools with specialized content may have certain advantages, especially since some colleges use field-specific literacy in their admissions criteria. For example, the SAT II subject exams, which require specific knowledge and skills (including an ability to rapidly decode field-specific content) are available as a supplemental test for use in undergraduate admissions, supporting the idea there is not one single threshold for acceptance into college. Different academic fields have various sorts of content requirements related to decoding and comprehending texts, writing coherently, and thinking critically within the traditions of that discipline. This way of viewing differences between fields has potential for informing a new type of discourse about academic preparation in high school. The SAT II subject exams pick up the content-specific aspects of preparation;[31] unfortunately, however, these exams do not yield the ethnic diversity of other methods used for college admissions, such as class rank.

The problems with understanding specialized content—usually thought to be acquired after students master basic requirements—are intertwined with issues of unequal access. Many schools do not offer the accelerated programs needed

TABLE 3.3
K–20 Perspectives on Literacy and Numeracy Skills

Academic level	Elementary	Secondary[a]	College	Professional preparation
Literacy	• emergent • decoding A and B • comprehension • composition • critical literacy	• reading and writing • argumentation • advanced decoding and literacy skills in a specialized field (market model)	field-type specific: • decoding • critical reading • literature analysis	literacy intensive: • arts/music • ministry • law/politics • journalism • humanities
Numeracy	• basic math	• advanced math, especially for social sciences (statistics) and STEM (calculus)	field-type specific: • math requirements and applications vary by field type	math intensive: • economics • medicine • engineering • sciences

[a]Some trade schools, similar to community colleges, can be entered after high school, and many students attending these schools receive remediation in basic and advanced math.

to acquire knowledge in the specialized subjects assessed on the SAT II exam, so the impact on inequalities can be magnified: students from schools that do not offer advanced courses are at an inherent disadvantage. In theory, requiring high standards for graduation or developing competitive niches can be partial remedies for this problem.

Some of our case-study high schools have developed specialized niches, which could lead to an integration of career content into the high school curriculum. Many urban school districts have historically had specialized high schools for the arts, the sciences, and technical fields, but these basic configurations are being reformulated in this new era of charter schools and of competition between public and quasi-private schools within cities. The newer, smaller schools provide opportunities to integrate content-specific approaches to literacy and numeracy into the core curriculum.

Within the liberal arts tradition, undergraduate students discover decoding in context:[32] comprehension, writing, and critical-thinking abilities and preparation fit with different major fields as part of the first two years of college. The ability to decode the meaning of concepts and symbols within a discipline influences a student's ability to complete a major in that field. The requirements of the social sciences vary substantially from those for the natural sciences and the humanities. For example, the types of college preparatory curricula (honors / advanced placement, college prep, or general) made a substantial difference in the choice of a major by the end of the third year in college among Indiana residents in the millennial cohort.[33] It is increasingly important for high school reformers to consider the forms of academic preparedness—in high school and the first two years of college—required for study in specific academic disciplines and related professions.

Different forms of preparedness can also be considered in college admissions, especially in universities that differentiate admissions by field or by their various undergraduate colleges.[34] Many universities consider applicants for engineering in a different pool from general admissions, routinely assessing their STEM preparedness. It is also common in the field of music to consider students' musical auditions as central to admissions decisions. Many universities vary the amounts of student-aid awards based on their applicants' preparedness in specialized subjects like music, the sciences, and so forth, often using the SAT II. Many also differentiate the amount of aid awarded, based on what has been offered by competitor institutions to which the student was admitted, or consider a preferred major as part of the award decision.[35]

While the mapping of collegiate literacy standards by field remains theoretical, it has sound logical foundations. With this background, we can return to the problem of advanced preparation in literacy for admission to college in the analyses below, as well as to the task of developing a K–16 frame on critical literacy and numeracy across the chapters of this book. The high schools discussed in chapters 1 and 2 had themes: Beta High School had an interpretive focus because the college preparation paradigm used in the school was rooted in the liberal arts; Remus High School was large and had multiple themes, but the CFES program we studied had aligned with the engineering unit (a technical-scientific specialization). In the remainder of this volume, we will use the typology of themes in our discussion of high school case studies.

Literacy Reform in High Schools

The K–20 framework for viewing literacy and numeracy skills (table 3.3) reveals that there should ideally be multiple standards for college preparation in literacy and numeracy, or at least flexibility in standards as they align with content niches. In our case-study analyses, we found that a dominant pattern of literacy education aligned with state standards.[36] In the following comparisons of public district and public charter high schools, we examine both the change processes in the field of English within the public charter and district high schools and the common patterns across both sectors. This approach provides a comparison of organizational barriers to change across systems, along with the forces within schools that enable change. For an in-depth case study, we examine patterns of literacy preparation in Sigma High School, an early college high school situated in a southwestern city, to show how they attempted to develop critical literacy using an approach that focused on writing across fields. Our Sigma case study demonstrates a commitment to embedding a focus on literacy—especially writing—within all parts of the high school curriculum, an approach consistent with the broader view of literacy used in our K–20 framework.

NYC Public High Schools

Both public district and charter high schools are highly dependent on state standards in the design of their curricula in English, social sciences, and other subjects. When standards change, schools rush to align their curricula with them, but an emphasis on complying with standards limits discourse within schools about critical literacy as a content challenge across subjects. Urban public high schools face additional constraints in efforts to innovate their curricula. In the context of urban education, teachers are often required to implement district mandates. They may play some role in deciding how to do this, such as developing complementary units and lessons and participating in curriculum-mapping processes. Yet they must be careful about making personal investments in reform initiatives that are not directly aligned with what has been approved by the district. Charter schools have some competitive advantages because they have the capacity and freedom to pursue strategies locally, without having to deal with a district-mandated curriculum.

Comparison of Literacy Reform in NYC District High Schools

Consistent with state standards, New York City requires six semester credits in English, and students must pass state exams; the curriculum and tests are aligned with CCSS. As summarized in table 3.4, the NYC district high schools were confronted by challenges to their literacy courses as they tried to adapt to changes in student-learning needs. There were also curriculum constraints, but the educators in these schools found ways around emergent challenges.

The English requirements in a core curriculum are problematic for schools seeking to provide an engaging English program aligned with other courses. An English teacher described the challenges of adapting courses to meet students' needs: "As an English teacher it is very difficult when you try to reference context or setting in books and the kids really are not learning about history right now, so it's just not really at the forefront of their minds." This comment, and others like it, illustrate how teachers must contend with curriculum compliance while also staying tuned in to the ways their students learn.

There was some flexibility in selecting books and adapting the curriculum in English classrooms. In Remus High School, which had an intensive, inquiry-based management process, teachers found that they could make adaptations to meet student-learning needs within its curriculum constraints. A teacher observed:

> One of the issues that really comes up is the fact that the population is changing, the curriculum needs to be modified, become multicultural, more so. Also, find new strategies, especially using technology to really reach these kids, because you're competing with large amounts of technology every minute. . . . Finding ways to tap into their [the students'] culture and finding ways, because they do not feel connected to it on a personal level, especially as an English teacher it's very difficult to get them involved. You do not have to just change the canon, you can use other strategies to bring in additional, like, what are the words I'm looking for . . . supplemental text that can bring it together.

These comments illustrate the critical role of curriculum adaptations within schools that seek excellence. Several English teachers in New York City consistently commented on this challenge. Those who thought the problem through—as was the case at Remus High School—found it necessary to supplement the state's curriculum.

Comparison of Public Charter High Schools

The four public charter high schools we visited were confronted by challenges because students entered 9th grade generally reading below grade level. Their English literacy skills were not seen to be as important as their math prepara-

TABLE 3.4

Adaptive Changes in English Education at Selected NYC District High Schools

Emergent challenges	Adaptations
Acme Collegiate Academy: a number of students enter with writing and reading skills in need of remediation	College-admissions essay writing taught in English class; CFES and a leadership class encourage mentoring to motivate students; smaller class sizes for English courses; award-winning student newspaper provides opportunities to sharpen college-readiness skills as students engage in investigative reporting, persuasive essay writing, and the creation of critical and argumentative stories
Onye Nkuzi High School: a number of students enter with writing and reading skills in need of remediation; English is the second language for many students; a state high school graduation test restricts the ability for study across literary genres and topics; students' concept of a paper is limited to a five-paragraph essay; only 30% complete homework; the state high school curriculum does not focus on writing skills and grammar	Students take a high school graduation exam after 10th grade, after which the focus of the English curriculum shifts to genres and topics (women's literature, romance, horror, etc.); college-admissions essay writing taught in English class; infusion of multiculturalism and technology into curriculum; sociology-based senior electives and the senior project focus on extended writing projects; the grading system allows parents and students to track progress; CFES and leadership courses encourage mentoring relationships that help motivate students
Remus High School: a number of students enter with writing and reading skills in need of remediation; English is the second language for nearly all of the students; courses are not rigorous, which hinders a successful transition to college	English enrichment offered after school; teachers provide individual tutoring; college-admissions essay writing taught in English class; well-developed assessment plan provides feedback to teachers about student progress; collaboration with CFES provides opportunities for CFES students to write and review college essays and work on spoken English in preparation for leadership summits
21st Century Technological Academy: a number of students enter with writing and reading skills in need of remediation; English is a second language for most students; students are unprepared to complete extended writing assignments (300–1000 words); lack of rigor in courses; curriculum reflects a linear understanding of skill development; small school budget for students who need AP courses	Partnered with an intervention program (New Visions); developed a literary design collaborative where students build skills by completing extended writing assignments in any discipline; college-admissions essay writing taught in English class; remapped the curriculum to allow clustering of skills, but also stand-alone courses; partnerships with colleges to offer AP courses

Note: At all schools, students were required to complete six semester credits and pass annual state exams, and common-core state standards were followed in the curriculum.

tion; as a result, a larger number of targeted inventions exist for math remediation, while critical literacy development is incorporated into classes on a more ad hoc basis. At Beta High School, for example, the language arts program lags behind the math and science departments in terms of identifying concrete indicators of student learning, as well as in timelines for when students must be able to demonstrate mastery of these indicators.

English education, like math education, is central to state and college-admissions tests (ACT and SAT); several states have adopted the ACT as their high school exit exam. Most states have taken steps to require more years of English for graduation. As already discussed, inner-city high schools face challenges related to the reading and writing readiness of their students on entry, as well as with the expectations of colleges. All of our selected charter schools went through a process of adapting their original strategies to meet these challenges (table 3.5).

At Sigma High School, it was evident that students with English as their second language had special learning needs. Sigma's ad hoc approach to the English curriculum had been challenged to provide more remedial support at the same time as the state stiffened regulations for English-language instruction. Sigma responded with a comprehensive approach, including an alignment of high school English with community college courses; the development of a school-wide rubric for writing; a new English sequence; remedial courses and seminars for writing; and the implementation of new strategies for students with limited English.

In contrast, Kappa High School had a coherent, sequenced English curriculum that was aligned with its technical themes, but it, too, ran into challenges with the learning needs of its students. Unlike the other schools, Kappa maintained control over the academic qualifications of students at entry and stiffened requirements when it went through a reorganization (chapter 1). After confronting these challenges, Kappa responded by altering sequences to fit both the learning needs of its students and the state's standards while also continuing to use backward mapping to maintain an alignment with college requirements. Kappa also developed a full K–12 program as a means of better ensuring the qualifications of students when they entered high school.

These case studies further illustrate how public charters had more freedom to adapt their literacy education programs. These schools responded to new state standards as they altered the curriculum and instructional methods to address the challenges they faced. Moreover, as public charters they were not constrained by a district-mandated curriculum as they developed their new strategies. Each of these schools also had external support from foundations as they made these adaptations, a luxury the typical public school does not enjoy.

TABLE 3.5
Adaptive Changes in English Courses at Public Charter Schools

Original approach	Emergent challenges	Adaptations
Alpha High School: ad hoc English course planning with no standard curriculum	Insufficient support for students entering with significantly below-grade-level reading skills; no systematic way of teaching reading, writing, and grammar	Adoption of standards-based English curriculum that conforms to national guidelines; all 9th and 10th graders required to take double blocks of English (an additional remediation course is available); instructors for 9th and 10th grade English classes have common planning periods to increase collaboration across sections
Beta High School: ad hoc English course planning with no standard curriculum	Students, in particular middle school students, lack basic literacy skills; curriculum lacks concrete power indicators of student learning	Teaching of writing is coordinated across content areas through the five-paragraph essay; implementation of a reading recovery program designed for students performing below grade level; most students take the English series (2 terms) at the local community college
Kappa High School: curriculum based on a career-focused approach and backward mapping from college courses; four units of English required; dual enrollment for senior English with a partner university	9th graders entered with English skills one to two years below grade level; scores on the state exam lagged behind state averages; unstable relationship with university partners; backward mapping of curriculum from college courses drives course focus down (research class or writing class based on 9th grade English requirements as well as agreement with college partner)	Aligned with state standards; college course content as specified by university partners; curriculum mapping is ongoing and teacher driven; integration of 9th grade seminar to boost acquisition of basic skills; development of common assessments of literacy skills; students are expected to be at college level by 12th grade
Sigma High School: ad hoc English course planning with no standard curriculum; maintained a literacy team	Many students were English Language Learners (ELL) and faced language barriers; literacy, reading, and understanding the textbooks were the biggest hurdles students had to overcome to succeed in their college-level classes; new state requirement for English immersion class	English curriculum is aligned with community college expectations; school-wide writing-assignment rubric; new course for ELL students to increase their English proficiency; new course sequence developed for grades 9–12; offers seminar courses focused on reading strategies; remedial reading recovery program was introduced during SY 2009–10 (all 9th graders now take this course); entire staff is part of the "literacy team"

Cross-School Patterns

None of the four charter schools we visited had a designated reading specialist on the staff and instead relied on English teachers to fill this role, despite the fact that teacher-training programs did not necessarily prepare the teachers for this level of instruction. At Alpha High School, the English department does not teach reading or reading comprehension, but an English teacher noted: "Honestly, I need to learn how to teach reading."

To address the gap in grade-level literacy expectations among 9th graders in the public charter high schools, administrators in all four of the schools we studied introduced intense remediation programs focused on basic-skills development. At Alpha High School, for example, the average reading level among entering 9th graders ranges from 4th to 8th grade level. Starting in AY 2002–3, 9th graders were required to participate in a five-week summer prep course. Additionally, in both the 9th and 10th grades, students have double blocks of English, meaning that they meet with their English class 90 minutes every day, instead of every other day, for the entire school year. There are also additional English-resource classes for students who need more remediation. At Alpha High School, it is possible for a student to be enrolled in essentially three English courses during both 9th and 10th grades.

Teachers at the four public charter high schools we visited, including those in their English departments, had a significant influence on the types of interventions the schools undertook and the curriculum they offered. In November 2009, Kappa High School implemented professional learning communities (PLCs) to enhance communication and collaboration among teachers within content areas. The leaders of the PLCs help facilitate a conversation among the teachers about how to improve student performance in the different content areas. Through this model, all teachers felt that they had a voice in the school's major decisions related to teaching and learning. For example, when Kappa's English department changed books in 2009, the department as a whole reached consensus about which textbooks to use.

One common pattern in all of these schools is incorporating responsibility for developing critical literacy skills across departments. In many schools, the burden lies primarily on its English department: English teachers must find ways to incorporate reading, writing, comprehension, and literature-content knowledge within a coherent curriculum. Embracing reading strategies and techniques that can be used across content areas and curricula allows the literacy burden to be shared more equitably. For example, Alpha High School lacks a systematic way of teaching reading, writing, and grammar. The assumption appears to be that the teaching of these subject areas is the responsibility of Alpha's English department and its English teachers. The department has not formally been tasked with this responsibility, however; instead, their emphasis is on an analysis of literature.

In contrast, administrators at Beta High School have adopted what they describe as a "holistic approach" to teaching reading, writing, and grammar. The curriculum initially focuses on the traditional five-paragraph paper, containing a thesis, support details with Modern Language Association (MLA) citations, and so on. The curriculum gradually becomes more advanced and the students' focus expands to analyzing the literature. During the earlier grades, language arts teachers try to select reading materials that complement other subjects, using a thematic approach. Teachers in these other subject areas incorporate writing exercises in their lessons to help reinforce the skills learned in language arts. This includes student summaries of what they learned in class, as well as other reflective exercises. Students learn to analyze the materials they read, take notes, and ask questions about the texts. Perhaps most importantly, the *language* used to teach writing is coordinated across content areas. Thus students know what a "five-paragraph essay" entails, regardless of the learning context.

Another challenge is transitioning students from basic literacy to college-level reading and writing over the course of four years of high school. The Beta High School curriculum is heavily balanced toward writing exercises that use the five-paragraph format. This pedagogy is a useful framework for teaching basic writing as well as for preparing students for the writing portions of standardized tests. College-level writing, however, demands a much more sophisticated presentation and development of ideas than the five-paragraph essay can capture.[37]

Case Study: Sigma High School

Sigma High School is an early college charter school in a major southwestern U.S. city with a large Latino/a population. Located within a community college campus, the teachers and school leadership have taken a strong advocacy position, focusing on providing education for many immigrant children who have been overlooked by the state's educational system. In our classification scheme (table 3.1), this school had an implicit critical orientation but not a thematic curriculum per se.

Given the strong alignment between the high school and college curricula, every student takes community college courses. The intended course sequence is for students to take English 9, English 10, and English 11 at Sigma, while preparing to take English 101 and English 102 at the community college during their senior year. One administrator put it this way: "They have to take college classes to graduate. They have to; they're here to take college classes." At Sigma, the teachers have to balance high school–level instruction, including supplemental grammar instruction in some instances, with the partner community college's reading and writing expectations. Teachers focus on providing a variety of challenging texts and advanced materials, while always keeping in mind that their students are in the process of completing four years of high school English.

One teacher described the goal of Sigma's English curriculum as being "to prepare the student to be able to read, write, and critically think at the college level." Another teacher stated: "We thought it would be silly for somebody to have English for just one semester and then not practice those skills. . . . I mean that's something we thought had to be continuous, whereas the other classes usually, they go every day, but they're done in half the time." This is essentially giving students a double dose of English, a common reform strategy used to provide low-achieving students with extra time and instruction.[38]

Not only do Sigma students spend a significant amount of time in English courses, they are also expected to apply reading and writing skills in all their courses. As a teacher observed: "Your reading and writing aren't independent of one another for the most part, so when we read, there's a writing component and when we write, there's a reading component." Students are expected to revise past essays, even while starting new writing assignments. An English teacher commented: "There's more multitasking: revising a past essay, while preparing a new one, while reading books in your spare time for our exhibition project at the end of the semester." Across all courses, teachers are building literacy tool kits for students. Examples of the tools include Cornell Notes, a standardized note-taking system; seminar courses that teach reading and test-taking strategies; and reading classes.

Teachers also use school-wide writing strategies that include requiring standardized document formats and assessing writing assignments using standardized rubrics. The teachers emphasize pre-writing strategies, including brainstorming and journaling, to help students discover what they want to write about.

The state's Department of Education expects all English teachers to teach writing using the following traits: ideas, organization, voice, word choice, sentence fluency, and conventions. All of the teachers at Sigma, regardless of content area, have been trained in these six traits. The English teachers took the lead in presenting the traits and providing professional development for the rest of the staff. For example, one session was on "This is how I would teach this trait in my classroom." After the session, all teachers in the school were expected to teach that trait. After the school started using these strategies, the writing scores on the state exam went up. According to Sigma's teachers, the key was stressing the traits across content areas, using the same rubric, and providing the training.

All teachers at Sigma use an in-house, school-wide writing rubric to assess student writing. The English teachers even developed school-wide editing marks to standardize corrections and have all students understand their teacher's annotations. The rubric was created to make sure everybody was on the same page—teaching the same, grading the same, and providing similar feedback. Students knew that in science or history their essay had to have the same type of headings and the same formats. One teacher stated: "We use those rubrics in all content areas on major assignments so the kids see that it's not just an English thing but it's also how I write in science." One of the teachers explained that the English teachers at Sigma decided: "Instead of just keeping it in the English department, we needed to practice across content areas so kids can write. You know that [state] test is huge for our students. If they can't pass that test, they can't graduate, so how are we going to get them to pass it?"

The teachers focus on teaching Sigma students skills they will be able to use as tools to prepare them for the types of lecture-based pedagogies they are likely to encounter in college-level instruction. Teachers make sure to incorporate student needs; for example, every Sigma student writes their college-admissions essay in their English class.

Each year, teachers become aware of and focus on the community college English course. They know what textbooks will be used, what types of rhetorical practices are expected, and what research skills are desired. The Sigma teachers try to replicate college expectations in the high school classroom. Knowing that students will have to use MLA citations in community college, it is also an expectation in Sigma's high school English classes. Students have to be able to read functional texts in order to understand the college textbooks, which are quite dense. The students develop their reading skills in seminar classes that focus on reading strategies. In addition, students in need of help attend a remedial-reading course; the intent is for students to only remain in the remedial-reading course during the 9th grade.

Teachers at Sigma had a lot of autonomy. One teacher, who had worked at the school for five years, stated: "So I pick a topic that I think might be interesting for them and then I select text that I haven't really worked with a lot of times before and use the summer to work with them [the texts], just to challenge myself, to keep myself fresh." The English teachers were familiar with the state's standards and aware that preparing students for the state test is important; that wasn't viewed as a burden. An English teacher noted: "When you look at the state standards, you know you just have to make sure you track them. . . . But I mean all those things are, if you're an English teacher, they're commonsense. You're teaching those aspects anyway. I'm aware of what they are and I plug the right things into the right areas, but I'm doing those things anyway." The school administers four benchmark tests throughout the year. The English teachers hand score "all 250 of them, four times a year." The results are put into a database.

Sigma consistently met or exceeded state standards between 2005 and 2008, but in 2009 the school fell behind. New challenges were introduced because of state requirements regarding limited-English students. Reading scores decreased, specifically in the areas of vocabulary, comprehension, and the historical/cultural aspects of literature. In order to meet score goals, the school recognized that it needed to provide additional support for English language learners (ELL). Sigma also had to contend with state-mandated changes to the English language development program. ELL students used to be mainstreamed into the classroom, but with support so they could understand the content areas. The state introduced an ELL assessment: if students do not pass the exam, they are removed from their content-area courses and placed into an English immersion class. Students are expected to go from being unable to speak any English to becoming fully proficient and able to pass the exam in two years, although many students enter the course able to speak some English.

Given the importance of student literacy, the school invested in Read 180, a reading recovery program for struggling readers, which all 9th grade students must take. Sigma teachers believe the most significant challenge they face is preparing students to understand college texts. When discussing students taking college courses, a teacher observed: "The writing really isn't all that, but it is reading and retaining and comprehending, then being able to spit it out on a multiple-choice test."

CHANGE PROCESS

Literacy has been the primary focus at Sigma for at least five years. Its teachers consistently stated that literacy, reading, and understanding the textbooks are the biggest hurdles students have to overcome in order to succeed at the college level. The school established a literacy team to tackle Sigma's literacy challenge and stressed literacy across the whole school. The process has evolved and now the whole staff is part of the literacy team.

At the start of SY 2009–10, Sigma's staff came together and recommended a reading course. The school's leaders told the staff to "figure out what you want to do, who's going to teach it" and said that if the teachers recommended a program and process, the school would find the money to do it. Previously, teachers were told that literacy should be handled in the classrooms and were informed that since teachers are "in the trenches" and know the school and their students best, they were the best equipped to work through a solution. New leadership brought new opportunities, as a teacher stated on behalf of her colleagues: "As a whole, we decided we needed an actual program, not relying on our own [individual ideas]." This led teachers to research the available programs and settle on the design for the new course, which uses a data-driven reading recovery program targeted toward schools that have a large number of students who need literacy help but do not have reading specialists or the knowledge or resources to address their students' literacy needs. The school pursued and received stimulus money to acquire the reading program.

Even though Sigma has consistently exceeded their reading targets on the state exam, literacy was emphasized in Sigma's school improvement plan in 2007–8. Critical literacy was identified as being first in the top three areas in greatest need of improvement. The school prioritized reading as second, with writing skills third.

While writing scores increased overall, the scores of African American, male, special education, and ELL students fell below the standard. Given the nature of the program and the rigor of college coursework, Sigma recognized that its students must demonstrate proficiency in writing at or above grade level. These test results led to new school-wide literacy and writing strategies, as well as professional-development initiatives.

In the immersion class now mandated by the state, ELL students at Sigma attend four class hours of reading, writing, listening, and speaking English daily. Teachers are expected to find ways to engage these students and keep them interested. Even though several of the teachers expressed concerns regarding the program, it seems to be supporting the ELL students' English acquisition. One teacher stated: "I was very anti this program. How can you segregate these kids? But the English side, the development is huge and they're back in their classes. They struggle here and there, they still need a little bit of extra time, they might need that little extra support, but they're doing pretty well, and they're in college classes as well." It is the school's expectation that, "whether you're ELL or not, you should be ready to go to college by the time you graduate."

CHALLENGES

The doubling-up strategy for English courses in Sigma appeared to be working, but state assessments and requirements for ELL students posed a problem. The teachers discussed four ongoing challenges:

1. *Missed opportunities for interdisciplinary units and backward curriculum mapping.* The teachers at Sigma seem to work individually, annually reinventing their curricula. One English teacher commented that the English teachers meet to align where there should be an appropriate amount of overlap in the courses, but they do not coordinate readings. As an example, he went on to say that one teacher focuses on grammar at the sentence level, while he emphasizes voice, word choice, and organization. He would like to build a humanities department and curriculum but has found that course scheduling and time have been impediments. A

curriculum-mapping process would ensure that the English curriculum is aligned and cumulative from 9th grade through graduation.

2. *Limited internal information on student reading scores.* A teacher noted that administrators think the caliber of students attending Sigma is increasing. Students take reading and writing benchmark assessments during orientation week, and they enter reading at a late 6th or early 7th grade level. Through the addition of the new 9th grade critical literacy course, it is likely that reading diagnostic exams will be introduced. Sigma's English teachers argue that they should have access to the students' reading scores.

3. *Literacy team meetings held without a reading specialist.* One teacher stated: "It would be nice to have an experienced reading specialist on board." Four teachers in the building are starting to work toward a reading-specialist endorsement. Given the school's literacy needs, adding a reading specialist to the staff or contracting reading consulting services might accelerate the desired student-literacy outcomes. As part of the 9th grade literacy course, a computer-based program was introduced, along with a dedicated reading lab; if there was a reading specialist teaching the course, student outcomes could be further improved.

4. *State mandates for ELL students.* Students are required to be in the ELL program and out of their content-area courses until they pass the English-assessment exam. According to one teacher: "Realistically, they could be in that pullout class for four years until they learn English, and now they know English, but they're a senior and then they have to go back and try to make up that work. So that's where it's difficult."

Conclusion

The central regulation of the curriculum in public systems differentiates the roles and functions of literacy education in public high schools—be they charters, specialized schools, or comprehensive college prep high schools—from a collegiate curriculum. Public district high schools, unlike Sigma and other public charters, usually have content constraints that separate advanced literacy from the content of the core subjects rather than integrate it into them. In most NYC district schools, core subjects have been codified into bits of testable subject matter, but teachers have room to integrate a culturally relevant curriculum in English education. Colleges rely on their students' ability to critically read and interpret content within subjects. Attempts to align the high school curriculum in English with collegiate instruction can be undermined by state efforts to regulate that curriculum. Despite these serious challenges and barriers, educators must continue to seek better ways to align high school literacy preparation and collegiate content requirements if the goal of improving high school graduation and college completion rates is to be realized.

Transforming public high schools from their historic comprehensive mission to a new mission of preparing every student for college has been complicated by the many notions of preparedness woven into the fabric of related discourses. From the vantage of contemporary K–12 policy, literacy is often viewed as the ability to pass a test, and that is a major motivating force in all of the high schools we examined. While there is reason to question whether the new literacy standards are well aligned with the tests states use in English, schools are faced with the challenge of meeting standards *and* preparing students for tests. While the new CCSS include content related to both direct instruction and critical schools of thought about advanced literacy education, the comprehensive nature of the standards could be a problem for students who enter high school with basic reading challenges.

There were differences in the language-education strategies used in the charter schools we visited. For several, partnerships with community colleges made it possible to place some emphasis on writing in all the courses, a contrast to the experiences of public schools. These charter schools found an alliance with a community college to be workable in literacy education. Even for charter high schools, however, state standards complicate efforts to provide a curriculum aligned with college preparatory expectations, because all of the students have to pass state exams.

After nearly three decades of federal efforts to raise educational standards, urban schools are not prepared to address critical educational challenges in literacy education. Rather than providing frameworks that guide improvements in literacy education, testing and standards inhibit the adaptability schools require to address the learning needs of their students, especially in public district schools. While the public charter schools had more flexibility in developing new strategies for addressing problems related to literacy and numeracy education, they, too, had their workable strategies undercut by state requirements. For example, Sigma High School had been outperforming the state average on tests using a critical literacy approach, but it was forced to change strategies to address new state policies regarding students for whom English was a second language and thus fell behind the state average in 2009.

Like the public district schools, the strategies for improvement in public charter schools often must focus on testing rather than on aligning education with their students' interests. The great irony in literacy education is that while the field of critical literacy strongly emphasizes the necessity of addressing the learning needs of students in the contextually situated learning environments in which they live, the structure and methods of the educational reform agenda undermine the capacity of educators to achieve these aims.

CHAPTER FOUR

College Knowledge

Urban high schools that successfully compete for students in urban markets have to provide information on colleges, student aid, and career pathways as part of the curriculum or as a co-curricular program. While most middle-class families have a residual knowledge of college and careers as part of the cultural capital that reproduces the middle class, many low-income students do not.[1] School counselors have traditionally supported college planning, but cuts in school funding have made it difficult for public high schools to maintain these positions. At the same time, the curriculum constraints make adaptations to include college knowledge difficult. Integrating college knowledge into the curriculum and the culture of schools represents a major challenge. After examining the evolving discourses on college knowledge, we analyze the NYC cases, which illustrate introducing college knowledge into schools with a constrained curriculum, and the charter schools, which show the potential of integrating college knowledge into a more flexible one.

Policies Influencing College Knowledge

Historical evidence supports the contention that early on, the federal TRIO programs improved access for underrepresented students.[2] These programs had an implicit *balanced approach to postsecondary encouragement* that provided information about college readiness, ensured access to adequate need-based student aid for low-income students, and developed social support services for students in high school and college, leaving it to universities to coordinate these services (i.e., local discretion). After federal grant funding declined and student-aid loans increased, an enrollment gap opened for minority students compared with majority ones.[3] In the context of growing inequality in the late twentieth century, when state programs were able to provide support for students and guarantee student aid (e.g., 21st Century Scholars, Washington State Achievers), they reduced inequality in college enrollment.[4] While balanced approaches to policy and practice that provide information, social support, and financial aid have long been advocated, they have been difficult to sustain.

We define college knowledge as a form of cultural capital students develop as they learn about and gain experience with navigating educational pathways.[5]

Given the realities of paying for college, especially the high costs and the inadequacy of financial aid at many two- and four-year colleges, low-income students need to develop a *deep* form of college knowledge that includes the capacity to understand financial-aid offers and their implications for jobs and loans during college; the repayment of student loans after college; and the linkages between career content in high school, possible fields of study during college, and prospective earnings in career pathways related to various fields of study. *Superficial* approaches to providing college information that simply encourage students to prepare, apply to college, and complete the free application for student financial aid (FASFA) without explaining more about the costs of higher education can be deceptive, leading to college dropout. When college dropouts return to their home communities with student debts to pay off, this deception becomes a form of locally constructed college knowledge, revealing the insidious nature of superficial approaches to providing college information.

State and federal projects that support balanced approaches to student-enrollment encouragement by colleges and nonprofit organizations actually have a long history in American higher education. We discuss the evolution of the balanced approach to access, illustrate the new face of poverty in the United States (using a survey of students involved in CFES programs across the country), and consider what constitutes trustworthy college knowledge when we reexamine the link between education and the promise of earnings sufficient to pay off college loans.

Is the Balanced Approach a Historical Artifact?

It has long been recognized that students from families without prior college experience benefit from encouragement during the college preparation and application process, along with support services during college. The original Title IV programs, as authorized by the Higher Education Act (HEA) of 1965, were not portable, like Pell grants now are.[6] Instead, federal funding was awarded to campuses based on applications that emphasized meeting the financial needs of low-income students. While the Pell grants provided students with more college choices—and the implementation of the Pell program corresponded with a decline in the enrollment gap across races[7]—the subsequent marketization of student aid reduced the coherence of these aid programs. We briefly review the original design of federal programs before reconsidering how balanced approaches have evolved.

THE ORIGINAL FEDERAL STRATEGY

The federal student-aid programs originally provided campuses with a capacity to integrate social support for underrepresented students with targeted need-based aid through the Educational Opportunity Grants (EOG), which formed the original HEA need-based grant program; college work study (CWS); and, if needed, federal National Defense Student Loans (NDSL).[8] HEA Title IV also included the TRIO programs:

- Talent Search provided outreach to encourage high-achieving, low-income students to enroll in college.
- Upward Bound provided encouragement and support for college preparation by low-income students.
- Specialized Services provided social support during college for low-income students.

To receive Title IV funding (EOG, CWS, NDSL, and TRIO), campuses wrote proposals making a commitment to align their aid programs with TRIO. Campuses had discretion in the administration of EOG to target grant aid to students in those programs. These policies encouraged balanced approaches to outreach and access by college campuses involved in TRIO programs. Between 1965 and 1975, college enrollment rates were the same for Whites, African Americans, and Hispanics, a strong indicator that the balanced approach equalized opportunity.[9]

In theory, at least, the marketization of aid by providing Pell grants as a quasi-entitlement improved student choice. In the middle 1970s, the most equitable period of college access, Pell grants were nearly fully federally funded (i.e., close to the authorized maximum award), as were the campus-based programs (CWS, NDSL, and EOG). This older approach of mixing comprehensive campus-based strategies and market models worked well, until aid programs were changed in the late 1970s and campuses were given discretion to redirect campus-based aid to middle-income students.[10] In the 1980s, the federal government cut back on campus-based programs, switched from requiring a grant application to implementing a formula for the distribution of campus-based aid, and shifted the emphasis in federal aid to students from grants to loans.[11] Over time, the balanced approach embedded in the original design of Title IV further declined as even larger amounts of federal funds flowed through market-based grants and loans.

THE RISE AND FALL OF STATE PROGRAMS

Indiana's 21st Century Scholars Program (developed in the early 1990s) provided social and academic support for low-income students and their parents, along with guaranteed grant aid equaling tuition for participating students who took the steps to prepare for college. Research on the program provided evidence of increased college enrollment rates for low-income students.[12] The adaptation of this model in Wisconsin, Oklahoma, Washington, and other states carried forward an approach that balanced social support and a commitment to student aid. The federal GEAR UP program included some of these features, but it is a small program, and funding for grants was so modest that it did little to mitigate the rising net costs of college facing low-income students.

A new federal program, Grants for Access and Persistence (GAP), was authorized in the Higher Education Act of 2008. This initiative, modeled after Indiana's 21st Century Scholars Program, authorized funding for states to develop new partnerships for student financial aid that supported access and persistence. The structure of the program required notifying low-income students of eligibility, providing last-dollar grants equaling tuition after other state and federal grants were sought, and instituting support services for retention at degree-granting institutions. As part of the GAP legislation, states were required to provide a "nonbinding estimate" of the award level they would provide under the program,[13] unlike the 21st Century Scholars Program, which provided a guarantee that the state award would cover estimated financial need as part of program design.[14] The federal GAP program would have ensured that students would receive an award through all their years of eligibility, in order to encourage degree attainment. The U.S. secretary of education was authorized to fund pilot programs under GAP, and a program was established with matching funds from foundations and other sources.[15] The creation of the federal GAP program illustrates an effort to improve persistence and completion, informed by research and rationalized in neoliberal terms but reflecting core classical liberal values.

Unfortunately, federal funding for GAP was eliminated as part of efforts to balance the federal budget. The few states that received pilot grants to begin to develop new partnerships through this federal initiative faced serious financial problems after these federal funds were cut, especially when the states had pledged grants as part of their pilot test of the program. While the award commitments to students under GAP were nonbinding, the information that grants would meet their financial needs for college encouraged students to apply and enroll in partner institutions, but both students and the partner colleges were essentially left high and dry when this federal funding ended.

Students Who Seek Uplift through Education

In recent decades the poverty rate has increased; paradoxically, so has the percentage of adults with college degrees. These developments raise questions about superficial notions of the links between college degrees, earnings, and debts that are included in most contemporary encouragement programs (i.e., information on college preparation, college applications, and financial-aid applications).

NEWLY EDUCATED AND POOR

After three decades of educational reform that promoted college during a period of decline in the middle class, it is time to rethink the relationships between

TABLE 4.1
Grade Levels of Respondents to CFES
2014 Surveys

	2014
6th grade	22%
7th grade	26%
8th grade	31%
9th grade	12%
10th grade	8%
Other	0%
Total number of responses	940

education and poverty. To illustrate the growing educational diversity of low-income families, we present analyses of the 2014 survey of College For Every Student Scholars. Respondents completed surveys at meetings in their schools.

With assistance from corporate foundations, CFES provides social support for college preparation and access to students across the nation. CFES is a non-profit organization that serves urban and rural schools with high poverty rates. Schools are encouraged to select low-income students who might not otherwise prepare for college (i.e., students with potential who are at risk) for the program. The 940 survey respondents were in grades 6 through 10, but they were primarily from middle schools (table 4.1).[16]

STUDENTS FROM HISTORICALLY
UNDERREPRESENTED POPULATIONS

Most students (64%) indicated that they were participants in the federal free or reduced-cost lunch program, a program available only to students from low-income families (table 4.2); only about one-quarter of the respondents indicated they had not participated in the program.[17] These responses affirm that CFES serves mostly low-income students.

If students from the different underrepresented minority groups are combined, that cohort forms the majority of CFES Scholars, although the single largest group of respondents was White / non-Hispanic, most of whom were from poor rural communities (table 4.3). These results further illustrate a focus on the involvement of underrepresented students.

The surprising finding, at least with respect to the major narratives about college access, is that 31% of the respondents lived in families that included an adult with a four-year degree or higher (table 4.4); another 25% were from families with at least one adult with some college education; and 16% were from families where adults had a high school education or less.[18] Since only about 30% of the U.S. population 25 years of age or older currently has a four-year degree,[19] the percentage of CFES Scholars reporting a family member who had completed

TABLE 4.2
Students Reporting Participation in Federal Free
and Reduced-Cost Lunch Programs

Free & Reduced-Cost Lunch	2014
Yes	64%
No	25%
Don't know	11%
No response	0%

TABLE 4.3
Race/Ethnicity of Respondents to CFES 2014 Surveys

	2014
White, not Hispanic	40%
African American	21%
American Indian or Alaskan Native	1%
Latino/a or Hispanic	14%
Asian / Native Hawaiian or other Pacific Islander	18%
Multiple categories or no response	5%

TABLE 4.4
Highest Educational Level of Families of CFES Respondents: Entire Sample, plus
Breakdown of Groups by Federal Free or Reduced-Cost Lunch (FFRL) Status

	All	FFRL yes	FFRL no	Don't know
Did not finish high school	6%	85%	6%	9%
High school diploma or GED	16%	68%	21%	11%
Some college (community college, technical or trade school)	25%	69%	22%	9%
Four-year degree (BA, BS) or higher	31%	53%	39%	8%
Don't know	23%	64%	18%	18%

2014 Breakdown by FFRL

college seems high, especially since the program focuses on low-income families. Given our findings on federal free and reduced-cost lunch (FFRL) programs and family education, we also examined family education by FFRL: the majority of respondents, including those from families with a four-year college graduate, were on FFRL.

Since the Great Recession of 2008, many college graduates have not found jobs consonant with their education, so it should not be a surprise that many students from families with adults who have some college education or a college degree live in poverty. This is consistent with Piketty's evidence-based proposition in *Capital in the Twenty-First Century*: the skills-based argument about poverty no longer holds up as an explanation for income inequality.[20]

The assertion that college completion corresponds with higher income—an underlying assumption in many rationales for policies promoting academic preparation and college success—is seriously problematic in the current economic context, especially given the rising net costs of college for low-income students. The percentage of youth going on to college has grown, even as states have implemented more stringent requirements for high school graduation. The CFES surveys reveal a population of students who are technically potential second-generation college students (i.e., most are from families with at least some prior college enrollment), but they still live in poverty (i.e., most qualify for FFRL programs).

The Great Recession eroded employment opportunities for college graduates, creating a new subculture of poverty: underemployed adults with college degrees. About half of the CFES Scholars who responded to the survey were potential first-generation college students, the group usually targeted for interventions through school-college networks, but many are from this new, more sophisticated class of economically disadvantaged children.

Even before the Great Recession, low-income students took much longer to complete college. Controlling for prior preparation, test scores, and other factors, low-income students in the high school class of 1992 who entered two-year colleges after high school were more likely to be still enrolled after six years than to have completed a degree or to have dropped out,[21] in part because college is so costly. Students who graduated from high school in 1992 are old enough to have children in middle school, which means we are starting to create cross-generation poverty among families with parents who persevered through the unfair K–12 and higher education systems.

Reframing College Knowledge

There is growing diversity in the educational backgrounds of families in poverty, which gives us reason to question the oft-made assumption that has dominated the logic behind reform rationales in K–12 and higher education in recent decades: low-income students will rise to the middle class and be able to pay off large student-debt burdens if they graduate from college. As need-based student financial aid has declined in value relative to the rising costs of college, additional theory- and research-based arguments have evolved for providing information about college pathways. We briefly consider how two major rationales for preparation have evolved before discussing how high schools adapt to the financial conditions facing low-income students aspiring to achieve social and economic uplift.

SOCIAL PROCESSES

Studies of social support and counseling in the 1990s built the argument that providing information on college opportunities and other social support improved college-enrollment opportunities for low-income students.[22] These studies essentially introduced issues related to social support into the discourse on college access, but they did not include student financial aid as an explicit issue that should be considered in interventions.

William G. Tierney and his graduate students have made substantial contributions to the literature on social support. Tierney's early work on outreach overlooked the roles of financial inequality and student aid; for example, neither *Preparing for College: Nine Elements of Effective Outreach*[23] nor *Increasing Access to College: Extending Possibilities for All Students*[24] included a discussion of the financial challenges facing students. But Tierney is a remarkable scholar who engages in dialogue when confronted with critiques of his research, such as missing variables. As a response, he edited *Financial Aid and Access to College: The Public Policy Challenges* as a special issue of *American Behavioral Scientist*.[25] He also collaborated on reframing social-support theory to include explicit considerations of poverty and financial aid.[26] This type of reconsideration is still needed in the theory and practice of social support for student outreach.

Such adaptive changes are also needed within school-college networks that focus on outreach and social support without addressing financial concerns. In interviews with students in rural schools in Florida and New York State, it was evident that students did not know much about the aid programs in their states.[27] This opened a dialogue about the financial context of poverty, resulting in a dramatic change: in the 2014 CFES survey, slightly over 90% of the respondents indicated that they knew about financial aid and scholarships (table 4.5). This awareness is also evident in our analysis of NYC public schools' strategies for using community resources.

The researchers and practitioners who work with social and cultural theories of change have demonstrated a willingness to reconstruct their strategies using empirical evidence that focuses explicitly on the financial, social, and academic challenges facing students from low-income families in a global period when higher education systems are privatizing at a rapid rate.[28] For example, CFES and Trinity College Dublin cohosted an international summit on college access for low-income students in the twenty-first century. In 2014, CFES partnered with Trinity College Dublin to initiate a global campaign called One Million More to help one million low-income youths attain college degrees by 2025 by leveraging the organizational knowledge, practices, and networks CFES has developed over two decades, along with the experiences both groups have had and the lessons they both have learned. Earlier, CFES had adapted its strategies to focus explicitly on work with community organizations to serve more low-

TABLE 4.5
CFES Scholars' Engagement in College and Career Pathways
Practices, 2014

	2014
CFES Scholar (self-identified)	93%
Talked to college student last year	71%
College students visited my school last year	63%
College representative visited last year	55%
Visited college campus last year	79%
I know about financial aid / scholarships	91%
I know the courses I need for college	72%
I talk with my family about college	81%
Need to improve grades for best college	92%

income students across the United States.[29] Trinity College Dublin pilot tested the CFES model through its outreach to high schools in low-income communities in Ireland and is using a research-based strategy for addressing the role of networks in promoting college pathways among working-class students.[30]

PARTIALLY RECONSTRUCTED PIPELINE RATIONALE

In its latest iteration, *The State of College Access and Completion: Improving College Success for Students from Underrepresented Groups*, a book edited by Laura Perna and Anthony Jones, integrates an emphasis on college affordability with college preparatory logic, but it also incorporates an emphasis on data systems, quasi-experimental analyses, and pathways for adults.[31] Indeed, this volume is a masterpiece that reconstructs the reform logic related to college preparation and the pipeline. Perna and Jones outlined six steps and solicited reviews of the literature related to each:[32] improve academic readiness, improve alignment, improve affordability, ensure awareness and knowledge, adapt to meet diverse student needs, and collect and use data (table 4.6). Their steps provide a partial reconstruction of the pipeline by adding student aid and considering adults along with the traditional-age students originally used by NCES to construct the pipeline. After three decades of high school reform, the percentage of adults with college preparation has increased nationally, so adults returning to higher education may be better prepared than in past decades.

As indicated above, there is a problem with even the modified pipeline model: many recent college graduates are underemployed or even unemployed.[33] The broadening of the social contexts of poverty in the United States to include many college graduates does not, however, diminish the importance of providing support for aspiring low-income college students. College financial aid has changed, necessitating large student loans for many and often resulting in substantial debts for both graduates and dropouts. Building college knowledge is of

TABLE 4.6
Reconstructed College Pipeline: New Rationales and Addition of Adult Learners

Steps	Summary of rationale
1. Improve academic readiness for college	Focuses on raising the proficiency levels of students (Conley, 2013; Perna, 2013); argues the courses provided to low-income students in urban schools are not as rigorous as those in high schools that use standards developed by teachers and postsecondary faculty
2. Improve the alignment across and within educational sectors and levels	Argues for using data systems and public accountability to ensure alignment between sectors (K–12, community colleges, and four-year colleges) using a standards-driven approach (Hearn, Jones, & Kurban, 2013; Hossler, Dunbar, & Schapiro, 2013; Perna, 2013)
3. Improve college affordability	Adds a focus on improving need-based grant aid in the set of rationales included in pipeline logics and encourages coordination among institutions, states, and federal programs (Hearn, Jones, & Kurban, 2013; Heller, 2013; Melguizo, Kienzl, & Kosiewicz, 2013; Perna, 2013)
4. Ensure early awareness and knowledge of college and financial aid	Argues that insufficient knowledge of student-aid programs affects aspiration and preparation and increases concerns about costs (Heller, 2013; Melguizo, Kienzl, & Kosiewicz, 2013; Perna & Kurban, 2013); early aid commitment programs recommended (e.g., Indiana's Twenty-First Century Scholars)
5. Adapt approaches to reflect diverse needs of current and prospective students	Expands the focus to include nontraditional-age students and adult career pathways (Bragg, 2013; Perna & Kurban, 2013); recognizes special learning needs of adults
6. Collect and use data to monitor access and completion and identify refinements needed in existing practices and policies	Urges the use of data systems that track students from K–20 to ensure alignment, recommend policy changes, and analyze impact using quasi-experimental methods (DesJardins & Flaster, 2013; Hearn, Jones & Kurban, 2013; Hossler, Dunbar, & Shapiro, 2013)

increasing importance because of the high net costs of college for low-income students in most states. Students need to be informed about the economic realities of different types of degrees, along with the costs of attending college.

Recontextualizing College Knowledge

The reconceptualization of the pipeline by Perna and Jones and the other scholars who contributed to their volume provides the beginnings of a new framework.[34] We agree that adding financial aid to the pipeline logic is crucial, as is a consideration of patterns of adult enrollment in college, but there are additional factors that should be acknowledged, including the claim that graduates can easily pay off their student debts. We identify some additional problems with the contemporary pipeline theory of change before examining actual practices in providing college knowledge as curriculum or co-curriculum in our case-study schools.

First, the infusion of career content into the curriculum of specialized high schools alters the paradigm of the academic pipeline to include career-specific knowledge. This development could hasten the demise of the liberal arts, general-education model for the first two years of undergraduate education (chapter 3). The economic value of social science and humanities fields has already come into question (chapter 2). Moreover, there is a serious problem that could shake the underpinnings of this new career-oriented model: because globalizing economies emphasize STEM education and careers (Organisation of Economic Co-operation and Development nations, as well as China and Brazil), there is an oversupply of STEM graduates. This is driving down compensation for STEM-educated labor both worldwide and in the United States, compounding the effects of the growing cost of a four-year degree and the debt load of many college graduates.

Second, it is crucial to rethink the links between high school and college relative to the demands placed on students entering college prepared for STEM fields. In the old liberal arts model, students would choose a major during their junior year, although STEM fields have long had more rigorous requirements for college admissions. Far more students change their majors out of STEM fields than change into them from other disciplines,[35] and academically underprepared students who enter college in STEM fields are often faced with a change in their major, transfer, or failure. Our Beta High School case study (chapter 2) illustrated that it may be necessary to rethink the 9–14 early college model if the goal is to prepare more students for STEM fields in four-year colleges. Sigma High School (chapter 3) focused on uplifting its student population to community college standards, but these students most likely would face serious academic challenges if they transferred to a four-year college in a math, science, or engineering major; this was also true at Kappa High School, which had developed a technology theme and related content (chapter 1). Preparing students for STEM fields may be counterproductive academically as well as economically.

Third, even with a good alignment between high school content niches and an undergraduate curriculum (an argument made by Perna and Jones,[36] as well as being part of the pipeline logic), the economic challenges of the labor market could undermine the aims of the STEM model. Some science fields, like biology, have a history of lower earnings than engineering and math.[37] It is entirely possible that graduates of high schools specializing in the humanities, social sciences, teaching, and some STEM fields will be at a disadvantage. At a minimum, students need to be coached about net costs and potential earnings as they review student-aid offers and consider fields of study. A way through this puzzle may be by tightly aligning high school and collegiate courses, as illustrated by our Kappa High School case study (chapter 1), but this option requires substantial financial resources and institutional commitment.

Fourth, these forces may necessitate a better-informed dialogue about college experiences and expectations across different types of colleges. In a market-based urban setting, high schools often have to adapt and change their niche-content specializations to appeal to students, as shown in our Onye Nkuzi High School case study (this chapter). The presence of market forces in high schools complicates efforts to create specialized pathways between high school and college. Marketing by colleges, trends in the appeal of majors, and expected earnings can alter these linkages. The market model of urban schools may be too fluid to establish tightly aligned pathways between high schools and colleges.

Fifth, it is crucial that students have realistic information about college costs if we expect to promote cross-generation uplift. There are already signs of poverty among college graduates, probably an artifact of their time-to-degree and financial hardships during college, in addition to the effect of the Great Recession. Perna and Jones's addition of student aid to the pipeline is a step forward.[38] Telling students to borrow to pay for college, consistent with the ACE rationale for preparation, is seriously problematic in the current higher education market. To ensure financial access, students with substantial financial need must, at a minimum, be made aware of their financial-aid options,[39] or, optimally, have a guarantee of financial aid (as in the 21st Century Scholars or Washington State Achievers models).[40] This, however, is not the current situation in most states, where the majority of low-income students face excessive debt and work burdens.

Sixth, it is crucial that organizers in nongovernmental organizations and colleges that engage in building partnerships to support college access pay attention to civic engagement and mentoring. William Sedlacek's noncognitive variables have long been used in holistic assessments for college admissions;[41] admissions personnel now look for indicators of an applicant's leadership, ability to navigate social and educational pathways, and capacity to deal with institutional racism. The Educational Testing Service has moved forward after conducting pilot tests of a new exam that measures students' strengths related to these long-standing indicators.[42] It is probable that low-income students will continue to need social support to build these types of skills and keep pace with more economically advantaged students in the college-admissions process. The rigid CCSS approach to the high school curriculum makes it difficult for public high schools to incorporate this support into their curriculum (chapters 1–3).

A Co-Curricular Approach to College Knowledge through CFES

CFES is a modestly priced reform model. It was developed as a student-support program funded on a school-by-school basis by private corporations with a vested interest in the regions in which the schools are located. After providing an overview of the flexible core practices in CFES, we discuss how these practices were adapted by the NYC public schools we studied and provide a brief illustrative case.

Flexible Core Practices

Most of the small urban schools we visited incorporated a school-wide, co-curricular support process. CFES has three core practices provided by school-college partnerships formed for each campus:[43]

- *Mentoring.* Relationships between CFES Scholars and their college student and graduate mentors, teachers, other adults, and peers foster personal and academic growth. Mentors are student advocates encouraging college preparation activities, fostering values clarification, providing career and college orientations, and building study skills that raise the CFES Scholars' sense of what is possible.
- *Pathways to college.* College partnerships allow CFES Scholars, many of whom are potential first-generation college students, to visit college campuses, interact with college students and faculty, and gain exposure to these institutions' admissions procedures, financial aid possibilities, and academic-program faculty. Additional exposure to college opportunities occurs through workshops for parents and CFES Scholars on how to choose a college and complete college-admissions and financial-aid applications. There are also summer on-campus programs to raise college aspirations and convince lower-income parents that financial obstacles are surmountable.
- *Leadership through service.* This key component of the CFES reform model builds students' leadership skills through school and service opportunities that empower them to broaden their horizons; learn leadership skills; take responsibility for others; and build self-esteem, resilience, discipline, and organizational skills.

Adaptations in NYC Public District Schools

Two of the four NYC district schools we visited were small enough so that all students could be involved in CFES. Both of these schools served college-bound students interested in the schools' college and career themes who had been admitted through a limited screening process. They included students from grades 9 through 12, organized into cross-grade groups. CFES functioned as a catalyst for change. Some of the patterns observed included:

- *Adaptation of practices learned through CFES.* School administrators, teachers, and students were able to attend CFES annual meetings to learn CFES practices from other schools in the network. Some of the NYC schools adapted these methods. Teachers described the "tremendous opportunity for schools" to develop new procedures and adjust their strategies for improvement.

- *Promotion of campus diversity in marketing students to colleges.* Many of the college partners created opportunities for CFES students to apply directly to their institutions, as did other colleges making presentations at CFES meetings. From the perspective of the urban high schools, these opportunities create new pathways to college for their students, while the colleges gain geographic and ethnic diversity.
- *Flexibility for schools.* School officials explained that CFES has "given us the opportunity to think broader than we would have otherwise." The CFES program is considered valuable because it does not dictate, but instead offers various models that can be applied to the schools' specific contexts. This is a marked contrast to the strategic, control-oriented approaches to reform used in many major initiatives undertaken by schools and states.
- *Development of targeted strategies.* Schools pick up ideas that enable them to focus on critical issues. For instance, Young Men's Leadership, an after-school mentoring program for the "most difficult" students, and a drug-awareness program were cited as examples of school-based programs growing out of CFES conferences.
- *Variation in CFES implementation strategies.* There was a lot of variation in the way the program was implemented at different campuses. At 21st Century Technological Academy (a small school on a large high school campus), CFES is in place at every level: from principal down through guidance counselor, CFES director, liaison, and teacher. At the other extreme, in Onye Nkuzi High School the CFES liaison seemed to be the sole driver of the process (see the case study below). These variations did not seem to affect school success with CFES.

The above observations illustrate that there is not one best way to go about creating a college-knowledge emphasis in high school. The core-practices approach enables schools to develop college-support processes, but the ways in which these practices are implemented are crafted in collaboration with each school. CFES program directors work closely with school liaisons and college partners to create annual plans. Each student is mentored by teachers or community members and, in turn, mentors younger students. College partners are actively engaged in programming at the schools. School leaders attend national and regional meetings where they learn about practices that have worked at other schools.

Case Study: Onye Nkuzi High School

Onye Nkuzi High School provides an illustrative case of the organizing process in CFES schools. Since becoming a school of choice in NYC, Onye Nkuzi attracts low-income students who aspire to complete college and find careers that uplift their families. We briefly look at how the Onye Nkuzi respondents compare with the entire group of respondents to the CFES survey before examining how the co-curriculum strategy for college knowledge developed in this school.

A total of 42 students in the 9th and 10th grades responded to the survey. Onye Nkuzi students were older than most of the other 2014 CFES respondents, who were in middle school (table 4.7).

Three-quarters of the Onye Nkuzi respondents were from low-income families eligible for federally subsidized lunches (table 4.8), a higher rate of poverty than is evident nationally for CFES. In addition, all respondents from Onye Nkuzi were from a minority group, a further contrast to the CFES general population (table 4.9)

The Onye Nkuzi respondents were from families with educational levels similar to the CFES respondents overall (table 4.10); most were from families with either some college (26%) or four-year degrees (31%), illustrating the new pattern of urban poverty. These students are clearly from families striving for cross-generation uplift, but their parents' gains in educational attainment did not lift them out of poverty.

TABLE 4.7
Grade Levels of Onye Nkuzi and All CFES Respondents

	Onye Nkuzi	All CFES
6th grade	0%	22%
7th grade	0%	26%
8th grade	0%	31%
9th grade	62%	12%
10th grade	38%	8%
No response	0%	0%
Total number of respondents	42	940

TABLE 4.8
Students Reporting Participation in Federal Free and
Reduced-Cost Lunch Programs at Onye Nkuzi Compared
with All CFES Respondents

	Onye Nkuzi	All CFES
Yes	76%	64%
No	14%	25%
Don't know	10%	11%
No response	0%	0%

TABLE 4.9
Race/Ethnicity of Onye Nkuzi Students Compared with
All CFES Respondents

	Onye Nkuzi	All CFES
White, not Hispanic	0%	40%
African American	31%	21%
American Indian or Alaska Native	0%	1%
Latino/a or Hispanic	48%	14%
Asian / Native Hawaiian or other Pacific Islander	14%	18%
No response	7%	5%

TABLE 4.10
Highest Educational Levels of Students' Families for Onye Nkuzi Students Compared
with All CFES Students

	Onye Nkuzi	All CFES
Did not finish high school	12%	6%
High school diploma or GED	10%	16%
Some college (community college, technical or trade school)	26%	25%
Four-year degree (BA, BS) or higher	31%	31%
Don't know	21%	23%
No response	0%	0%

PATHWAYS TO COLLEGE AND CAREERS

The challenges of developing a compelling theme to attract students and providing realistic information about college costs converged at Onye Nkuzi. The school continues to be a landing place for students in the option pool who are interested in careers in education, as well as for transfer students from closed schools or students who did not have a good experience at their original school. When the principal (who was an excellent leader) realized that the admissions process was delivering some students who hadn't chosen the school and weren't necessarily interested in the theme, he responded by adding the liberal arts academy to meet their needs.

With the addition of the liberal arts school, students were able to explore a wide range of options for majors in college. For example, a student commented: "I think I want to get a degree in medicine—biology major or pre-med—or I want to do journalism. I haven't decided yet." The next student in the same focus group added: "I've always wanted to own my own business or actually travel the world and be like a hotel critic so you're getting paid to go on vacation." Clearly these students were still figuring out what they wanted to do, although they did not mention the school's theme in discussing their future plans.

TABLE 4.11
CFES Scholars' Engagement in College and Career Pathways Practices
for Onye Nkuzi Students Compared with All CFES Respondents

	Onye Nkuzi	All CFES
CFES Scholar (self-identified)	76%	93%
Talked to college student last year	57%	71%
College students visited my school last year	57%	63%
College representative visited last year	45%	55%
Visited college campus last year	57%	79%
I know about financial aid / scholarships	98%	91%
I know the courses I need for college	88%	72%
I talk with my family about college	83%	81%
Need to improve grades for best college	98%	92%

TABLE 4.12
Plans after High School: Onye Nkuzi Students Compared
with All CFES Respondents

	Onye Nkuzi	All CFES
Go to Work	2%	6%
Go to a trade or technical school	0%	2%
Attend a two-year or community college	0%	7%
Attend a four-year college or university	67%	65%
Don't know, more than one response, or no response	31%	21%

Educators in the school also indicated that family concerns about potential earnings were a factor in the change: shifting to a general liberal arts theme would make it clear to families that their children would have choices about majors and careers. The majority of both overall and Onye Nkuzi respondents self-identified as CFES Scholars (table 4.11). A very high percentage of the Onye Nkuzi students knew about the courses and grades they would need for college, and virtually all knew about student financial aid.

Students described their involvement in CFES as a process of "joining" the group. One student said: "I heard about it my freshman year. I actually had [teacher's name] for my life-skills class. So in the life-skills class he said, 'You're a good student, you should join CFES.' So once I joined I went on college trips." The activities through CFES gave students opportunities to learn about career paths. While some students used their involvement to broaden their interests, as the student's comments above illustrate, others found that their initial liking for teaching was intensified through their involvement. For example, another Onye Nkuzi student reflected: "I want to be a 1st grade elementary school teacher. I want to go to college. I really do."

About two-thirds of the overall CFES and Onye Nkuzi respondents indicated that they planned to go to a four-year college after high school (table 4.12), but a higher percentage of Onye Nkuzi students either didn't know their plans, had more than one response, or did not respond.

An overarching concern at Onye Nkuzi was that both its students and their parents wanted to learn about college options. One teacher mentioned the concerns students and parents had about costs: "They're aware that there are scholarship opportunities out there, but they don't have the confidence to know that 'I can get that.'" Onye Nkuzi teachers recognized that their students had to work through personal challenges to have an opportunity to attend a good four-year program, and that high grades would help them earn grant and/or scholarship funding. Finding realistic pathways for students was a crucial concern for teachers and administrators at Onye Nkuzi: "We always try to set up meetings, you know, we've had in the past, we've had our guidance counselor, our senior advisor come and do a presentation about the FAFSA and talk to kids about financial aid and scholarship opportunities. But for the most part it's something that we definitely need to work and focus more on, because financial aid is a huge issue."

ENGAGEMENT IN CFES SOCIAL SUPPORT

The social support offered through CFES is more comprehensive than that provided by most school-college networks. Two-thirds of the Onye Nkuzi CFES students were acquainted with college dropouts, a higher percentage than for all CFES respondents (table 4.13). Students reported having either adult or student mentors and that their mentors engaged them in talking about college. Most found it easy to talk with their mentors.

The CFES program director at Onye Nkuzi described their approach to working with colleges: "We always have, you know, sessions where somebody will come in and they'll explain, you know, the admissions process, they'll talk about financial aid, they give a run-down on basically all aspects of what the

TABLE 4.13
CFES Scholars' Engagement in Mentoring and Social Support for Onye Nkuzi Students Compared with All CFES Respondents

	Onye Nkuzi	All CFES
I know college dropouts	67%	51%
Talked with older student about problems	48%	38%
Older student is a mentor	50%	42%
Adult mentor (teacher, counselor, other)	43%	63%
Mentor makes it easy to ask questions	71%	72%
Teachers encourage college plans	83%	88%
Mentor encourages me to think about college	81%	74%
I am a mentor	10%	45%

kids would need to know for college and, you know, we bring all kids there. We bring freshmen, sophomores, juniors, and seniors." He also tried to build ongoing partnerships with colleges: "Every time I try to set up a visit I tell them, like, 'Listen, trust me, you want freshmen, you want sophomores,' because those kids, especially these inner-city kids, they go to that campus, it's the first one they've ever seen, that sticks in their mind."

LEADERSHIP THROUGH SERVICE

The Onye Nkuzi leadership team realized that they could build on community connectivity as they addressed their students' concerns about college costs (table 4.14). For example, a teacher reflected on the factors that attracted students to the school: "We have a really good community base where the teacher-student rapport has always been very strong at our school so, you know, a lot of times you'll find siblings, you know, brothers and sisters coming to the school because they know the good opportunities that have been offered for their brothers and sisters."

A student observed: "We also go to an elementary school once a year and teach kids about college to start off. We do activities with them like face painting. We read to them and we feed them stuff." Volunteering in lower-grade schools was commonly practiced. Events and activities were often organized by students and helped them build an awareness of community and social issues as an integral part of their high school education, at the same time as they provided experiences that could help the students with college admissions. Social networking offers students an opportunity to learn from each other, a key skill for group cooperative learning in college. A student commented: "So it starts to rub off on you and you start competing with higher standards." There was also a cross-grade approach to student leadership, illustrated by the relatively high

TABLE 4.14
Student Involvement in Engaged Leadership Practices by Onye Nkuzi
and All CFES Respondents

	Onye Nkuzi	All CFES
Involved in service activities	45%	47%
Sport team	10%	47%
Students seek my opinion	88%	78%
See self as a leader	81%	80%
Band/chorus	5%	45%
Community service through school	74%	76%
Worked with other students on out-of-class projects	67%	62%
Worked with other students to solve problems	59%	68%
Served as a mentor or coach to younger students	13%	40%
Organized activities for student groups	21%	30%
Learned about project planning and teamwork	69%	59%

percentage of Onye Nkuzi students who had older students as mentors and who talked with older students about their problems.

Teachers and administrators helped the students consider specific challenges they would face. For example, one Onye Nkuzi teacher expressed a sentiment widely echoed across our interviews: "I know in the past, and we've recently, one of our best students, our most hard-working student, top five in the class, and she was undocumented, and she wasn't even able, she wasn't able to apply for the Posse scholarship, which she very well could have won." To help with this problem, Onye Nkuzi informed undocumented immigrant students that they could receive college credits through the City University of New York (CUNY) system.

Integrating College Knowledge into the Curriculum in Charter Schools

Each of the public charter high schools we visited viewed college access and success as key elements of their mission and purpose. Recognizing the challenge of preparing first-generation college students for higher education, each school prioritized preparation for and enrollment in college as a central part of the school's design. The schools emphasized academic rigor and high standards through a college preparatory curriculum for all students.

Integrating College Knowledge

The public charter schools exude an attitude of "We will do whatever it takes to make sure our students are successful." High expectations and standards are important, but what makes these schools different is the support and resources they provide to help students and families access postsecondary institutions. The freedom to align the curriculum with career content has the additional benefit of blending in information about college and career pathways related to their school's themes.

These charter schools integrated college prep courses with their thematic content. Sigma High School uses seminar courses as a "touchstone" for the student's college classes. The seminar teacher is expected to help the students navigate their community college courses. In addition, Alpha, Beta, and Sigma use high school graduation requirements to support student development of college-readiness skills. Through Alpha's classes and a portfolio requirement, Beta's gateways, and Sigma's senior capstone, students learn about self-management and organization, which apply when they complete their personal statements and college applications.

Three of the charter high schools we studied—Beta, Sigma, and Kappa—integrated a college curriculum into their academic programs for all students at the high school level. An emphasis on college was integral to the daily life of students at these campuses, as is evident in the discussion of curricular subjects in chapters 1, 2, and 3. A member of the Sigma leadership team reflected: "We aligned our graduation requirements to the university admission standards when we transitioned to an early college. And we're a little bit ahead of the curve on that as far as [the state] is concerned." Alpha provides a college counselor, an assistant for the college counselor, and an alumni coordinator. Beta uses a strong advisory model: every teacher is expected to also be an advisor, and this school has even turned great teachers away because they were not interested in serving in an advisory capacity.

Our Alpha case study offers a distinctive model: collaborating with a foundation-sponsored program to provide an explicit emphasis on college preparation and college applications as a co-curricular process, similar in many respects to CFES core practices. One principal described this activist approach: "We might have a couple that are going to be college bound regardless of what we do. I would say for 99% of them, we're doing some sort of intervention to make that happen." This statement could easily have been made by any of the leaders from our four innovative public charter schools. Through their engagement in the academic curriculum and co-curricular programming at their high schools, the students' educational trajectories changed.

Case Study: Alpha High School

Alpha High School grew out of the experience of law students and professors in the community-advocacy law center at a major private university who, while teaching at a neighborhood high school, witnessed how limited opportunities stunted the academic and social development of its students. They saw an opportunity to use legal principles as teaching tools to educate and empower the students they encountered. They collaborated with education experts and community members to create a school that would provide committed students with the academic and youth-development resources they needed to succeed and become actively involved citizens. Alpha's charter was granted in 2001, and the school welcomed its first class that same year. Alpha has worked diligently to provide a college preparatory education to students in a long-underserved community. Located in the most impoverished neighborhood of a major city, Alpha strives to educate students facing significant barriers to learning: the community has the highest rate of poverty (36%) and the lowest high school (66%) and college (8%) graduation rates in the city.

Alpha's mission is to prepare students to succeed in college and engage in a democratic society. In practice, these values translate into a college preparatory curriculum for all students, with a focus on law and the skills successful lawyers need to develop: the ability to solve complex problems; think critically; and advocate persuasively for themselves, their clients, and their communities. In order to accomplish this mission, Alpha integrates a rigorous curriculum with in-school and after-school support programming, such as academic tutoring, personalized mentoring, and one-on-one college guidance.

Academic rigor and high standards are woven into the fabric of the school's culture. In addition to developing a curriculum aligned with social justice and its state's educational standards, Alpha has a comprehensive approach to family engagement and college planning, including a cohesive four-year college-knowledge building process.

PARENTAL OUTREACH

Alpha encourages family involvement from day one, recognizing that the role of parents/guardians is crucial in their students' success. An Alpha administrator explains: "If you look at kids who come from different circumstances, they have social capital and they have parents who know how to navigate the system. Our kids don't necessarily have that structure and so it's providing some of those same things that other kids they're competing with have, but just in a different format."

The admissions process at Alpha is based on a common application and a lottery. Parents are required to sign a parent compact that outlines expectations for the school, the student, and the student's family in the educational process. According to the Alpha website, parents are asked to:

- monitor attendance;
- ensure that students complete their assigned homework;
- provide all necessary supplies;
- attend all portfolio presentations and open houses;
- participate (as appropriate) in decisions relating to their child's education;
- stay informed about their child's education by promptly reading all notices from the school received either from their child or by mail;
- communicate with teachers and the school's administration; and
- participate (to the extent possible) in the parent-teacher organization.

This school is highly focused on parental involvement and fulfillment of these expectations. About 90% of the families attended at least one Alpha event, indicating a high level of engagement. A full-time parent-involvement coordinator maintains contact with the parents and organizes monthly parent-teacher organization (PTO) meetings. During the 2008–9 academic year, the college-access program sponsored two college nights where students and their parents could work on college applications. Alpha regularly communicates with parents using letters and flyers and, in some cases, personal phone calls and home visits. Parents receive tri-quarterly progress reports from teachers and alert notices if their child is failing to make adequate progress.[44] Ongoing communication mechanisms for engaging the students' parents include:

- monthly update letters that contain schedules of all open houses, upcoming PTO meetings, a school calendar, and other school events;
- two progress reports per quarter, as well as quarterly report cards;
- invitations to attend annual portfolio panel presentations;
- opportunities to become members of the board of trustees;
- monthly PTO meetings with on-site childcare; and
- a variety of social and informative activities, such as poetry night, potlucks, and a college financial-aid workshop.

The school requires all teachers to maintain a call log documenting they have made at least 15 parent contacts per month. Alpha provides parents with access to NetClassroom, an online tool that allows them to track their child's attendance, conduct, and grades.

COLLEGE-ACCESS PROGRAM

Alpha is the only high school in their area of the city that offers an extensive college-access program. The school employs a full-time college counselor, who is responsible for coordinating all activities directly related to college going, such as college visits, financial-aid workshops, and application preparation. Due to the overwhelming nature of the position, an assistant was hired to help with scholarship applications. This staffing addition enabled the college counselor to focus on the seniors' needs.

The college counselor works as a liaison with the College Access and Success Program (CASP), a foundation-funded scholarship program that provides a significant last-dollar award, ensuring financial aid for selected Alpha students; supplemental in-school college counseling; and support to students, ranging from the college-application process through college completion. The foundation uses a unique set of strengths-based indicators for the selection of high school juniors as CASP Scholars. A representative from the program provides in-school college counseling. Key components of CASP include SAT preparation, college advising, college visits, parent workshops, and mentoring while a student is in college. Alpha also maintains strategic partnerships with a citywide college-access program that provides supplemental in-school counseling, up to $2000 in last-dollar awards for eligible students not funded by CASP, and a community internship program that allows advanced Alpha seniors to dually enroll in first-year college courses.

Alpha has an enviably strong track record thus far in college-acceptance rates. Across 10 graduating classes, 100% of their graduates have been accepted into college, and two out of three of their alumni/ae graduate from college, well above the national average of 54%. Alpha students benefit from the school's relationship with CASP. Starting in spring 2007, students were eligible to apply for the CASP Scholar Awards program, established by the school's partner foundation to increase high school and college graduation rates among Title I students. In the class of 2008, 29 students received CASP Scholar awards, a last-dollar award of up to $9700 per year for up to five years if they attend a four-year college or university.

THE COMPREHENSIVE COLLEGE-PREPARATION PROGRAM

Students enrolled at Alpha receive support services across all four years of high school to help them prepare for college and build their knowledge of college options. During their freshman and sophomore years, students and their families are introduced to college planning as part of a summer program. Throughout the 9th and 10th grades, the college counselor imparts information on postsecondary education options during advisory periods. Students visit at least one college during their freshmen and sophomore years. Parents have the opportunity to attend evening and weekend workshops on the college-application and financial-aid processes.

All juniors are required to participate in a half-year SAT preparation course, based on the Cambridge curriculum. Alpha also provides Kaplan online access and other support for test preparation. Alpha has set a goal that by 2015, 75% of their students will score at least 800 (in combined math and verbal) on the SAT and 25% will score at least 1000. Juniors also receive introductory instruction on college planning and access, go to college fairs, and make at least one college visit.

All seniors participate in the year-long senior seminar, cotaught by the college counselor and the CASP advisor, that meets for 90 minutes twice a week. The course is modeled on the College Summit curriculum, which walks students through the process of completing college applications, drafting personal statements, and preparing for the transition to college life. In addition, the college counseling staff helps seniors with every step of their college-application process, including writing essays, securing recommendations and fee waivers, and ensuring that their paperwork is in order. Many of these activities are accomplished during the senior seminar.

ALUMNI

In SY 2006–7, the college counselor and a member of the Development Office began providing services to Alpha alumni/ae. A school leader describes the reason why this was necessary: "We would find out, kind of after the fact, that they [Alpha alumni/ae] had failed classes, or dropped out, or what have you, and because we didn't know about it or even know they were on the road to dropping out, we had no ability or opportunity to intervene and try to help the student for whatever reason they were being challenged at the college level, try to get them the help they needed so that they could stay in school and be successful."

In SY 2007–8, a formal alumni-coordinator position was created to track graduates' progress in college through monthly contacts and care packages. The coordinator works individually with alumni/ae to assist them in managing the transition to college and helps connect them with resources and emergency funding (if needed).

High Schools in Transition

There is a growing body of literature that emphasizes the integration of college-preparation content into the high school curriculum, which is proving to be a major challenge. It is a widely held assumption that students will prepare for college if they have information on college options. When we examined the experiences of high schools that have had some success in building college-going cultures, we realized that more than information is needed.

At three of the four public charter schools we visited, the high school curriculum was integrated with college experiences in ways that developed college knowledge. At the other schools we studied, there were co-curricular programs established that included mentoring, service opportunities, and college visits. Whether developed through a school-based methodology or through adaptation of practices provided by external support organizations (both were evident at Alpha High School), these schools created a sequence of practices that support student learning about college.

CFES partnerships played a key role in the NYC public district high schools, as did the partnerships developed with local and national colleges. The curriculum alignment was deeper than meeting requirements for graduation; it also included offering courses in collaboration with colleges. While much of the literature and current educational policies emphasize a high school curriculum aligned with college-admission standards, many of the schools we visited had gone beyond that and were deeply engaged in a collaborative delivery of educational opportunities. These new policies offered opportunities for high schools and colleges to explore integrated approaches to providing an undergraduate curriculum. Yet as our Beta High School case study (chapter 2) illustrated, partnerships in advanced math education between high schools and community colleges can inhibit the preparation for math in four-year colleges. There is a need to carefully craft strategies for curriculum alignment.

The schools that used a wraparound co-curricular process—CFES schools and Alpha High School—illustrate that there are many variations in strategies for supplying college-going support. Indeed, Alpha has multiple methods of providing college knowledge: curriculum integration, student-support services, and guaranteed financial aid. Thus, while both the urban district schools and public charter schools used as our case studies had external support from foundations and other sources, only Alpha High School provided additional student aid for low-income students, a reform evident in only a few schools nationally.[45]

Conclusions

The policy literature has placed a strong emphasis on providing information about colleges and college applications as a means of encouraging college preparation and enrollment. All too frequently, however, reform advocates conclude that applying for financial aid is enough to counter concerns about costs. Nonetheless, if need-based grants are not sufficiently funded, as is increasingly the reality across the United States, low-income students will not be able to pay for college. Students in this situation may be faced with high levels of work while attending and student debt, often resulting in a delayed degree—or no degree at all. Federal need-based grants are woefully inadequate, and most states simply do not make up the difference for low-income, college-prepared students.

State financial-aid programs can guarantee grant aid for low-income students, as was once the case with the model pioneered by Indiana in its 21st Century Scholars Program, but in practice few states have been able to stick with this strategy, not even Indiana. States like New York have a history of substantial funding for need-based aid, but these systems fall short of providing an aid guarantee of the type provided by Alpha High School, which had a school-based grant program developed in partnership with ample funding from a supportive foundation. Our Onye Nkuzi case study illustrates that even with New York State's relatively generous need-based grant program, students still have concerns about college costs *after* they learn about student financial-aid programs. Many students also knew about the limitations of a college degree, because they had parents who had navigated the postsecondary system and were still in poverty.

The public charter schools aligned their curricula with college applications: Kappa High School (chapter 1) had collegiate courses for all students; Beta High school (chapter 2) developed a curriculum that taught students to write college essays; Sigma High School provided community college credits for most students (chapter 3); and Alpha High School offered an introduction to social justice and law curriculum for all students (this chapter). Thus all four of the charter schools we visited had developed strategies that aligned college pathways with college access, college credit, and/or career pathways and content. In addition, several of the NYC public district schools developed similar strategies: Remus High School had a CUNY partnership that offered college courses to students in engineering and medical specializations; and Acme Collegiate Academy developed a course that helped students prepare for the essay portion of college applications.

In addition to college preparation courses in math and other fields, college knowledge includes both career-related content and trustworthy information on student aid. Our Alpha High School case study provides a rare example of a high school ensuring that its students will be able to pay for college, along with a curriculum oriented toward a collegiate specialization. The rest of the high schools we examined developed strategies for encouraging their students to apply for student aid. Our Onye Nkuzi case study illustrates that students struggle with the prospects of paying for college, even when they gain realistic information about the net costs of college. Inequality in college access, based on finances, merits the attention of high school reformers and college-access providers/partners, who often overlook the difficult realities of financial access to colleges for low-income students.

CHAPTER FIVE

Toward Equitable Transformation

There has been progress toward transforming high school education in the United States. Most states have raised high school graduation requirements. Typically, there was an initial period of decline in graduation rates following implementation, but that has reversed in most states as they gained experience with the new requirements.[1] The new common standards (i.e., CCSS) attempt to define a rigorous curriculum for all students. Most of the rationales for reform, including the recent conceptualization that links career and technical education with college preparatory content, make questionable assumptions about education, income, and debt repayment, based on an optimistic prognostication of returns to education that should be tempered with realistic evidence about underlying causes of the growing inequality in educational opportunity and income. If more students are graduating from high school prepared for college and more students are attaining at least some amount of higher education—thanks to the past three decades of reform—why have educational and income inequalities grown during this same period?

There is not a simple explanation for the relationships among growth in income inequality, improved rigor in high schools, and college attainment over the past three decades. Throughout this volume, we've been critical of the simplistic application of correlations in policy advocacy. For decades, school reformers have simply assumed that raising educational quality (i.e., standards and requirements for graduation) would reduce income inequality, and some studies have confirmed this (chapter 2). But the issue is not that simple, because global economic conditions, tax and spending policies in nations, and many other factors contribute to the growth in income inequality.[2]

Adding career content to college prep does little to alter the underlying problem with income distribution. This would not be as serious an issue if student debt was not mortgaging the futures of so many low-income college students, graduates, and dropouts. While gains in education are obviously not the cause of income inequality, the rationales used for educational reform and new methods of financing higher education have seriously mislead families. As a concluding chapter, we explain how deceptive reform rationales may have come about, discuss how schools adapted to the contradictory goals of educational reform, and offer possible next steps.

Inequality and Urban School Reform

Educational reformers and social science researchers assume a positive association between educational reform and cross-generation economic development.
From the creation of land grant colleges,[3] to the development of public K–12
education from local Protestant school systems,[4] to the G.I. Bill after World
War II,[5] and on through the Great Society reforms,[6] increased public investment in education had indeed corresponded with economic progress. A recent
mistake has been in assuming that educational reforms are causally linked to
cross-economic uplift; in truth, economic uplift is also related to egalitarian
economic and social policies, as well as many other factors.[7] Education contrib-
utes to economic revitalization, but without progressive economic policies, it is
unlikely that educated citizens will transform national economies. For example,
both China and India already had an educated labor force before a globalization of corporations brought these nations new employment opportunities and
increased personal income.[8] In the United States. the grand theory of public
investment in services broke down in the 1980s as neoconservatives argued that
government was the problem, taxes were too high, and the private sector could
provide public services—including education—better than the federal and state
governments. At the same time, neoliberals argued for increased rights and standards in education, health care, and social services, but without resisting cuts
in taxation (particularly at higher-income levels) and decreases in public investment in education.

Through our analyses of policy discourses involving alliances of researchers
and political agents and the ways in which successful schools navigated the con-
tested terrain of school reform in urban markets, we've gained insight into how
deceptive rationales for educational reform evolved. We've also seen how well-
intended reforms within schools can actually *contribute* to educational inequality, even though they have successfully improved the education of motivated
and able students from low-income families. First, we focus on people left out
of the reform strategies used in urban schools. Second, we look at the emergence of educated poor families despite their active engagement in economic
and social uplift across generations. Third, we reconsider the ways educational
reform links to inequalities in education and income. We then conclude this
section by refining our research-based theory of change, one that was developed
through a series of studies on college preparation, access, choice, and persistence
over the past decades.[9]

Students Left Behind

Nationally, there is an oft-expressed concern that school-choice schemes in NYC
and other cities leave many low-income students behind, tracked into schools
that have been unable to improve.[10] An examination of change processes in

schools that navigated successfully through the complex terrain of educational reform revealed some of the mechanisms that perpetuate educational inequality. The literature on educational inequality correctly identifies a persistent correlation between poverty and low levels of educational attainment. The sad reality, however, is that while reforms that raise educational standards and use market mechanisms recognize that poor families deserve high-quality education, the implementation of these reforms often denies the most challenged students access to schools that are engaged in elevating their position in local quality rankings.

We briefly summarize the patterns reproducing inequality that are evident in the public charter and NYC district schools we studied before focusing on the challenges of uplift for the truly disadvantaged.

PUBLIC CHARTER SCHOOLS

Charter schools face difficult choices about retaining all students as they seek to develop an engaging and rigorous curriculum. The ones we visited provided four distinctive models: a social-justice-themed urban school guaranteeing student financial aid (Alpha); a liberal arts high school promoting access to four-year colleges for low-income students (Beta); a new-generation technical high school offering college-level courses to low-income students (Kappa); and an early college high school, situated on a community college campus, serving mostly immigrants (Sigma). Urban low-income students constitute the majority in all four schools, and these schools adapted their curriculum to meet their students' perceived needs, but they left some of the most-challenged students behind.

Alpha and Beta High Schools used lottery systems for admission, with no consideration of prior achievement. Both schools, however, sought to provide a rigorous curriculum that would help students qualify for a four-year college, including elite private institutions. Alpha required more advanced math courses for graduation than the schools in the public school district in which Alpha was situated, leading to some of its students transferring to schools with a less-rigorous curriculum.

Beta High School started out with an early college model, using local community college courses for advanced math, but when it became clear that its students had trouble in undergraduate engineering programs, it developed a more rigorous in-school math curriculum. The teachers recognized the tradeoff of losing motivated students who struggled with the rigor of Beta's program, but those students could go to local public schools.

Kappa High School faced a similar challenge but had more flexibility. This school upgraded its curriculum and developed a new admissions scheme. Students who did not have the level of preparation they needed were asked to take an additional year of middle school before entering high school, and after implementing this screening process, Kappa rose in its state's ranking. Some students did not want to repeat a grade level, however, and instead chose a different high school, where they could make normal progress.

Among our charter school case studies, Sigma High School was the most committed to serving students left behind by the traditional educational system: inner-city immigrants who sought access to the American dream of uplift. The core strength of Sigma's approach was to align content with the values of uplift in the Latino/a community it served. The school navigated through the restrictive requirements of literacy education to offer a curriculum that was engaging and also yielded high test scores. Their 9–14 model required adaptation, but it eventually met their goal of uplifting its minority population, although Sigma did not aim to prepare its graduates for elite private colleges. Unfortunately, the state's stand of denying undocumented immigrants the right to pay lower in-state tuition rates was restrictive, and it was one reason some Sigma students dropped out, often to no known high school.

NYC PUBLIC DISTRICT HIGH SCHOOLS

The NYC district schools we visited considered prior achievement along with demographics and other factors when determining whether students would be admitted to their school of choice. This approach created an implicit competition among schools for high-achieving students who would help them realize gains in competitive school rankings. While these schools did not have the same freedom to adapt their curriculum that was evident in charter schools, the public district schools used the social support provided through CFES as part of their competitive strategy.

Three of the schools we studied were small high schools that attracted low-income students with high-enough test scores to be considered for their school of choice. All three schools offered content themes that would attract students' and parents' interest because of links to career paths. The two schools that offered a STEM-oriented curriculum (Acme Collegiate Academy and 21st Century Technological Academy) tapped into their students' interest in careers with potentially high earnings. In contrast, Onye Nkuzi High School started with a teaching theme, but, as its students learned about a wider range of college options, it developed a liberal arts theme. While it is possible that teaching would pay as well as many other career pathways, the most-competitive schools offered gateways to fields thought to generate higher earnings.

The fourth, Remus High School, was a medium-sized comprehensive school composed of specialized houses, three of which are labeled "academies." The medical, humanities, and engineering academies were highly competitive within the NYC school-choice system, so even though some of their students came or were placed into the general program called "academic professions," the school could compete in the overall rankings, Remus was also competitive because students admitted to its specialized academies were on track and had parents who were involved enough to inform themselves about the high school application process, do the research, and go through the steps of completing the forms and submitting them. Remus chose to center their CFES program on its engineering academy, in part to improve their competitive position.

UPLIFT CHALLENGES

The schools we studied contended nobly with complicated issues related to rigorous standards and competition for rankings within accountability systems. The educators we interviewed were consistently committed to uplifting the opportunities for urban children who lived in poverty. There was substantial evidence—both from our case studies and from the information on student achievement—that these schools were successful in navigating the complex terrain of urban school reform. Even so, each of the schools left students behind.

The NYC public district and national charter schools we studied illustrate the new tiered system of urban education that replaced tracking. Most of the schools had rigorous programs that attracted students ready to meet the challenges of college preparation and of attendance at top-level colleges. Within the public system, at least in NYC, there were schools that served any student, along with schools that focused on attracting high-quality students and offering a thematic curriculum. In all our case-study schools except Sigma and the general catch-all house at Remus, admission standards were high enough and the curriculum tough enough that many students could not make the grade.

It is crucial to realize that a significant number of students are left out of the improved urban schools because they are not admitted or drop out, sometimes ending up without a high school diploma. While our case-study schools did not consider severely challenged students, we think it is essential to recognize this as an imperfection in the emerging urban systems.

Upward Mobility and Urban Poverty

Reforms over the past three decades using market models attempted to uplift urban education, but inequalities persisted. In *The Darwin Economy: Liberty, Competition, and the Common Good*, Robert Frank notes a fundamental flaw in the rating schemes: no matter how you rate schools, at least 50% of the student population will attend schools in the lower half of the quality rankings.[11] Some urban schools, like the charter schools we studied, promoted uplift and raised their competitive positions in local school-choice schemes. These improving schools had support from foundations (especially the charter schools) and community-based organizations. Since most urban schools do not have this supplemental form of assistance, only a minority can become competitive. Thus better efforts to involve community groups are needed, including more programs like CFES.

It has also become clear that educational inequality is no longer the paramount cause of income inequality, which has been overlooked in the more recent rationales for educational reform and college access. In addition, many college graduates struggle to find employment matching their knowledge and skills. In *Aspiring Adults Adrift: Tentative Transitions of College Graduates*, Richard Arum and Josipa Roksa report on a research cohort of graduates now struggling to make it in the U.S. version of the global economy.[12] Our hunch is that for more than a decade, college graduates from low-income families have often scrabbled to find suitable employment. The implicit promise in college-access rationales of better earnings often proved false, especially for those students who took excessive time to attain their degrees.[13]

EDUCATED BUT STILL IN POVERTY

CFES serves schools in urban and rural communities with substantial portions of their populations living in poverty. Most self-identified CFES Scholars are from low-income families eligible for federally subsidized lunch programs, but a relatively high percentage of CFES Scholars come from families with prior college experience. Of course, such a small-scale survey provides no definitive proof, but it suggests that the concept of educational reform as a remedy for economic inequality—one subscribed to for the past thirty years—is not necessarily borne out in the current American economy. Analyses of our school case studies and the survey of CFES Scholars reveal that many families are trying for cross-generation social and economic uplift through educational attainment, which no longer appears to be a direct route. For this generation of strivers, the links between educational opportunities and opportunities in the workforce seem especially crucial because of both the global and U.S. economies.

This illustrates an unintended consequence of the three-decade mantra to raise high school graduation standards as means of increasing college access: some students make it through the educational and financial barriers to a college education, but educational gains don't always provide a pathway out of poverty. Today, about 20% of the poor have attained college degrees, a substantially higher percentage than in 1980, but the percentage of the population that is poor has increased during the last thirty years, two points Piketty's analysis of the American economy make abundantly evident.[14] The logics used to rationalize reform—the ideas that education offers a route out of poverty and that gains in education revive local economies—seem desperately in need of revision.

ECONOMIC RESTRUCTURING TRUMPS SCHOOL REFORM

The newest rationale for urban school reform explicitly links career content with college preparatory content under the logic of college *and* career ready. We argue that this logic is predicated on analyses of earnings by field and projections of demand for skilled labor that may be false. The growing number of educated families in poverty suggests one downside to perpetuating this misapprehension, but there are other risks that merit the attention of researchers and policymakers allied in promoting this rationale.

First, in the current economy it is possible that a transformation of the skill level of labor will not be accompanied by jobs that lift people out of poverty. For decades before globalization took off in the 1980s, India and other developing nations had well-educated, unemployed, skilled professionals,[15] including China, which had rapidly expanded its postsecondary education in science and engineering (S&E) fields. This global pool of technically trained labor, which drives down pay for jobs in these fields in the United States and China, suggests that there may be a surplus of S&E-educated workers.[16]

Once international corporations learned how to exploit the educated workforce in India and other developing nations, skilled jobs began to move to those countries, where employers could pay workers much less. It is probable that corporations will be attracted back to the United States when this country has a sufficient surplus of educated labor, but the earnings for these professions will not be as high as are currently projected. Already there is evidence of an excess supply of lawyers;[17] doctors facing difficulties paying off their educational debt, given the regulation of health-care costs;[18] and firms putting engineers and other technicians on contract instead of hiring them outright, so the employers don't have to provide benefits. In other words, the promise of high-paying jobs could be cruelly deceptive.

Second, the large debt burden often acquired for postsecondary education can make it difficult for many technically trained people—those who get stuck in low-paying jobs that require some postsecondary education—to pay back their student loans. The "We are the 99%" protest included a number of college graduates with a significant amount of student debt and limited job prospects.[19] The substantial cost of postsecondary education is a serious problem, constraining lifetime family capital formation due to debt repayment and a restricted earnings potential. We are not suggesting that the proponents of CTE or of college and career readiness are intentionally being deceptive, but it is important that current and future policy reports do not just provide glossy renditions of utopian images of educational opportunities and economic development. While we agree that postsecondary education is vitally important for individual and family well-being, it is also crucial to have public integrity and to be morally responsible when promoting educational policy agendas and providing information to students. Educators can adopt a practice of emphasizing the realities of debt-based student aid while also promoting preparation for and access to elite colleges. Honesty is the best policy with respect to college information for low-income students.

We found that partnerships with community-based organizations played a crucial role in the uplift of both charter and district high schools. It may be that since public funding is not adequate to provide a quality education in economically challenged communities, ties have been broken between neighborhoods and their schools. Joint ventures between schools and community-based organizations rebuild this missing connectivity in a way that is compatible with markets systems.

In the NYC district high schools we visited, all of which are involved in CFES, district control constrained their ability to align the mandated curriculum with individual school themes. Community partnerships provided mechanisms for adaptive change in these schools, and thus illustrate why community connectivity is important. CFES core practices emphasize participating in community service, building strong linkages through mentorships, and creating knowledge of postsecondary pathways through partnerships with colleges. These joint ventures connect communities with their schools and engage students in their communities. Given the current educational policy emphasis on markets and standards, corporations, nonprofit organizations, colleges, and other local resource centers need to form partnerships that support students and promote community development by empowering the students in their communities. Existing federal and state programs may illuminate the pathway, but with these initiatives' limited funding to support educational improvement and the development of community partnerships, they cannot solve the problem by themselves.

A Research-Based Theory of Change

In recent decades, educational policy has shifted away from systematic concepts of reform and instead presented fragmented arguments about specific reform strategies. Based on the research in this volume, along with other studies using a critical social frame to examine policy on 9–16 education,[20] we developed and refined a theory of change, with linkages between interventions and educational outcomes (fig. 5.1), that focused on the pathways ahead for low-income students if they make it through the educational system. The topic of adults returning to school to pursue a higher education is beyond the scope of this book, but it is another important issue, given the rapid pace of change in U.S. labor markets.[21]

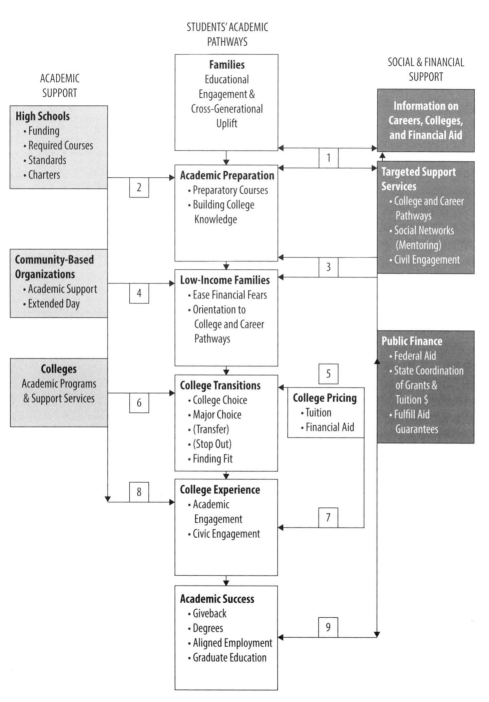

STUDENTS' ACADEMIC
PATHWAYS

ACADEMIC
SUPPORT

SOCIAL & FINANCIAL
SUPPORT

Families
Educational
Engagement &
Cross-Generational
Uplift

High Schools
• Funding
• Required Courses
• Standards
• Charters

**Information on
Careers, Colleges,
and Financial Aid**

1

2

Academic Preparation
• Preparatory Courses
• Building College
  Knowledge

**Targeted Support
Services**
• College and Career
  Pathways
• Social Networks
  (Mentoring)
• Civil Engagement

**Community-Based
Organizations**
• Academic Support
• Extended Day

4

Low-Income Families
• Ease Financial Fears
• Orientation to
  College and Career
  Pathways

3

Colleges
Academic Programs
& Support Services

6

College Transitions
• College Choice
• Major Choice
• (Transfer)
• (Stop Out)
• Finding Fit

5

College Pricing
• Tuition
• Financial Aid

Public Finance
• Federal Aid
• State Coordination
  of Grants &
  Tuition $
• Fulfill Aid
  Guarantees

8

College Experience
• Academic
  Engagement
• Civic Engagement

7

Academic Success
• Giveback
• Degrees
• Aligned Employment
• Graduate Education

9

Figure 5.1. Research-Based Theory of Change: How Interventions Link to Attainment

ACADEMIC PATHWAYS

The original educational attainment logic used by the U.S. Department of Education focused on family background, preparation during high school, and college choices. This was on a par with the status-attainment model of social research, and studies typically found that students in families with low socio-economic status were less likely to raise their status. The USDE research went beyond these older concepts to argue that inequality was caused by differences in academic preparation (e.g., algebra and geometry courses, and college applications prepared in the fall of a student's senior year) and in parents' education. These were deceptive arguments (chapter 2), because parents' education was highly correlated with family income in the 1980s and 1990s, but that is no longer the case. Thus continuing to use parents' education obfuscates the role of income in student tracking in high schools and in families' ability to pay for college applications and the net costs of college.[22]

Through subsequent studies using national and state databases and qualitative research, our academic-pathway construct was refined to recognize the following:[23]

- Low-income students did not enter high school with the same level of academic capital as did students from middle- and upper-income families. The former lacked knowledge about college and careers, as well as trustworthy information on college costs and career earnings.
- Rather than considering fall applications to colleges as a necessary step to gaining access, it was important to view college enrollment in broader terms. Not all colleges require students to apply in the fall, an implicit assumption in some of the models.[24] Community colleges and proprietary schools have open enrollment that allows application as part of an individual's registration for courses. Changes in majors and transfers from one college to another can also be factors in the process of finding an academic fit for students with the financial freedom to make these choices.
- Prior socialization—including supplemental support for and civic engagement of low-income students without the same level of academic capital as their wealthier peers—was important in students' academic and social engagement during college. Research on college students emphasizes how vital both civic and academic engagement are for them.[25] Studies on low-income students have found that when these students have guaranteed grant aid and minimal work and student-loan burdens, they are more likely to engage with their peers in study groups and projects, as well as to take internships (academic engagement), get involved in volunteer activities, and support the academic preparation of younger students (civic

engagement). The USDE studies overlooked the ways in which ability to pay influences academic engagement.[26]

·   Finally, an emphasis on career-connected education, along with the consequences of student debt, also means paying attention to the quality of employment *after* college, which has implications for student involvement in giving back to their communities, including pulling up peers in those neighborhoods.

ACADEMIC INTERVENTIONS

The standards and markets movements shifted policymakers' attention away from the promotion of financial aid as a mechanism for access that predominated in the 1960s and 1970s. In particular, USDE research was used to argue instead for raising graduation requirements and instituting new standards that aligned the curriculum and standardized tests (fig. 5.1, left-hand side). The early arguments for K–12 markets were essentially void of information on college access, yet standards and markets reinforce inequality in this area. The charter schools we studied had to meet the graduation requirements for their states, but they were not forced to adopt a curriculum aligned with the state standards, thus giving them greater flexibility to find engaging methods of instruction. The NYC public high schools that sought to rise in their district's choice schemes lacked this curriculum flexibility, so they focused instead on social networks that could provide support for their low-income students. Both types of schools strove to improve outcomes within educational markets that curtailed opportunities for low-income students through attrition (dropouts and transfers) or through admissions screening based on achievement. As noted above, not only does the combination of markets and standards create troublesome binds, especially for public district schools, but the implementation of both policies tends to squeeze out low-income students (fig. 5.1, linkage 2).

Providing academic support for students through assistance with homework assignments, thus extending the learning time in a student's day, and involving parents in planning for college (i.e., college visits) improve the chances that high school students will go on to college. Community-based organizations can offer these services, a mechanism used in Indiana's 21st Century Scholars Program, a support program for willing low-income students in the state who were in federally subsidized lunch programs. Research on the 21st Century Scholars Program found that family engagement in the above two activities (fig. 5.1, linkage 4) was significantly associated with a student's enrollment in a four-year college.[27] Although we did not specifically study organizations that gave this type of assistance in the Indiana project, CFES provided social support in the NYC public district schools we visited, which helped build academic capital.

FINANCIAL AND SOCIAL INTERVENTIONS

The American Council on Education (ACE) argued that telling students about financial-aid applications and college requirements was sufficient to improve enrollment by underrepresented students,[28] a rationale aligned with the math-advocacy research for the USDE (chapter 3).[29] This approach can sideline low-income students (fig. 5.1, linkage 1), especially if the information is superficial and does not address the realities of college affordability and the difficulties of navigating the net costs of college through loans and work in addition to grants. In our discussion of college knowledge (chapter 4), we examined how this simplistic approach can reinforce inequality.

We also observed how community organizing and social support increased the chances that low-income students would prepare for college (fig. 5.1, linkage 3). We discussed how the pathways practices should be broadened to include a focus on providing realistic and trustworthy information about student aid (fig 5.1, linkage 9). Our reconfigured theory of change also notes some of the ways in which finances influence college transitions (fig. 5.1, linkage 5) and a student's ability to engage academically and civically during college (fig. 5.1, linkage 7). Having an opportunity to talk with college students can help high school students build their understanding of these critical aspects of navigating through college (fig. 5.1, linkage 8). As we discussed in chapter 4, there has been a history of federal programs (HEA Title IV) that provide colleges with mechanisms to integrate outreach, as well as academic support for prospective students and assistance for students during college (fig. 5.1, linkage 6).

There is also a long-term impact of a high-work plus high-debt burden. The more low-income students work and borrow to go to college, the more likely they are to stop out or drop out (fig. 5.1, linkage 9). In addition, a high-debt burden for college graduates limits their ability to derive a benefit from modest income gains, keeping more families with skilled workers in poverty despite their educational gains.[30] The higher-than-expected percentage of CFES students living in low-income families with a history of college experience (chapter 4) illustrates this troubling aspect of the current policy trajectory.

The Failure of Policy Alliances

With this recontextualization of educational policy as background, it is easier to figure out why reform alliances failed both education in general and low-income students in particular. In *The Death and Life of the Great American School System: How Testing and Choice Are Undermining Education*, Ravitch provided a rare example of candid introspection by researchers and policymakers who had collaborated on the development of market and standards policies.[31] She not only discussed how these policies have not produced their intended outcomes, but also rather pointedly criticized their failure to consider evidence contrary to positions advocated by many of the policy alliances. Our discussion above of people who are left behind in educational reforms provides a short summary of one of the problems created by the market and standards approaches. Building on insights from analyses that took a hard look at such policies, we now briefly examine how conflicting assumptions in policy rationales, the false claims perpetuated for over three decades since the public release of *ANAR*, and the methods researchers use can reinforce closed-minded approaches to public policy on education.

Conflicting Reform Rationales

After World War II and up through the Cold War, public policy in education and on many other topics used a systems approach that relied on grand theories (e.g., human capital), a process that routinely oversimplified social problems. Critics of this methodology suggested combining policy research with advocacy, an approach proposed originally by Charles Lindblom and David Cohen in *Usable Knowledge: Social Science and Social Problem Solving.*[32] Researchers who worked in this frame were instrumental in supporting a new federal role that addressed challenges but overlooked total-system problems, viewing these latter obstacles as an early manifestation of the neoliberal approach.[33] A similar issues-oriented advocacy approach was used in *ANAR* and subsequent reforms. Combining social problem solving with political advocacy has created difficulties because (1) it has resulted in deeply conflicted policies; (2) policy rationales seldom consider how systems as a whole are working and instead narrowly focus on specific issues; and (3), as Ravitch notes,[34] most members of policy alliances fail to reflect on the unintended consequences of policies—based on the alliances' rationales—that were adopted by schools and by state and federal governments. We briefly summarize a few examples of equivocal educational policies illustrating this pattern.

DISCORD BETWEEN PIPELINE STANDARDS AND ENGAGED-LEARNING LOGICS IN PRACTICE

The CCSS follows decades of top-town, standards-driven reform. There is a growing body of literature advocating engaging approaches to teaching and the empowerment of teachers while critiquing central control. This literature provides cogent political analyses while also addressing curriculum issues in high school classrooms, a topic usually left to content specialists in school districts and teacher-education programs.

For example, in *Deeper Learning: How Eight Innovative Public Schools Are Transforming Education in the Twenty-First Century*, Monica Martinez and David McGrath advocate methods that empower students, teachers, and their communities.[35] They use case studies from across the United States to illustrate this teaching model. Their approach involves a discussion of student-learning needs, often across subjects, but these authors do not address the pedagogical-content challenges teachers face as they try to provide engaging curriculum. Empowerment within middle and high schools is needed, as our case studies illustrate, but this conflicts with the top-down approach to standards-driven reform used in most large school districts.

In another example, David Kirp's *Improbable Scholars: The Rebirth of a Great American School System and a Strategy for America's Schools* (based on his study of schools in Union City, New Jersey) also advocates for an engaging approach to student learning and an empowering approach to reform, addressing challenges related to a thematic curriculum and to market competition.[36] His work focuses mostly on elementary schools and classrooms, along with the politics of change in a moderate-sized urban community across the river from New York City, using a critique of NYC schools as a counter case while also acknowledging the strong funding base for public education in New Jersey, especially in Union City (one of the locales included in Martinez and McGrath's book).

Our case studies illustrated the challenges teachers encounter as they try to provide content and pedagogies that engage their students in learning advanced subject matter while also responding to a mandated curriculum, all the while competing for students in urban markets. Our Beta High School case study illustrated the complexity of offering an engaging curriculum for advanced math. Beta's educators examined many 9–14 math options before deciding that they needed to tackle the problem of preparing their students for advanced subjects by developing their own math curriculum. Sigma High School was an outstanding example of the ways in which educators contended with restrictive state requirements as they developed an engaging critical-literacy approach to language education suitable for their low-income population, which has limited prior preparation in English. The public charter schools we visited had more flexibility to try out new approaches for meeting state standards while responding to their students' learning needs; in contrast, the NYC district schools faced a constrained curriculum, as is the case in most public school districts. The CCSS only modestly modify some standards—which have evolved over decades—and provide only a limited opportunity to change the trajectory of content and teaching within district-based public schools.

Unlike other publications advocating engaged learning, for this book we dug beneath the surface of the problem, looking at high schools competing in urban markets. Both the public charter schools and the NYC district schools we studied developed strategies for improving their test scores. The charters had more flexibility in adapting their curricula, which made it possible for them to integrate a thematic curriculum (e.g., Kappa in engineering technology, Alpha in social justice and pre-law), as well as to respond to specialized learning needs (e.g., Beta in math, Sigma in literacy). Three of the charters made tough choices about rigor that, unfortunately, influenced some entering students to move back to the public system or out of education altogether.

In the large NYC public high school system, the selection criteria embedded in the school-choice scheme provided a sorting mechanism that incentivized schools to engage in constructing co-curricular adaptations (to provide social support for students undergoing a complex process of educational, social, and economic uplift) and in marketing their school concepts to middle school students. The co-curricular adaptations improved these schools' competitiveness and enabled them to attract students with a greater capability for high scores on standardized tests. The strategic adaptations we observed in the curriculum and co-curriculum, however, tended to enable only those students willing to engage in the uplift process. Sigma stood out as a school that managed to improve its competitive position while also adapting its curriculum to fit the most-challenged students in the community.

FACING UP TO UNINTENDED CONSEQUENCES

Relatively narrow arguments have been used to advocate for a pipeline approach (e.g., advanced math requirements) and college access (submission of college and student-aid applications). Not only were these arguments based on misleading claims, but they left out crucial elements of the college knowledge students would need to navigate collegiate pathways. It is incumbent on researchers and policymakers who work in the policy alliances to revise their rationales and recognize the unintended consequences of the policies they advocate. Many of the current problems could have been anticipated had alternative theories been considered when these individuals and groups were designing their research, conducting analyses of their findings, and crafting policy arguments.

For example, had early proponents of college prep thought more seriously about the role cutbacks in financial aid had played in the reopening of an enrollment gap in the early 1980s,[37] a more thoughtful approach would have been possible in their advocacy for advanced math education. More critically, it is unfortunate that subsequent researcher-advocates perpetuated their predecessors' line of reasoning,[38] while overlooking research conducted on the same databases used in their own advocacy studies. Simply considering alternative explanations, a process of thought taught in inferential statistics, could have averted serious subsequent problems.

Severe economic and social challenges were also left out of the initial conceptions of college knowledge promoted by ACE and the U.S. Department of Education. In the 1990s and early 2000s, policy alliances promoted raising standards and using loans to offer need-based aid. These logics had been carefully crafted by neoconservatives in the 1980s as a strategy for reducing the federal cost of higher education.[39] Within groups promoting these rationales, researchers who would raise critical social issues were accused of "blaming the victim."[40] Fortunately, social critical scholars developed qualitative research looking at topics related to class reproduction that illuminated inequality in the educational system, and (as discussed in chapter 4) the social critical research community was more open to testing concepts related to financial need than many policymakers in government agencies.[41] This breakthrough stimulated a broader conversation about college access that brought interventions focused on student support and financial aid back into the policy and practice of college outreach and school-college networks, exemplified in the evolving CFES core practices (chapter 4).

As early as 1965, the federal TRIO programs and campus-based aid (i.e., HEA Title IV) provided a set of mechanisms colleges could use to offer academic and social support along with strategies that would reduce family concerns about costs. These programs worked extremely well in reducing inequality in educational access until the early 1980s, when the policy conversations shifted.[42] While there were a few notable examples of large-scale state programs that offered guaranteed grant aid, academic encouragement, and social support— especially Indiana's 21st Century Scholars and Washington State Achievers[43]— neoconservative arguments about cutting taxes prevailed in Washington, D.C., so this strategy fell victim to the budget reconciliation process.

Social justice advocates in school-college networks now face the challenge of providing *realistic* information about student aid and the labor market. At this point, as our Onye Nkuzi case study illustrates, aspiring low-income middle school students require this information to choose an appropriate high school: public, private, or niche. Schools navigate toward missions that appeal to students in markets where students have limited information about the linkages between academic fields and careers.

There is also a *veil of ignorance* around the new poverty levels of college graduates.[44] The overly simplistic notion that students should apply for student aid and take on debt to attend college because they will earn more when they graduate is deceptive and troubling, given the employment problems now encountered by college graduates. At a minimum, information about college costs, forms of student aid, and correlations between careers and earnings is essential college knowledge.

Deceptive Claims Used by Political Ideologues

Ideology, by definition, is based on belief, as is religion, but it is important to at least be introspective on the meaning of belief in both domains.[45] Political ideologies are particularly troublesome when they manipulate research findings through the political vetting process and the crafting of alliances. Neoliberals bought into reforms—such as raising standards—that did not have a hefty price tag, which then make it easier for the neoconservatives to dominate at budget time. *It does not matter what programs and funding levels are authorized in legislation regarding education when the annual budget process does not fund them.*[46] It is especially difficult for educational advocates to contend with the strategies used by neoconservatives,[47] and it is particularly important that educational researchers, practitioners, and policy advocates consider what is true and what is false in policy discussions.

There are many erroneous claims (sometimes called proofiness) in the policy sphere.[48] For example, statisticians obfuscated the links between smoking and cancer for many years. Some of the deceptive assertions that have influenced policies accelerating inequality in educational attainment include (but are not limited to) the following:

- *Deception 1: Monetary inputs don't make a difference, so regulate outcomes.* This argument was proposed by Chester Finn when, as an assistant U.S. secretary of education, he promoted the standards movement and market models.[49] These arguments made it easier to cut federal educational budgets and can often be heard when states rationalize tax cuts.
- *Deception 2: Urban educational markets will improve urban schools.* This argument evolved from neoconservatives, who encouraged educational researchers to use Milton Friedman's *Capitalism and Freedom* as a framework for educational finance and policy. In his book, Friedman argued that vouchers were a better way to fund public education,[50] and this argument was widely accepted by the Reagan administration.[51] Chubb and Moe's *Politics, Markets, and America's Schools* included a study of NYC schools and developed an argument for markets,[52] but there was no proof of success in that book, because the strategy had not yet been tried. Decades of reform initiatives followed, but, as we discussed in chapter 1, the evidence that markets are somehow better than public schools proved to be erroneous.[53]
- *Deception 3: Raising the minimum course requirements for high school graduation will eliminate inequality in college preparation.* We examined the evolution of this claim in relation to arguments about the math pipeline (chapter 2). This was a classic case of the misuse of correlational studies to make a policy argument. As we illustrated, the CCSS literature perpetuates this myth by providing talking points to rationalize increasing requirements, based on expected future earnings.
- *Deception 4: Private returns from college loans justify the use of student loans instead of grants.* The notion that returns to the individual borrowers provide

a basis for emphasizing loans dominated finance policy by the 1990s,[54] reinforcing the shift from student grants to loans.[55] The student-aid research community ended up promoting this rationale with studies that compared average debt with average earnings.[56] This research further reinforced ACE reports encouraging borrowing.[57] From studies conducted for, but not released by, the U.S. Department of Education, it had long been known that college debt was problematic for low-income students. While these studies were eventually published as academic articles,[58] literature advocating loans prevailed in policy and practice. Elizabeth Warren is currently leading an initiative to reduce governmental profits from the interest rates charged on federal student loans;[59] instead of providing subsidies to low-income students through need-based grants, the U.S. government is now making money on its loans to college students.

- *Deception 5: Providing information about student aid and encouraging college applications will eliminate inequality in college access.* The pipeline and loan rationales converged with research on access to create a problematic alliance promoting college and financial-aid applications without encouraging a realistic assessment of these aid awards in relation to college costs (chapter 4).

In some instances there was evidence that these claims were misleading when the logics were first framed, but the real public deception was the persistent marshaling of evidence to bolster these claims and ignore research that contradicted the policy positions that were taken. Had there been a willingness to consider alternative explanations, it may have been possible to reduce inequality while also improving high schools. Our case studies illustrate that some high schools did just that, despite policies that were contradictory, but it required supplemental resources from foundations and the involvement of community organizations.

Educational Research Contributed to Deceptive Rationales

Researchers in the social and political sciences, economics, and education often inadvertently—and perhaps sometimes intentionally—support political rationale building based on erroneous premises. In some instances, the governmental agencies and foundations funding these studies use the vetting process to shape findings in ways that promote narrow conceptions of educational problems and/or potential solutions. In other cases, investigators are engaged in the policy arena and actively use their research to advance their own strongly held views.[60] In fact, the political vetting of policy studies resembles the academic-review process for journals and dissertation committees. The theory behind such reviews is that they reduce errors—and indeed, this process is essential to the quality of academic and policy research of various types—but the practice is highly prone to political influence. To untangle this, we briefly discuss how theory and methods can contribute to these problems.

THEORY PROBLEMS

There have always been conflicting views within academic fields. In the mid-twentieth century, grand theories like human capital and social attainment were widely used in systematic approaches to policy. As these overarching constructs broke down as frames for policy, competing ones emerged. Unlike Thomas Kuhn's concept of paradigms in science—that a dominant theory will be widely accepted until its core precepts are proven wrong[61]—the humanities and social sciences have long been accustomed to competing arguments. For example, Marxist theory has been an alternative to Western functionalist theory in the social sciences and, as we discussed in chapter 4, the emergence of critical social theory informed and broadened general scholarship on access in the 1990s. The truth, however, is that whatever theoretical narrative dominates, something important is usually left out.

To illustrate the problem of conflicting theories in education, we reconsidered the debates about literacy education (chapter 3). For many decades there was tension between instruction using sound-letter (phonics) methods and whole-word meanings. While this debate would last throughout the twentieth century, neoconservative policymakers promoted phonics in part because the whole-language and critical literacy communities often used more social critical theories in their research. For example, in 1998 the National Academy Press released *Preventing Reading Difficulties in Young Children*, a "scientific" review of studies that reinforced the political dominance of phonemic approaches.[62] During this period, research in Indiana illustrated that (1) phonic approaches were associated with higher test scores, but also with increased retention of students in grade level and special education referrals; (2) critical literacy methods were associated with improved academic progress in early grades; and (3) approaches that included a balance of phonemic and critical literacy methods improved both scores and students' academic progress.[63]

As we documented in chapter 3, the CCSS literacy standards reach a new reconciliation between the phonics-comprehension and the critical literacy schools of thought. As we also noted, however, these newer standards can make it difficult to adopt socially critical literature in the curriculum. Our Sigma High School case study illustrated how a charter school improved the advanced literacy test scores for its immigrant students by using socially relevant literature. State standards, coupled with a district-controlled curriculum, however, created barriers to this type of adaptation in the NYC public schools. In the charter schools we studied, it was easier for educators to have the freedom to try out approaches that would both meet standards *and* engage students. Literacy educators in the NYC district schools we visited expressed frustration with their system's curriculum because it constrained their ability to use culturally relevant texts. Instead, some worked around the system—using CFES core practices to create a co-curriculum—to provide balanced, culturally situated learning.

This literacy example illustrates some of the complex ways in which competing theories can influence policy and practice and create barriers for low-income students. We provided similar examples related to market models and the emergence of competitive, thematic niches (chapter 1), the development of engaged advanced math (chapter 2), and the creation of school-based strategies for college knowledge that address student concerns about costs, such as Alpha High School's guarantee of financial aid (chapter 4). The capacity to make these adaptive changes rests largely on the moral consciousness of educators who must enhance or adapt practices to provide engaging learning opportunities and realistic information about college costs and educational pathways to careers that enable students to pay off their student-loan debts. This can be risky for educators if they don't have the opportunity to work within communities of practitioners who share their commitments to social justice.

METHODS PROBLEMS

There have also been longstanding debates about research methods in relation to public policy and educational practice. Both qualitative and quantitative methods have evolved over time, as have the various conflicting contentions between generic types of methods. We do not attempt to enter into these debates as part of this concluding chapter, but instead try to explain what we've learned about how both of these methodologies influence policy and practice related to college preparation.

Quantitative research emphasizes experimental methods and statistics that permit conclusions about causal relationships between interventions and outcomes.[64] Most of the quantitative research on higher education assumes that it's possible to determine such relationships between interventions and outcomes. *The problem is that when random experiments—widely considered as the gold standard in educational, economic, and policy research—are replicated, they seldom prove that an intervention results in the same outcome, because: (1) the conditions must be exactly the same in the new context; (2) the patterns of engagement among the practitioners involved must be the same; and (3) the students must be the same.* Despite these limitations, causal research is still being touted as the most valid methodology.

For example, when the ACSFA commissioned reviews of NCES studies of the college-access pipeline, they chose to focus on difficulties with processes[65] rather than the problems with the use of theory and policy logics.[66] The next wave of ACSFA-funded research, however, used quasi-experimental methods on student-record data and concentrated on promoting causal research practices (such as using data systems to track students from grades K through 20) to ensure alignment, recommend policy changes, and analyze the impact of a particular policy.[67]

As early as 1998, *Preventing Reading Difficulties in Young Children* promoted experimental design over other types of quantitative and qualitative research (chapter 3).[68] One experiment—using randomized groups to test the effects of phonics—played a pivotal role in the overall analysis, finding that students who were taught phonics had higher scores on tests. The report also acknowledged extensive research on Reading Recovery (RR),[69] a one-on-one approach to reading intervention based on the work of Marie Clay,[70] but this research did not rise to the same standards because it used qualitative methods.

Social critical research focuses on contexts, implementation, and the enthusiasm of its practitioners. There have been attempts to use quantitative methods to examine inequalities in educational outcomes,[71] but qualitative investigators have been more likely to conduct research with a social critical focus. In our school case studies, for example, we examined qualitatively how educators addressed challenges arising from the implementation of standards in market settings. We found that what happened when such standards were put into practice was different from what had been assumed by most of the educational research that informed these standards. The context was far from that of the investigators' hypothetically unfettered markets—especially with regard to the NYC public schools' constrained curriculum—so the theories that drove the reforms were largely miscast as being frameworks to guide urban educational reform. We believe social critical analyses can inform policy and practice *in tandem* with empirical analyses using functional theories from the social sciences, economics, and education, rather than serve as a complete replacement for them.

Pragmatic Approaches to Policy and Practice

The intersection between policy on educational reform and professional practice in urban school markets is far more complex than that portrayed in the policy literature or in educational research on teaching advanced content. The shift to competitive markets fundamentally altered the context for community control of schools through a district's organizational structures. Market systems and regulated public accountability incentivize public school educators to seek competitive advantages (e.g., higher test scores, as measured by the accountability system), yet their schools serve many students whose educational interests do not mesh well with the mandated curriculum. Since it is unlikely that these conditions will change in the near future, we suggest an alternative approach to research on the policy and practice of school reform, along with practical actions for improving high schools, including the involvement of community-based organizations.

Research Supporting Educational Reform

A wide range of theories and methods can and have been employed in research on college preparation, access, and success. If there is an overarching problem in the use of research to make policy arguments, it is the failure to systematically consider alternatives and competing explanations. While the factors examined in a research project may explain some of the variance among outcomes, it is incumbent on investigators to explore other interpretations. That foundational tenet of both quantitative and qualitative research is often overlooked in studies that build policy rationales and test teaching methods. It is important to consider various avenues and different forms of reasoning in both policy and practice.

It is essential for social science researchers to consider social, economic, and educational theories when interpreting findings from studies on college preparation, access, and success. Our research-based theory of change illustrates a framework for identifying factors influencing student outcomes (figure 5.1), an approach that integrates social, economic, cultural, and educational theory with investigations into educational improvement. When educational researchers began to consider the role of preparation in access, they shifted the focus of their investigations away from social and economic explanations, going against the well-established policy-research tradition of considering preparation, social background, and college costs in studies of college access.[72] This started when the Reagan administration commissioned the study that promoted the "algebra explanation" for inequality,[73] a faulty premise because there had been no decline in the teaching of algebra that would account for the gap that opened up in college access for African Americans and Hispanics compared with Whites. On the other hand, need-based grants *had* declined,[74] but data on social background and financial variables for the students were not included in this particular report. In the waves of USDE-funded research that followed,[75] the failure to take these factors into account had serious consequences for social justice in the United States, as we have discussed throughout this volume. At the very least, balanced research that considers a range of explanations for problems can inform wise policy and practice. A myopic investigative approach can set changes in motion that undermine fairness, which is precisely what happened in this instance.

A critical-empirical method—considering diverse types of evidence and claims—can and should be used in policy development and practice within schools, colleges, and financial institutions participating in educational programs and reforms.[76] This involves using competing functionalist and social critical theories to examine emergent problems and their possible causes. In educational practice, trying out alternative solutions after examining potential underlying causes provides a strategy for adaptive change.[77] The adjustments made by the schools in our case studies as they created competitive niches (chapter 1), offered advanced math to students who did not receive quality elementary school preparation (chapter 2), and put together an engaging literacy curriculum (chapter 3) illustrate decisions that openly considered social critical issues. These schools developed strategies, assessed the results, and made adaptive changes contending with the contradictions that emerged from raising standards while implementing competitive markets.

Practical Strategies

1. *Encourage open discourse in policy and practice.* The development of policy alliances that maintain silence about or actively engage in resistance to evidence that contradicts their claims has been a problematic aspect of reforms promoting college preparation, access, and success over the past three decades. Ravitch discussed and demonstrated an open approach to policy research,[78] and we also encourage policymakers, professors, and practitioners to consider and evaluate *all* available information, not just prior research and study results that support their claims. It is possible to both pursue goals and reflect on contrary evidence, a form of broadly inclusive strategic thought and action that is needed in both policy and practice.[79] Reflecting on contradictory evidence can inform the types of adaptive changes that are necessary to improve practice and outcomes, as is evident from the analyses of our case studies.

2. *Relax curriculum constraints to support engaged learning of advanced subjects, especially in thematic high schools in urban markets.* The notion of constraining a high school curriculum as a means of improving achievement was derived in part from research on Catholic high schools,[80] but stiffer requirements coupled with high standards and central control of the curriculum have created unequal competition in urban markets. The CCSS advanced literacy standards provide some flexibility for choosing texts that relate to students' interests and integrate literacy education with career themes. This is a step in the right direction, but more innovation is needed, including developing and pilot testing engaging approaches to math instruction in algebra and geometry; allowing more flexibility in public district schools so themes can be integrated into the curriculum in small high schools; promoting greater student engagement; and providing better social support for students and educators. It is also essential that educational leadership, teacher education, and curriculum specialization in education and the disciplines it covers demonstrate and encourage adaptive and reflective methods of engaging students.

3. *Provide educators with opportunities for academic preparation in advanced*

subjects. The college preparatory and career ready curriculum, as currently defined by the CCSS, requires teachers to master new subject matter and develop pedagogical skills to teach it. It is extremely important to address the level of content expertise and the capacity of those who are to present the material to students when new requirements are introduced. For example, raising high school standards for graduation to include advanced math for all students caused serious problems in urban high schools, because most math instructors were not prepared to teach this level of mathematics and most teacher-education programs did not provide sufficient numbers of new teachers trained in the subject matter. When public school districts ease their constraints so instructors can come up with methods that meet their students' learning needs, district administrators need to increase the time allocated for professional development to support the teachers as they create curricular materials and hone their craft, as well as provide time for the individual schools to make the necessary changes.

4. *Reconstruct the alignment of K–12 education with labor markets and college pathways.* Career and technical education and STEM pipeline theories have oversimplified the challenges facing low-income families as they engage in social and economic uplift. It is apparent that entry into the middle class is a cross-generation project for many low-income households. As students gain exposure to advanced subjects, their career interests can change. If urban high schools continue to emphasize career content, it is crucial that middle and high schools encourage learning about alternative career and educational pathways. While a constrained curriculum ensures general preparation for college, it limits the capacity of district schools to provide career-aligned content in advanced courses. District schools need more flexibility to compete with charter schools that integrate career content with advanced subjects, yet it is also important to ensure that students have options and opportunities to change their specialization in high school, just as they do in college. Rigid graduation requirements can undermine efforts to create viable pathways.

5. *Integrate knowledge of college costs, career pathways, and debt management into academic and social support in high schools.* Given the substantial debt and work burden associated with attaining a four-year degree, as well as technical jobs that don't always have sufficient incomes to pay off student debt, some college choices no longer provide pathways out of poverty. These conditions can discourage families' engagement in education as a strategy for cross-generation economic uplift, especially if the information they receive is deceptive, mistakenly espousing the supposition that a college education will guarantee economic success. We have been encouraged by the adaptive changes we observed in NYC public district schools as they promoted learning about educational and career pathways, provided opportunities for student engagement in the community, and encouraged a thoughtful analysis of postsecondary educational expenses

and the aid packages offered by colleges. Supplying realistic information about college costs in relation to career pathways can provide a context and content that engages students in learning advanced subjects. Social support through mentoring, the involvement of students in local civic activities, and college outreach to schools—patterns of practice evident in the NYC high schools we visited—added real-world aspects, based on reliable information, to the social construction of market niches. This type of practicality is a necessary part of educational improvement in urban high schools.

6. *Encourage and test new approaches to engaged learning in urban schools.* Several factors have undermined schools' efforts to improve student achievement, especially in advanced math. The most critical challenge is to educate current and new generations of teachers in advanced topics and engaging methods of instruction. Raising graduation requirements without investing in professional education for teachers created a decline in educational outcomes, although this was later followed by gradual recovery and improvement.[81] Finding qualified teachers is challenging in urban areas. Sending new college graduates out to teach in cities, the approach used by Teach For America, is troublesome because the new teachers usually are not prepared in the advanced content they will be expected to convey to students and lack teaching experience in general. Once they obtain the knowledge and experience they need, their obligations to the program will be over, and most will move forward with their careers in places outside the city. Community-based organizations can provide help to ensure that students' homework is completed, in addition to support groups for parents, strategies that proved somewhat successful for Indiana's 21st Century Scholars,[82] but it has been difficult to sustain this exemplary program. Initiatives are needed that encourage and assist educators to develop more engaging teaching methods, as well as ones that provide academic support for students learning advanced subject matter.

7. *Organize community engagement in schools.* Both the public charter and NYC district schools we studied had assistance from a combination of foundations, corporations, community organizations, colleges, and community activists. In the small NYC district high schools we visited, CFES core practices provided mechanisms for engaging students with their communities and promoting new concepts of educational uplift. Foundations funded educational innovations in all of the public charter schools we examined, but many community-based charters lack these resources. External funding can play a central role in a school's success, but not all schools can receive the levels of financial aid evident in three of the charter schools we visited (Alpha, Beta, and Kappa). It is crucial to develop new avenues where communities can nurture their schools and to engage local groups in helping to build new pathways to college and careers. The support provided by CFES in the NYC district schools illustrates a low-cost

strategy for organizing a community to foster its students' academic preparation and college opportunities. Policymakers, educators, and professionals in businesses and community organizations should explore ways of building partnerships that bolster local schools.

8. *Provide trustworthy information on college costs and career pathways.* Given the misguided claims that have driven public policy in recent decades, it is not surprising that many college-prepared students end up with little or no college education or delayed college enrollment, and a high-debt burden after college, whether they graduate or not. These conditions are especially problematic for low-income students, who can be misled by claims promoting improbable dreams. Integrating realism into the process of providing information to students is essential, even though it is not as hopeful as asserting that college will ensure uplift. It is crucial to prepare students in a trustworthy manner to successfully navigate college and career pathways.

9. *Use comprehensive and cohesive interventions.* There are a range of strategies colleges can use for outreach, admissions, and academic support to assist low-income students as they navigate from high school into and through college.[83] Colleges typically have bridge programs, support services, research opportunities, and academic assistance that, if combined in coherent ways, could provide more equitable access to higher education. Colleges and universities can partner with urban school systems to offer support for teacher development, conduct research that buttresses reforms, and build diverse pathways to college. Some high schools have been placed on college campuses after structuring agreements between the campuses and the schools, which is a viable approach (as illustrated by our Remus, Kappa, and Sigma case studies). As the market system of urban education evolves, however, flexibility is required to restructure these agreements to encourage engaged student learning and address new educational requirements.

Conclusion

Market and standards trajectories have converged to create worrisome obstacles for urban high schools seeking to make positive educational changes. Standards-driven reforms have imposed new content requirements, but few urban high schools have teachers with the necessary educational background to teach them. Linking advanced materials in math and English to career content remains a largely untested concept, posing serious challenges for urban school districts as they attempt to meet the college and career ready standards. Some school districts restrict their curriculum as a means of meeting the new standards, while charter schools have the freedom to test various strategies for change, but their outcomes are rarely better than those of the constrained district high schools. The chaos created in the urban high school market by these policies is truly troubling. We conclude that the challenges facing urban high schools have not been solved by the issue-focused advocacy of educational-reform alliances, but instead have been created or exacerbated by them. Yet the policy trajectories of market-based school choice and college and career preparatory standards continue onward in urban education. Therefore, it is crucial that policymakers, researchers, educators, student advocates, and philanthropists organize to support schools as they make the necessary adaptations. In particular, policymakers and advocates should be more perceptive about the barriers facing urban schools instead of pursuing quick-fix remedies that can further degrade the will and hope of urban families and the educators who work with their children.

It is crucial for researchers to consider how urban market systems actually work and the ways in which cultural contexts influence educational choices by families. The notion that there are "best practices" that can be easily replicated seems the antithesis of the type of adaptive change that is needed in urban schools. Community organizations and philanthropists are also integral factors in the struggles to improve educational opportunity for low-income urban children. Social support and financial aid are essential to break through the barriers in this savagely unequal system. It is time for notions of equality and the public good to be revived in the communities and schools within our troubled cities.

Introduction

1. U.S. Department of Education, 1983.
2. Ravitch, 2010.
3. St. John, 2013.
4. St. John, et al., 2013.
5. B. Freidman, 2005; Piketty, 2014, Stiglitz, 2012.
6. Meyer, et al., 2013.
7. St. John & Bowman, in press.
8. Moses & Cobb, 2001.
9. St. John, 1994b, 2003, 2013; St. John, et al., 2013.
10. Rawls, 1971, 1999.
11. St. John, 2003, 2013.
12. Perna & Jones, 2013.
13. Trent, Gong, & Owens-Nicholson, 2004.
14. St. John, et al., 2013.
15. Advisory Committee on Student Financial Assistance (hereafter cited as ACSFA), 2001, 2013.
16. Meyer, et al., 2013; St. John & Bowman, in press.
17. The Affordable Care Act, commonly known as Obamacare, is an exception, although it emphasizes raising standards for health care and insuring individuals through the private insurance system, which is vastly different from the public health-care model in most other nations that depends more directly on public funding.
18. There was also a movement toward direct federal lending, initiated during the Clinton administration. This approach shifted the banking role to the federal government because it was less expensive than subsidies to private lenders. For histories of this period of federal student aid, see Fossey & Bateman, 1998; Hearn & Holdsworth, 2004.
19. Piketty, 2014.
20. Adelman, 1999; Conklin, Curran, & Gandal, 2005.
21. Choy, 2002a, 2002b; King, 2002.
22. Davis, 1997; Hartle, Simmons, & Timmons, 2005.
23. Strogatz, 2010, p. 8.
24. Warren, 2014.
25. Piketty, 2014.
26. St. John, Kim, & Yang, 2013.
27. Meyer, et al., 2013.

28. G. Becker, 1975; Levin & McEwan 2000; Theobald, 2003.
29. Heller, 1997; Leslie & Brinkman, 1988; McPherson, 1978.
30. Carnes, 1987; Chubb & Moe, 1990; Finn, 1988a, 1988b, 1990a, 1990b.
31. St. John, et al., 2013.
32. Bourdieu, 1974, 1977; Bourdieu & Passeron 1990.
33. McDonough, 1997; Winkle-Wagner, 2010.
34. St. John, Hu, & Fisher, 2011.
35. Winkle-Wagner 2012.
36. While we recognize that it is also possible to consider the role of policy in schools, including informal policies developed through practice (as documented by St. John, 2009a, 2009b, 2013), we distinguish governmental policy from these school-level processes in this volume. By using the term "policy" to refer to governmental decisions and the term "practice" to describe local adaptive behaviors by educators within schools, we can illuminate better how locally distinctive schools emerge.
37. Schultze, 1968; Weathersby & Balderston, 1972.
38. Hearn, 1993, 2001; Lindblom, 1959; Wildavsky, 1979.
39. W. Becker, 2004; Heller, 2004.
40. ACSFA, 2001, 2008, 2010, 2013.
41. King, 1999a, 1999b, 1999c.
42. Hartle, 1998; Hartle, Simmons, & Timmons, 2005.
43. St. John, et. al., 2013.
44. Ravitch, 2010.
45. St. John & Meyer, 2013a, 2013b
46. Piketty, 2014; Stiglitz, 2012.
47. Orfield & Eaton, 1997; Orfield, et al., 2007.
48. Kneebone, Nadeau, & Berube, 2011.
49. We had the opportunity to visit four rural high schools and four NYC high schools as part of our selection process. In addition to questions about the curriculum, we asked about educator involvement in CFES core practices: pathways to college, mentoring, and leadership through service. The four NYC schools provided essential information needed for this book on urban high schools. We completed a separate paper from interviews done in the four rural high schools (Dalton, Bigelow, & St. John, 2012).
50. Eckes & Rapp 2006; Ravitch, 2010; U.S. Department of Education, 2004.
51. Commission on the Skills of the American Workforce, 2007.
52. Hoffman, et al., 2007.
53. Commission on the Skills of the American Workforce, 2007.
54. Hoffman, et al., 2007.
55. Cupiak, in press.
56. Meyer, et al., 2013; Rong & Chen, 2013.
57. Gonzales, et al., 2009.
58. Oakes, 1985/2005.
59. Adelman, 1999; Berkner & Chavez, 1997; Pelavin & Kane, 1990.
60. Lumina Foundation, 2014.
61. Curto, Fryer, & Howard, 2011.
62. Kahlenberg & Potter, 2014.

Chapter 1 · Market Niches

1. Schultze, 1968; Weathersby & Balderston, 1972.
2. Lindblom & Cohen, 1979.
3. Ravitch, 2010.
4. Coleman, 1966.
5. Jencks, 1972.
6. National Center for Education Statistics, 2009.
7. Alvis & Willie, 1987; Willie 1976. Magnet schools are elementary and middle schools that often have a specific focus (e.g., science and math), with students applying from across the district. Students are channeled into specific higher-level schools (e.g., from a science-based middle school into a science-based high school).
8. For more information on the Lusher School, see http://en.wikipedia.org/wiki/Lusher_Charter_School/ [downloaded Nov. 7, 2010]; www.youtube.com/watch?v=MrG8abBS1Fg/ [downloaded Nov. 7, 2010].
9. Wong, 2003.
10. Comprehensive School Reform Quality Center, 2006.
11. Education Resources Institute, 1997.
12. Jordan, et al., 2000.
13. Toch, 2003.
14. Ravitch, 2010.
15. Hoffman, et al., 2007.
16. M. Friedman, 1962.
17. Hansen & Weisbrod, 1969.
18. Newman, 1971.
19. Gladieux & Wolanin, 1976.
20. St. John & Masten, 1990.
21. Chubb & Moe, 1990.
22. Metcalf, et al., 2004; Witte, 2000.
23. Metcalf & Paul, 2006.
24. Peterson, 1998; Peterson & Howell, 2004; Peterson, et al., 2003.
25. Kolderie, 1992; Vergari, 1999.
26. Eckes & Rapp, 2006, 2007; Ravitch, 2010.
27. Kahlenberg & Potter, 2014.
28. Ravitch, 2010.
29. U.S. Department of Education, 1983.
30. Siddle Walker & Snarey, 2004.
31. Conklin, Curran, & Gandal, 2005; Kirp, 2014.
32. Argyris & Schön, 1974; St. John, 2013.
33. Ravitch, 2010.
34. St. John, 2006, 2012.
35. Chubb & Moe, 1990.
36. Peterson, et al., 2003; Ridenour & St. John, 2003.
37. Ridenour & St. John, 2003; St. John & Ridenour, 2001.
38. Kahlenberg & Potter, 2014.
39. St. John & Ridenour, 2001.

40. St. John & Ridenour, 2002.
41. Ridenour & St. John, 2003.
42. Piketty, 2014.
43. St. John, 2003, 2006, 2013; St. John, Daun-Barnett, & Moronski-Chapman, 2013.
44. Piketty, 2014.
45. DiMaggio & Powell, 1983.
46. It is possible for schools to provide college preparation plus a specialization as a means of contending with the new pressures. At the same time, college preparation itself can be a specialized niche, as was the case with some of the small charter schools we visited.
47. Oakes, 1985/2005.
48. St. John & Mirón, 2003.
49. Partnership for 21st Century Skills, 2011. Partnership for 21st Century Skills stresses mastery of core subjects, including global awareness and environmental literacy; learning and innovation skills, such as critical thinking; information, media, and technology skills; life and career skills, such as self-directedness; and productivity and accountability.

Chapter 2 · Math Problems

1. U.S. Department of Education, 1983.
2. Pelavin Associates, a small policy research firm in the 1980s, had a policy-studies contract with the U.S. Department of Education. At that time, St. John was an associate in the firm and was responsible for developing new work on higher education. This narrative draws from his experience and has previously been documented (St. John, 1994b, 2003). Eventually Pelavin Associates, a highly successful and growing policy research firm, became part of the American Institutes for Research.
3. By the time the gap opened, higher education policy researchers had already begun to address the problems created by shifting student aid from low-income to middle-income students (e.g., St. John & Byce, 1982).
4. Heller, 1997; Jackson & Weathersby, 1975; Leslie & Brinkman, 1988; McPherson, 1978. We cite these studies because of their wide review of available information.
5. After eventually leaving the firm, St. John published his studies in higher education journals (e.g., St. John, 1989, 1991)—an option since they had been submitted to the government and thus were not copyrighted—although USDE policies for reviews are now more restrictive than they were at the time. The reviews sponsored by the ACSFA (ACSFA, 2003; W. Becker, 2004; Heller, 2004) have created higher statistical standards that were used in the USDE reports discussed in this section.
6. Pelavin & Kane, 1988, 1990.
7. St. John, 1989, 1991.
8. Adelman, 1999; Berkner & Chavez, 1997.
9. W. Becker, 2004; Heller, 2004.
10. William Goggin was an economist at ACSFA, while Brian Fitzgerald was its director. Both had previously been hired by Pelavin Associates to work on the minority enrollment gap study. Around the time when it became apparent that this study would not consider student aid, they left the firm to take positions at the newly formed ACSFA. Goggin and Fitzgerald had witnessed the deception in the reporting of statistics first hand, but it was over a decade before the issue was addressed in a formal report (ACSFA, 2001).
11. Choy, 2002a, 2002b.

12. ACSFA, 2003.

13. U.S. Department of Education, 2006.

14. ACSFA, 2013.

15. Barghaus, et al., 2013.

16. G. Hoachlander, 1997, 1999.

17. Berkner & Chavez, 1997; Choy, 2002a, 2002b.

18. W. Becker, 2004; Heller, 2004.

19. St. John, Daun-Barnett, & Moronski-Chapman, 2013.

20. National Research Council, 2011.

21. Daun-Barnett, 2008; St. John, 2006.

22. See, for example, Silver 2000; Silver, Smith, & Nelson, 1995.

23. Achieve, et. al., 2013.

24. Carnevale, Smith, & Strohl, 2013.

25. Hoffman, et al., 2007.

26. Carnevale, 2007.

27. B. Friedman, 2005; Meyer, et al., 2013; Stiglitz, 2012.

28. Chambers, 1994.

29. Silver, Smith, & Nelson, 1995.

30. Stein, et al., 2009.

31. House & Telese, 2008.

32. Graham & Fennell, 2001.

33. Boaler, 2002.

34. Moses & Cobb, 2001; Perry, et al., 2010.

35. Moses & Cobb, 2001; Perry, et al., 2010.

36. Furner & Robinson, 2004.

37. Antonijević, 2006.

38. Gonzales, et al., 2009.

39. House & Telese, 2008.

40. Shen & Tam, 2008.

41. Ongaga, 2010.

42. Allensworth, et. al., 2009.

43. Jabon, et al., 2010.

44. Klein, 2003.

45. Boaler, 2002.

46. Based on weighted Regents' Exam pass rates.

47. There is enough flexibility in the system for students to be advanced to the appropriate level if they achieve competence quickly in the preparatory course.

48. See http://stateimpact.npr.org/ohio/tag/teacher-evaluation/.

49. Kappa High School and Sigma High School are described more fully in chapter 3, as part of the discussion of critical literacy.

50. Sigma High School targeted its support on Hispanic students, some of whom did not have legal access to other public high schools, due to their immigration status.

51. Klein, 2003.

52. Nisar, 2012.

53. We examine English-education strategies at Sigma High School in chapter 3, as an example of another approach to engaged learning.

Chapter 3 · Advanced Literacies

1. This definition of critical literacy is further developed within this chapter to represent a different type of standard than has been used in K–12 reforms over the past three decades. The direction of reform toward content-aligned tests can lead to a knowledge gap between requirements for tests and the types of critical thinking necessary to be successful in college.

2. Bowen, 2011; Sedlacek, 2004.

3. National Center for Education Statistics (hereafter cited as NCES), 2009.

4. Ibid.

5. Snow, Burns, & Griffin, 1998.

6. Au & Raphael, 2000; Meacham, 2000.

7. Baugh, 2009.

8. Snow, Burns, & Griffin, 1998.

9. The idea that speech and language acquisition vary across social, cultural, and racial groups is firmly established in the literature on reading, as noted from the review above. In addition, language and numeracy differences matter across academic fields in higher education, just as they do in the professions.

10. NCES, 2009. NAEP scores for math rose for 9- and 13-year-olds, but not for 17-year-olds. Since SAT scores in math rose, however, there is less national concern about test scores in high school math.

11. St. John, Loescher, & Bardzell, 2003, p. 29.

12. Manset-Williamson, et al., 2002; St. John, Loescher, & Bardzell, 2003.

13. Spradlin, et al., 2005.

14. Snow, Burns, & Griffin, 1998.

15. St. John, Loescher, & Bardzell, 2003.

16. For example, entry into engineering and other technical fields requires more substantial advanced math (e.g., calculus II), along with knowledge of specialized content areas that intersect with basic engineering.

17. On general education, see Bell, 1966. On useful arts, see Cheit, 1975.

18. Goodchild, 1997.

19. Common Core State Standards Initiative, n.d.

20. Franzak, 2006.

21. Gutiérrez, Zitiali Morales, & Martinez, 2009.

22. Lee, 2009.

23. Pearson, Moje, & Greenleaf, 2010.

24. Smart, Feldman, & Ethington, 2000; Spokane, 1996.

25. St. John, 2009b.

26. This statement is adapted from St. John, 2009b, pp. 58–59. The sequence of frames was altered from the original—where the order was critical, interpretive, social, and technical-scientific—as we developed our argument about the roles of literacy and numeracy. We changed the sequence because the social sciences now have a greater emphasis on math than do critical interpretive fields.

27. Bolman & Deal, 1991/1997.

28. Nussbaum, 2011; Ravitch, 2010.

29. Rex, 2006a, 2006b.

30. St. John & Musoba, 2010.

31. Chapa & Horn, 2007; Oakes, 2003. The debates about the use of tests for college admis-

sions are now intertwined with the topic of racial representation (Bowman & St. John, 2011). The use of noncognitive variables in admission decisions provides one means of improving diversity (e.g., Sedlacek, 2004); class rank is another option (e.g., Chapa & Horn, 2007). There are also merit-aware methods that adapt test scores based on school context (St. John & Chung, 2004; St. John, Simmons & Musoba, 2002).

32. While phonemic (i.e., sound-letter) decoding remains important in college, especially as it relates to enunciation and key terms, decoding at a collegiate level refers to understanding meanings in context. In college, as in the professions, it is important to know the specific meanings of contextualized and specialized terms. The key role of decoding is not widely used in discussions of liberal arts education. In contrast, the concept of deconstructing theory, an advanced form of critical analytics related to decoding, is vitally important in the social sciences and the humanities.

33. St. John & Musoba, 2010. In the Indiana model, levels of preparation were generally thought of as being related to ability. High school students interested in the arts or music, however, can opt out of the honors track so they can take more courses in these areas. The honors diploma required an additional course each in math, science, and language over the college preparatory diploma. Given the extensive requirements in this type of proscribed model, some students can't get the preparation they need for specialized fields.

34. Hossler, 2004.

35. Hossler, 2004; Singha, 1997.

36. There are certainly other possible ways to structure high school literacy education. Our examples emerged from the case studies.

37. Ransdell & Glau, 1996.

38. Comprehensive School Reform Quality Center, 2006.

Chapter 4 · College Knowledge

1. McDonough, 1997; McDonough & Calderone, 2006.

2. St. John, 2003.

3. St. John, et al., 2013.

4. St. John, 2003; St. John, et al., 2013.

5. St. John, Hu, & Fisher, 2011.

6. Pell grants were introduced as Basic Educational Opportunity Grants (BEOG) in 1972 under the reauthorization of HEA Title IV.

7. St. John, 2003.

8. For histories of these programs, see Gladieux & Wolanin, 1976; St. John, 2003.

9. St. John, 2003.

10. St. John & Byce, 1982.

11. Hearn, 1993; St. John, 1994b.

12. Hossler & Schmit, 1995; Hossler, Schmit, & Vesper, 1999; St. John, 1991; St. John, Musoba, & Simmons, 2001, 2003.

13. HEA 2008, 122 STAT, p. 3221.

14. St. John, Fisher, et al., 2008.

15. Oliver, 2009.

16. Since the CFES survey was not administered using random selection, we make no claims about whether this group of respondents is statistically representative of the larger population of CFES Scholars in middle and high schools across the United States.

17. Some students did not know if they were in the program.
18. About one-quarter of the respondents did not know the answer to this question.
19. U.S. Census Bureau, 2012.
20. Piketty, 2014.
21. St. John, 2006.
22. Levine & Nidiffer, 1996.
23. Tierney, Corwin, & Colyar, 2005.
24. Tierney & Hagedorn, 2002.
25. Tierney, Venegas, & De La Rosa, 2006.
26. Tierney & Venegas, 2007.
27. Dalton, Bigelow, & St. John, 2012.
28. Meyer, et al., 2013; St. John, Kim, & Yang, 2014.
29. Dalton & St. John, in review.
30. McCoy, et al., 2014.
31. Perna & Jones, 2013.
32. Ibid.
33. Weissman, 2012.
34. Perna & Jones, 2013.
35. St. John & Musoba, 2010.
36. Perna & Jones, 2013.
37. St. John, 2004.
38. Perna & Jones, 2013.
39. Hoxby & Turner, 2013.
40. St. John, Hu, & Fisher, 2011.
41. Sedlacek, 2004.
42. St. John & Bowman, in press.
43. Dalton, Bigelow, & St. John, 2012.
44. A parent-satisfaction survey is distributed at the end of the school year.
45. St. John, Hu, & Fisher, 2011.

Chapter 5 · Toward Equitable Transformation

1. St. John, et al., 2013.
2. B. Friedman, 2005; Piketty, 2014.
3. Thelin, 2004.
4. Reese, 2005.
5. Bound & Turner, 2002.
6. St. John, 2013.
7. B. Friedman, 2005; Piketty, 2014; Stiglitz, 2012.
8. B. Friedman, 2005; T. Freidman, 2005.
9. St. John, 2003; St. John, Daun-Barnett, & Moronski-Chapman, 2013; St. John & Musoba, 2010.
10. Kahlenberg & Potter, 2014.
11. Frank, 2011.
12. Arum & Roksa, 2014.
13. Research on the 1992 high school cohort reveals long-term periodic enrollment as a pattern for many low-income undergraduates (St. John, 2006).

14. Piketty, 2014.
15. Irizarry, 1980.
16. Marginson, in press.
17. See www.bls.gov/ooh/legal/lawyers.htm#tab-6/.
18. There are ways of getting part of the college-loan debt forgiven (e.g., see www.lrp.nih .gov/about_the_programs/index.aspx), especially for students choosing professions linked to loan forgiveness (e.g., education and health in urban and rural areas). There are also some income-based loan repayment plans that provide a measure of relief during the first years, but they do not reduce the total debt and could increase the total amount paid.
19. Stiglitz, 2012.
20. St. John, 2003, 2006, 2013; St. John, Daun-Barnett, & Moronski-Chapman, 2012; St. John, Hu, & Fisher, 2011; St. John & Musoba, 2010. Our research-based theory of change has evolved over a series of comprehensive reviews and policy studies. The cited books moved forward iterations of this framework, building toward the current volume.
21. Perna & Jones, 2013.
22. St. John, 2003.
23. St. John, Hu, & Fisher, 2011; St. John & Musoba, 2010.
24. Berkner & Chavez, 1997.
25. Kuh, et al., 2005.
26. St. John, Hu, & Fisher, 2011.
27. Fisher, 2013; St. John, Hu, & Fisher, 2011.
28. King, 1999a, 1999b, 1999c.
29. Choy 2002a; 2002b.
30. St. John (2006) found that both poverty and debt burden were negatively associated with college completion by students who initially enrolled in community colleges. Grubb (1996) identified the problems caused by a high-debt burden for midskilled workers with limited income. These conditions have gotten worse in more recent decades (St. John, et al., 2013).
31. Ravitch, 2010.
32. Lindblom & Cohen, 1979.
33. Turnbull, Smith, & Ginsburg, 1981.
34. Ravitch, 2010.
35. Martinez & McGrath, 2014.
36. Kirp, 2014.
37. Pelavin & Kane, 1988.
38. Adelman, 1999; Berkner & Chavez, 1997.
39. This is not an unfounded claim. St. John 1994b, 2003 has discussed his experiences as a researcher at policy tables where this idea and others were designed and tested. Based on this, his subsequent work has emphasized the moral aspects of policy and practice (St. John 2009a, 2009b, 2013), in an attempt to reconcile his inner angst and regret for having been part of these processes.
40. Not only did St. John often hear these statements in policy conversations, but reviewers frequently also voiced this type of comment, making it difficult to raise critical issues. The federal vetting process screened out all such arguments, while academic reviewers were somewhat more accepting of well-reasoned, research-based arguments (e.g., St. John, 1989, 1991, 1994b).

41. McDonough & Calderone, 2006; Tierney, Venegas, & De La Rosa, 2006.

42. St. John, 2003.

43. St. John, et al., 2013.

44. Rawls (1971, 1999) uses this concept in his theory of justice, a concept that is particularly appropriate for this policy and social problem.

45. St. John, 2009a, 2009b.

46. Evans, 1971; St. John, 1981, 1994b, 2003.

47. Neoconservative arguments about funding and markets are often characterized as "managerialism" and "neoliberal" in the literature on education, especially in comparative literature (e.g., Meyer, 2013; Rizvi, 2004). We take the position that it is crucial to distinguish neoconservative arguments about public finance from neoliberal arguments promoting standards and accountability. Advocates for education may get monetary commitments in enacted legislation but they can lose these funds during the governmental budgeting process if they are naïve about the political strategies used in public finance. See Warren, 2014.

48. For a more in-depth discussion of proofiness in education, see St. John, Daun-Barnett, & Moronski-Chapman, 2013, a text that uses this concept as part of their review of the research base for federal educational policy.

49. Finn 1990a, 1990b.

50. M. Freidman, 1962.

51. For example, St. John was asked to read Milton Friedman's (1962) book when he was conducting his study of federal returns on student aid (St. John & Masten, 1990), but instead St. John used human-capital theory and cost-benefit theory to more carefully craft the presentation of his findings. Rather than arguing for dismantling public funding for higher education, the position implicit in Friedman's argument from 1962, St. John carefully bound his analyses to spending on and returns from federal grants, based on logics and the methods developed by G. Becker, 1975; Levin & McEwan, 2000.

52. Chubb & Moe, 1990.

53. Ravitch, 2010.

54. Pasque, 2007, 2010.

55. Fossey & Bateman, 1998; Hearn & Holdsworth, 2004.

56. Davis 1997, 2000

57. King, 2002.

58. St. John, 1990a, 1990b, 1991.

59. Warren, 2014.

60. In the preceding notes for this chapter, we have given examples of the ways in which political views shape and influence research findings. This is a common part of the research process. Even in dissertation committees—symbolic of academic freedom—committee members' views influence how emerging academics make arguments.

61. Kuhn, 1962/1976.

62. Snow, Burns, & Griffin, 1998.

63. Manset-Williamson, et al., 2002; St. John, Loescher, & Bardzell, 2003.

64. Manset-Williamson, et al., 2002.

65. W. Becker, 2004; Heller, 2004.

66. St. John, 2003.

67. DesJardins & Flaster, 2013; Hearn, et al., 2013; Hossler, Dunbar, & Shapiro, 2013.

68. Snow, Burns, & Griffin, 1998.

69. The RR program, based on meaning-oriented letter-sound relationships (a form of phonics) tailored interventions to the individual or the group by selecting appropriate books, a method emphasizing professional discretion and expertise over uniform approaches.

70. Clay, 1991, 1993.

71. St. John, 2007; Stage, 2007.

72. Jackson, 1978; Manski & Wise, 1983.

73. Pelavin & Kane, 1988, 1990.

74. St. John, 1989, 1991.

75. Adelman, 1999; Berkner & Chavez, 1997; Choy, 2002a, 2002b.

76. St. John, 1994a, 2003, 2007, 2013; St. John & Mirón, 2003.

77. St. John, 2009a, 2009b, 2013.

78. Ravitch, 2010.

79. Argyris & Schön, 1974; St. John, 2013.

80. Bryk, Lee, & Holland, 1995.

81. Daun-Barnett & St. John, 2012.

82. St. John, Fisher, et al., 2008.

83. St. John, et al., 2013.

Achieve, College Summit, NASSP, & NAESP. (2013). *Implementing the common core state standards: The role of the secondary school leader.* Washington, DC: Author.

Adelman, C. (1999). *Answers in the tool box: Academic intensity, attendance patterns, and bachelor's degree attainment.* Washington, DC: National Center for Education Statistics.

Advisory Committee on Student Financial Assistance. (2001). *Access denied: Restoring the nation's commitment to equal educational opportunity.* Washington, DC: Author.

Advisory Committee on Student Financial Assistance. (2003). *Review of NCES research on financial aid and college participation* and *Omitted variables and sample selection issues in the NCES research on financial aid and college participation.* Reports prepared for ACSFA by D. Heller & W. E. Becker. Washington, DC: Author.

Advisory Committee on Student Financial Assistance. (2008). *Apply to succeed: Ensuring community college students benefit from need-based financial aid.* Report prepared for ACSFA by the [ACFSA] Advisory Committee on Student Financial Assistance. Washington, DC: Author.

Advisory Committee on Student Financial Assistance. (2010). *The rising price of inequality: How inadequate grant aid limits college access and persistence.* Report prepared for Congress and the Secretary of Education by the [ACFSA] Advisory Committee on Student Financial Assistance. Washington, DC: Author.

Advisory Committee on Student Financial Assistance. (2013). *Inequality matters: Bachelor's degree losses among low-income Black and Hispanic high school graduates.* Policy bulletin for HEA reauthorization. Washington DC: Author.

Allensworth, E., Nomi, T., Montgomery, N., & Lee, V. E. (2009). College preparatory curriculum for all: Academic consequences of requiring algebra and English I for ninth graders in Chicago. *Educational Evaluation and Policy Analysis, 31*(4), 367–391.

Alvis, M. J., & Willie, C. V. (1987). Controlled choice assignments: A new and more effective approach to school desegregation. *Urban Review, 19*(1), 67–88.

Antonijević, R. (2006). Achievements of Serbian eighth grade students in science. *Institute for Educational Research, 38*(2), 333–355.

Argyris, C, & Schön, D. A. (1974). *Theory in practice: Increasing professional effectiveness.* San Francisco: Jossey-Bass.

Arum, R., & Roksa, J. (2014). *Aspiring adults adrift: Tentative transitions of college graduates.* Chicago: University of Chicago Press.

Au, K. H., & Raphael, T. E. (2000). Equity and literacy in the next millennium. *Reading Research Quarterly, 35*(1), 170–188.

Barghaus, K. M., Bradlow, E. T., McMaken, J., & Rikoon, S. H. (2013). Assessing and measuring workforce readiness: A discussion toward development of a universal and valid measure. In L. W. Perna (Ed.), *Preparing today's students for tomorrow's jobs in metropolitan America* (pp. 37–56). Philadelphia: University of Pennsylvania Press.

Baugh, J. (2009). Linguistic diversity, access, and risk. *Review of Research in Education, 33*(1), 272–282.

Becker, G. S. (1975). *Human capital: A theoretical and empirical analysis, with special reference to education* (2nd ed.). New York: National Bureau of Economic Research.

Becker, W. E. (2004). Omitted variables and sample selection in studies of college-going decisions. In E. P. St. John (Ed.), *Public policy and college access: Investigating the federal and state roles in equalizing postsecondary opportunity* (pp. 65–86). Readings on Equal Education 19. New York: AMS Press.

Bell, D. (1966). *The reforming of general education: The Columbia College experience in its national setting.* New York: Columbia University Press.

Berkner, L. K., & Chavez, L. (1997). *Access to postsecondary education for the 1992 high school graduates.* Washington, DC: U.S. Department of Education, Office of Educational Research and Improvement.

Boaler, J. (2002). Learning from teaching: Exploring the relationship between reform curriculum and equity. *Journal for Research in Mathematics Education, 33*(4), 239–258.

Bolman, L. G., & Deal, T. E. (1991/1997). *Reframing organizations: Artistry, choice, and leadership.* San Francisco: Jossey-Bass.

Bourdieu, P. (1974). The school as a conservative force: Scholastic and cultural inequalities. In J. Eggleston (Ed.), *Contemporary research in the sociology of education.* London: Metheun.

Bourdieu, P. (1977). *Outline of a theory of practice* (trans. R. Nice). Cambridge, MA: Cambridge University Press.

Bourdieu, P., & Passeron, J.-C. (1990). *Reproduction in education, society, and culture* (trans. R. Nice). London: Sage.

Bowen, W. G. (2011). Foreword. In T. Walsh (Ed.), *Unlocking the gates: How and why leading universities are opening up access to their courses.* Princeton, NJ: Princeton University Press.

Bowman, P. J., & St. John, E. P. (2011). *Diversity, merit, and higher education: Toward a comprehensive agenda for the 21st century.* Readings on Equal Education 25. New York: AMS Press.

Bound, J., & Turner, S. (2002). Going to war and going to college: Did World War II and the G.I. bill increase educational attainment for returning veterans? *Journal of Labor Economics, 20*(4), 784–815.

Bragg, D. D. (2013). Pathways to college for underserved and nontraditional students: Lessons from research, policy, and practice. In L. W. Perna & A. Jones, *The state of college access and completion: Improving college success for students from underrepresented groups* (pp. 34–56). New York: Routledge.

Bryk, A. S., Lee, V. E., & Holland, P. B. (1995). *Catholic schools and the common good.* Boston: Harvard University Press.

Carnes, B. M. (1987). The campus cost explosion: College tuitions are unnecessarily high. *Policy Review, 40,* 68–71.

Carnevale, A. P. (2007). Confessions of an education fundamentalist: Why grade 12 is not the right end point for anyone. In N. Hoffman, J. Vargas, A. Venezia, & M. S. Miller (Eds.), *Minding the gap: Why integrating high school with college makes sense and how to do it* (pp. 15–26). Cambridge, MA: Harvard Education Press.

Carnevale, A. P., Smith, N., & Strohl, J. (2013). Postsecondary education and economic opportunity. In L. W. Perna (Ed.), *Preparing today's students for tomorrow's jobs in metropolitan America* (pp. 93–120). Philadelphia: University of Pennsylvania Press.

Chambers, D. l. (1994). The *right* algebra for all. *Educational Leadership, 51*(6), 85–86.

Chapa, J., & Horn, C. L. (2007). Is anything race neutral? Comparing "race-neutral" admissions policies at the University of Texas and the University of California. In G. Orfield, P. Marin, S. M. Flores, & L. Garces, *Charting the future of college affirmative action: Legal victories, continuing attacks, and new research* (pp. 157–172). Los Angeles: Civil Rights Project, UCLA School of Education, http://escholarship.org/uc/item/2f20k3hn/.

Cheit, E. F. (1975). *The useful arts and the liberal tradition.* New York: McGraw-Hill.

Choy, S. P. (2002a). *Access & persistence: Findings from 10 years of longitudinal research on students.* Washington, DC: American Council on Education.

Choy, S. P. (2002b). *Nontraditional undergraduates: Findings from "The Condition of Education, 2002."* Washington, DC: National Center for Education Statistics.

Chubb, J. E., & Moe, T. M. (1990). *Politics, markets, and America's schools.* Washington, DC: Brookings Institution.

Clay, M. M. (1991). *Becoming literate: The construction of inner control.* Portsmouth, NH: Heinemann.

Clay, M. M. (1993). *Reading recovery: A guidebook for teachers in training.* Portsmouth, NH: Heinemann.

Coleman, J. S. (1966). *Equality of educational opportunity.* Washington, DC: U.S. Department of Health, Education, and Welfare.

Commission on the Skills of the American Workforce. (2007). *Tough choices, tough times: The report of the new Commission on Skills of the American Workforce.* Washington, DC: National Center on Education and the Economy.

Common Core State Standards Initiative. (n.d.). Students who are college and career ready in reading, writing, speaking, listening, & language. *English language arts standards: Introduction,* www.corestandards.org/ELA-Literacy/introduction/students-who-are-college-and -career-ready-in-reading-writing-speaking-listening-language/.

Comprehensive School Reform Quality Center. (2006). *CSRQ report on middle and high school comprehensive school reform models.* Washington, DC: American Institutes of Research, www.air.org/files/MSHS_2006_Report_Final_Full_Version_10-03-06.pdf.

Conklin, K. D., Curran, B. K., & Gandal, M. (2005). *Action agenda for improving America's high schools.* Washington, DC: Achieve, Inc., and National Governors Association, www .achieve.org/files/actionagenda2005.pdf.

Conley, D. T. (2013). Proficiency approaches for making more students college and career ready. In L. W. Perna and A. Jones (Eds.), *The state of college access and completion: Improving college success for students from underrepresented groups* (pp. 77–95). New York: Routledge.

Cupiak, Y. Z. (in press). *On the nexus of local and global: Chinese higher education and college students in the era of globalization.* Issues in Globalization and Social Justice 3. New York: AMS Press.

Curto, V. E., Fryer, R. G., & Howard, M. L. (2011). It may not take a village: Increasing achievement among the poor. In G. D. Duncan, & R. J. Murnane (Eds.), *Whither opportunity? Rising inequality, schools, and children's life chances.* New York: Russell Sage Foundation.

Dalton, R., Bigelow, V., & St. John, E. P. (2012). College for every student: A model for postsecondary encouragement in rural schools. In R. Winkle-Wagner, P. J. Bowman, &

E. P. St. John (Eds.), *Expanding postsecondary opportunity for underrepresented students: Theory and practice of academic capital formation* (pp. 181–204). Readings on Equal Education 26. New York: AMS Press.

Dalton R., & St. John, E. P. (in review). College for every student: Building a research partnership supporting an access network. In E. P. St. John, K. Lijana, & G. M. Musoba, (Eds.), *Using action inquiry in education reform: Organizing guide for improving pathways to college.* Sterling, VA: Stylus Press.

Daun-Barnett, N. (2008). Preparation and access: A multi-level analysis of state policy influences on the academic antecedents to college enrollment. PhD diss., University of Michigan.

Daun-Barnett, N., & St. John, E. P. (2012). Constrained curriculum in high schools: The changing math standards and student achievement, high school graduation, and college continuation. *Education Policy Analysis Archives, 20*(5), http://epaa.asu.edu/ojs/article/view/907/.

Davis, J. S. (1997). *College affordability: A closer look at the crisis.* Washington, DC: Sallie Mae Education Institute.

Davis, J. S. (2000). *College affordability: Overlooked long-term trends and recent 50-state patterns.* USA Group Foundation New Agenda Series, Vol. 3, No. 1 (November). Indianapolis: USA Group Foundation.

DesJardins, S. L., & Flaster, A. (2013). Non-experimental designs and causal analyses of college access, persistence, and completion. In L. W. Perna & A. Jones (Eds.), *The state of college access and completion: Improving college success for students from underrepresented groups* (pp. 190–207). New York: Routledge.

DiMaggio, P. J., & Powell, W. W. (1983). The iron cage revisited: Institutional isomorphism and collective rationality in organizational fields. *American Sociological Review, 4*(2), 147–160.

Eckes, S., & Rapp, K. (2006). Charter school research: Trends and implications. In E. P. St. John (Ed.), *Public policy and equal educational opportunity: School reforms, postsecondary encouragement, and state policies on postsecondary education* (pp. 3–36). Readings on Equal Education 21. New York: AMS Press.

Eckes, S., & Rapp, K. (2007). Are charter schools using recruitment strategies to increase student body diversity? *Education and Urban Society, 40*(1), 62–90.

Education Resources Institute. (1997). *Missed opportunities: A new look at disadvantaged college aspirants.* Washington, DC: Institute for Higher Education Policy.

Evans, J. (1971).View from a state capitol. *Change, 3*(5), 40–45.

Finn, C. E., Jr. (1988a). Prepared statement and attachments: Hearing before the Subcommittee on Postsecondary Education, Committee on Education and Labor, House of Representatives, 100th Congress, 1st Session, No. 100-47, September 25. Washington, DC: Government Printing Office.

Finn, C. E., Jr. (1988b). Judgment time for higher education: In the court of public opinion. *Change, 20*(4), 35–38.

Finn, C. E., Jr. (1990a). The biggest reform of all. *Phi-Delta-Kappan, 71*(8), 584–592.

Finn, C. E., Jr. (1990b). Why we need choice. In W. L. Boyd & H. J. Walberg (Eds.), *Choice in education: Potential and problems* (pp. 3–20). Berkeley, CA: McCutchan.

Fisher, A. S. (2013). *When did public become the new private? Grappling with access to postsecondary education for low-income students.* PhD diss., University of Michigan.

Fossey, R. E., & Bateman, M. E. (Eds.). (1998). *Condemning students to debt: College loans and public policy.* New York: Teachers College Press.

Frank, R. (2011). *The Darwin economy: Liberty, competition, and the common good.* Princeton, NJ: Princeton University Press.

Franzak, J. K. (2006). Zoom: A review of the literature on marginalized adolescent readers, literacy theory, and policy implications. *Review of Educational Research, 27*(2), 209–248.

Friedman, B. M. (2005). *The moral consequences of economic growth.* New York: Vintage.

Friedman, M. (1962). *Capitalism and freedom.* Chicago: University of Chicago Press.

Friedman, T. L. (2005). *The world is flat: A brief history of the twenty-first century.* New York: Farrar, Straus, and Giroux.

Furner, J. M., & Robinson, S. (2004). Using TIMSS to improve the undergraduate preparation of mathematics teachers. *Curriculum Journal, 4,* 10–21.

Gladieux, L. E., & Wolanin, T. R. (1976). *Congress and the colleges: The national politics of higher education.* Lexington, MA: Lexington Books.

Gonzales, P., Williams, T., Jocelyn, L., Roey, S., Kastberg, D., & Brenwald, S. (2009). *Highlights from TIMSS 2007: Mathematics and science achievement of U.S. fourth- and eighth-grade students in an international context.* Washington, DC: National Center for Education Statistics.

Goodchild, L. F. (1997). Contemporary Undergraduate Education: An Era of Alternatives and Reassessment. *Theory into Practice, 36*(2), 123–131.

Graham, K. J., & Fennell, F. (2001). "Principles and Standards for School Mathematics" and teacher education: Preparing and empowering teachers. *School Science and Mathematics, 101*(6), 319–327.

Grubb, W. N. (1996). *Working in the middle: Strengthening education and training for the mid-skilled labor force.* San Francisco: Jossey-Bass.

Gutiérrez, K. D., Zitiali Morales, P., & Martinez, D. C. (2009). Remediating literacy: Culture, difference, and learning for students from nondominant cultures. *Review of Research in Education, 33,* 212–245.

Hansen, W. L., & Weisbrod, B. A. (1969). *Benefits, costs, and finance of public higher education.* Chicago: Markham.

Hartle, T. W. (1998). Clueless about college costs. *Presidency, 1*(1), 20–27.

Hartle, T. W., Simmons, C. A. M., & Timmons, B. H. (2005). *What every student should know about federal aid.* Washington, DC: American Council on Education.

Hearn, J. C. (1993). The paradox of growth in federal aid for college students, 1965–1990. In J. C. Smart (Ed.), *Higher education: Handbook of theory and research,* vol. 9 (pp. 94–153). New York: Agathon Press.

Hearn, J. C. (2001). Access to postsecondary education: Financing equity in an evolving context. In M. B. Paulsen & J. C. Smart (Eds.), *The finance of higher education: Theory, research, policy, and practice* (pp. 439–460). New York: Agathon Press.

Hearn, J. C., & Holdsworth, J. M. (2004). Federal student aid: The shift from grants to loans. In E. P. St. John & M. D. Parsons (Eds.), *Public funding of higher education: Changing contexts and new rationales* (pp. 40–59). Baltimore: Johns Hopkins University Press.

Hearn, J. C., Jones, A. P., & Kurban, E. R. (2013). Access, persistence, and completion in the state context. In L. W. Perna & A. Jones, *The state of college access and completion: Improving college success for students from underrepresented groups* (pp. 166–189). New York: Routledge.

Heller, D. E. (1997). Student price response in higher education: An update to Leslie and Brinkman. *Journal of Higher Education, 68*(6), 624–659.

Heller, D. E. (2004). NCES research on college participation: A critical analysis. In E. P. St. John (Ed.), *Public policy and college access: Investigating the federal and state roles in equalizing postsecondary opportunity* (pp. 29–64). Readings on Equal Education 19. New York: AMS Press.

Heller, D. E. (2013). The role of finances in postsecondary access and success. In L. W. Perna & A. Jones, *The state of college access and completion: Improving college success for students from underrepresented groups* (pp. 96–114). New York: Routledge.

Hoachlander, E. G., Kaufman, P., Levesque, K., & Houser, J. (1992). *Vocational Education in the United States: 1969–1990*. Washington, DC: National Center for Education Statistics.

Hoachlander, G. (1997). Organizing mathematics around work. In L. A. Steen (Ed.), *Why numbers count: Quantitative literacy for tomorrow's America*. New York: College Entrance Examination Board.

Hoachlander, G. (1999). Integrating academic and vocational curriculum: Why is theory so hard to practice? *CenterPoint 7*, http://ncrve.berkeley.edu/CenterPoint/CP7/CP7.html.

Hoffman, N., Vargas, J., Venezia, A., & Miller, M. S. (Eds.). (2007). *Minding the gap: Why integrating high school with college makes sense and how to do it*. Cambridge, MA: Harvard Education Press.

Hossler, D. (2004). Refinancing public universities: Student enrollments, incentive-based budgeting, and incremental revenue. In E. P. St. John & M. D. Parsons (Eds.), *Public funding of higher education: Changing contexts and new rationales* (pp. 145–163). Baltimore: Johns Hopkins University Press.

Hossler, D., Dunbar, A., & Shapiro, D. T. (2013). Longitudinal pathways to college persistence and completion: Student, institutional, and public. In L. W. Perna & A. Jones, *The state of college access and completion: Improving college success for students from underrepresented groups* (pp. 140–165). New York: Routledge.

Hossler, D., & Schmit, J. (1995). The Indiana postsecondary-encouragement experiment. In E. P. St. John (Ed.), *Rethinking tuition and student aid strategies* (pp. 27–39). San Francisco: Jossey-Bass.

Hossler, D., Schmit, J. L., & Vesper, N. (1999). *Going to college: How social, economic, and educational factors influence the decisions students make*. Baltimore: Johns Hopkins University Press.

House, J. D., & Telese, J. A. (2008). Relationships between student and instructional factors and algebra achievement of students in the United States and Japan: An analysis of TIMSS 2003 data. *Educational Research and Evaluation, 14*(1), 101–112, doi:10.1080/13803610801896679.

Hoxby, C., & Turner, S. (2013). *Expanding college opportunities for high-achieving, low income students*. SIEPR Discussion Paper No. 12-014. Stanford, CA: Stanford Institute for Economic Policy Research, http://siepr.stanford.edu/?q=/system/files/shared/pubs/papers/12-014paper.pdf [retrieved November 6, 2014].

Irizarry, R. L. (1980). Overeducation and unemployment in the Third World: The paradoxes of dependent industrialization. *Comparative Education Review, 24*(3), 338–352.

Jabon, D., Narasimhan, L., Boller, J., Sally, P., Baldwin, J., & Slaughter, R. (2010). The Chicago Algebra Initiative. *Notices of the American Mathematical Society, 57*(7), 685–687.

Jackson, G. A. (1978). Financial aid and student enrollment. *Journal of Higher Education, 49*(6), 548–574.

Jackson, G. A., & Weathersby, G. B. (1975). Individual demand for higher education: A review and analysis of recent empirical studies. *Journal of Higher Education, 46*(6), 623–652.

Jencks, C. (1972). *Inequality: A reassessment of the effect of family and schooling in America.* New York: Basic Books.

Jordan, W. J., McPartland, J. M., Legters, N. E., & Balfanz, R. (2000). Creating a comprehensive school reform model: The Talent Development High School with Career Academies. *Journal for Education of Students Placed at Risk, 5*(1/2), 159–181.

Kahlenberg, R. D., & Potter, H. (2014). *A smarter charter: Finding what works for charter schools and public education.* New York: Teachers College Press.

King, J. E. (1999a). Conclusion. In J. E. King (Ed.), *Financing a college education: How it works, how it's changing* (pp. 198–202). Westport, CT: American Council on Education / Oryx Press.

King, J. E. (1999b). Crisis or convenience: Why are students borrowing more? In J. E. King (Ed.), *Financing a college education: How it works, how it's changing* (pp. 165–176). Westport, CT: American Council on Education / Oryx Press.

King, J. E. (1999c). *Money matters: The impact of race/ethnicity and gender and how students pay for college.* Washington, DC: American Council on Education.

King, J. E. (2002). *Crucial choices: How students' financial decisions affect their academic success.* Washington, DC: American Council on Education.

Kirp, D. L. (2014). *Improbable scholars: The rebirth of a great American school system and strategy for America's schools.* Oxford: Oxford University Press.

Klein, D. (2003) A brief history of American K–12 mathematics education in the 20th century. In J. M. Royer (Ed.), *Mathematical cognition* (pp.175–225). Greenwich, CT: Information Age.

Kneebone, E., Nadeau, C., & Berube, A. (2011). The re-emergence of concentrated poverty: Metropolitan trends in the 2000s. *Metropolitan opportunities series*, Brookings Institution, www.brookings.edu/papers/2011/1103_poverty_kneebone_nadeau_berube.aspx.

Kolderie, T. (1992). Chartering diversity. *Equity and Choice, 9*(1), 28–31.

Kuh, G. D., Kinzie, J., Schuh, J. H., & Whitt, E. J. (2005). *Student success in college: Creating conditions that matter.* San Francisco: Jossey-Bass.

Kuhn, Thomas. (1962/1976). *The structure of scientific revolutions.* Chicago: University of Chicago Press.

Lee, C. D. (2009). Historical evolution of risk and equity: Interdisciplinary issues and critiques. *Review of Research in Education, 33*(1), 63–100.

Leslie, L. L., & Brinkman, P. T. (1988). *The economic value of higher education.* New York: Macmillan.

Levin, H. M., & McEwan, P. J. (2000). *Cost-effectiveness analysis: Methods and applications* (2nd ed.). Thousand Oaks, CA: Sage.

Levine, A., & Nidiffer, J. (1996). *Beating the odds: How the poor get into college.* San Francisco: Jossey-Bass.

Lindblom, C. E. (1959). The science of "muddling through." *Public Administration Review, 19*(2), 79–88.

Lindblom, C. E., & Cohen, D. K. (1979). *Usable knowledge: Social science and social problem solving.* New Haven, CT: Yale University Press.

Lumina Foundation. (2014). *College bound communities: The smartest cities make student suc-*

cess a shared mission. Lumina Foundation Focus, Summer 2014. Indianapolis: Author, http://focus.luminafoundation.org/summer2014/.

Manset-Williamson, G., St. John, E. P., Hu, S., & Gordon, D. (2002). Early literacy practices as predictors of reading related outcomes: Tests scores, test passing rates, retention, and special education referral. *Exceptionality, 10*(1), 11–28.

Manski, C. F., & Wise, D. A. (1983). *College choice in America.* Cambridge, MA: Harvard University Press.

Marginson, S. (in press). Education, innovation, and East Asian development miracles. In W. G. Tierney (Ed.), *Education and poverty.* Baltimore: Johns Hopkins University Press.

Martinez, M., & McGrath, D. (2014). *Deeper learning: How eight innovative public schools are transforming education in the twenty-first century.* New York: New Press.

McCoy, S., Smyth, E., Watson, D., & Darmody, M. (2014). *Leaving school in Ireland: A longitudinal study of post-school transitions.* ESRI Research Series 36. Dublin: Economic and Social Research Institute, www.esri.ie/publications/search_for_a_publication/search_results/view/index.xml?id=3944/.

McDonough, P. M. (1997). *Choosing colleges: How social class and schools structure opportunity.* Albany: State University of New York Press.

McDonough, P. M., & Calderone, S. (2006). The meaning of money: Perceptual differences between college counselors and low-income families about college costs and financial aid. *American Behavioral Scientist, 49*(12), 1703–1718, doi:10.1177/0002764206289140.

McPherson, M. S. (1978). The demand for higher education. In D. W. Breneman & C. E. Finn, Jr. (Eds.), *Public policy and private higher education* (pp. 143–146). Washington, DC: Brookings Institution.

Meacham, S. J. (2000). Literacy at the crossroads: Movement, connection, and communication within the research literature on literacy and cultural diversity. *Review of Research in Education, 25*(1), 181.

Melguizo, T., Kienzl, G., & Kosiewicz, H. (2013). The potential of community college to increase bachelor's degree attainment rates. In L. W. Perna & A. Jones, *The state of college access and completion: Improving college success for students from underrepresented groups* (pp. 140–165). New York: Routledge.

Metcalf, K. K., & Paul, K. M. (2006). Enhancing or destroying equity? An examination of educational vouchers. In E. P. St. John (Ed.), *Public policy and equal educational opportunity: School reforms, postsecondary encouragement, and state policies on postsecondary education* (pp. 37–74). Readings on Equal Education 21. New York: AMS Press.

Metcalf, K. K., West, S. D., Legan, N., Paul, K. M., & Boone, W. J. (2004). *Evaluation of the Cleveland Scholarship and Tutoring Program: Technical and summary reports, 1998–2003.* Bloomington: Indiana University, School of Education.

Meyer, H.-D. (2013). Reasoning about fairness in access to higher education: Common sense, normative, and institutional perspectives. In H.-D. Meyer, E. P. St. John, M. Chankseliani, & L. Uribe (Eds.), *Fairness in access to higher education in a global perspective: Reconciling excellence, efficiency, and justice* (pp. 15–40). Rotterdam, The Netherlands: Sense Publications.

Meyer, H.-D., St. John, E. P., Chankseliani, M., & Uribe, L. (2013). The crisis in access to higher education: A crisis of justice. In H.-D. Meyer, E. P. St. John, M. Chankseliani, & L. Uribe (Eds.), *Fairness in access to higher education in a global perspective: Reconciling excellence, efficiency, and justice* (pp. 1–14). Rotterdam, The Netherlands: Sense Publications.

Moses, R. P., & Cobb, C. E., Jr. (2001). Racial equations: Civil rights from Mississippi to the Algebra Project. Boston: Beacon Press.

National Center for Education Statistics. (2009). *NAEP 2008 trends in academic progress.* Washington, DC: Author, http://nces.ed.gov/nationsreportcard/pdf/main2008/2009479_1 .pdf.

National Research Council. (2011). *Successful K–12 STEM education: Identifying effective approaches in science, technology, engineering, and mathematics.* Washington, DC: National Academies Press.

Newman, F. (1971). *Report on higher education.* Washington, DC: Government Printing Office.

Nisar, H. (2012). Does variation in the autonomy granted to charter schools affect their impact on student achievement? *National Center for the Study of Privatization in Education,* www.abtassociates.com/Articles/2012/Does-Variation-in-the-Autonomy-Granted-to -Charter-.aspx.

Nussbaum, M. C. (2011). *Creating capabilities: The human development approach.* Cambridge, MA: Belcamp Press.

Oakes, J. (1985/2005). *Keeping track: How schools structure inequality.* New Haven, CT: Yale University Press.

Oakes, J. (2003). Critical conditions for equity and diversity in college access: Informing policy and monitoring results. *UC/ACCORD: University of California All Campus Consortium on Research for Diversity,* www.escholarship.org/uc/item/427737xt/.

Oliver, I. (2009). College access challenge grant: The federal policy climate explained. Powerpoint presentation, *HCM Strategists,* www.wiche.edu/info/cacg/meetings/boulder09/ oliver.pdf [retrieved March 11, 2011].

Ongaga, K. O. (2010). Students' learning experiences in an early college high school. *Peabody Journal of Education, 85*(3), 375–388.

Orfield, G., & Eaton, S. E. (1997). *Dismantling desegregation: The quiet reversal of Brown v. Board of Education.* New York: Free Press.

Orfield, G., Marin, P., Flores, S. M., and Garces, L. M. (2007). *Charting the future of college affirmative action: Legal victories, continuing attacks, and new research.* Los Angeles: Civil Rights Project, UCLA School of Education, http://escholarship.org/uc/item/2f20k3hn/.

Partnership for 21st Century Skills. (2011). Overview. *Framework for 21st century learning,* www.p21.org/our-work/p21-framework/.

Pasque, P. A. (2007). Seeing more of the educational inequalities around us: Visions toward strengthening relationships between higher education and society. In E. P. St. John (Ed.), *Confronting educational inequality: Reframing, building understanding, and making change* (pp. 37–84). Readings on Equal Education 22. New York: AMS Press.

Pasque, P. A. (2010). *American higher education, leadership, and policy: Critical issues and the public good.* New York: Palgrave.

Pearson, P. D., Moje, E., & Greenleaf, C. (2010). Literacy and science: Each in the service of the other. *Science, 328*(5977), 459–463.

Pelavin, S. H., & Kane, M. B. (1988). *Minority participation in higher education.* Washington, DC: Pelavin Associates.

Pelavin, S. H., & Kane, M. B. (1990). *Changing the odds: Factors increasing access to college.* New York: College Board.

Perna, L. W. (2013). Conclusions: Improving college access, persistence, and completion; Lessons learned. In L. W. Perna & A. Jones, *The state of college access and completion:*

Improving college success for students from underrepresented groups (pp. 140–165). New York: Routledge.

Perna, L. W., & Jones, A. (2013). *The state of college access and completion: Improving college success for students from underrepresented groups.* New York: Routledge.

Perna, L., & Kurban, E. L. (2013). Improving college access and choice. In L. W. Perna and A. Jones (Eds.), *The state of college access and completion: Improving college success for students from underrepresented groups* (pp. 10–33). New York: Routledge.

Perry, T., Moses, R. P., Wynne, J. T., Cortes, E., & Delpit, L. E. (Eds.). (2010). *Quality education as a constitutional right: Creating a grassroots movement to transform public schools.* Boston: Beacon Press.

Peterson, P. E. (1998). School choice: A report card. *Virginia Journal of Social Policy and Law, 6*(1), 47–80.

Peterson, P. E., & Howell, W. G. (2004). Efficiency, bias, and classification schemes: A response to Alan B. Kreuewger and Pei Zhu. *American Behavioral Scientist, 47*(5), 699–717.

Peterson, P. E., Howell, W. G., Wolf, P. J., & Campbell, D. E. (2003). School vouchers: Results from randomized experiments. In C. M. Hoxby (Ed.), *The economics of school choice.* Chicago: University of Chicago Press.

Piketty, T. (2014). *Capital in the 21st century* (trans. A. Goldhammer). Cambridge, MA: Belknap Press of Harvard University Press.

Ransdell, D. R., & Glau, G. R. (1996). Articulation and student voices: Eliminating the perception that "high school English doesn't teach you nothing." *English Journal, 86*(1), 7–21.

Ravitch, D. (2010). *The death and life of the great American school system: How testing and choice are undermining education.* New York: Basic Books.

Rawls, J. (1971). *A theory of justice.* Cambridge, MA: Belknap Press of Harvard University Press.

Rawls, J. (1999). *A theory of justice* (revised ed.). Cambridge, MA: Harvard University Press.

Reese, W. J. (2005). *America's public schools: From the common school to "No Child Left Behind."* Baltimore: Johns Hopkins University Press.

Rex, L. A. (2006a). Acting "cool" and "appropriate": Toward a framework for considering literacy classroom interactions when race is a factor. *Journal of Literacy Research, 38*(3), 275–325.

Rex, L. A. (Ed.) (2006b). *Discourse of opportunity: How talk in learning situations creates and constrains interactional ethnographic studies in teaching and learning.* Discourse and Social Processes Series. Cresskill, NJ: Hampton Press.

Ridenour, C. S., & St. John, E. P. (2003). Private scholarships and school choice: Innovation or class reproduction? In L. F. Mirón & E. P. St. John (Eds.), *Reinterpreting urban schools reform: Have urban schools failed, or has the reform movement failed urban schools?* (pp. 177–206). Albany: State University of New York Press.

Rizvi, F. (2004). Globalisation and the dilemmas of Australian higher education. *Access: Critical Perspectives on Communication, Cultural, and Policy Studies, 23*(2), 33–42.

Rong, L., & Chen, R. (2013). Educational development in China: Policy and access. In E. P. St. John, J. Kim, & L. Yang (Eds.). *Privatization and inequality: Comparative studies of college access, education policy, and public finance.* Issues in Globalization and Social Justice 1. New York: AMS Press.

St. John, E. P. (1981). *Public policy and college management: Title III of the Higher Education Act.* New York: Praeger Press.

St. John, E. P. (1989). The influence of student aid on persistence. *Journal of Student Financial Aid, 19*(3), 52–68.

St. John, E. P. (1990a). Price response in enrollment decisions: An analysis of the High School and Beyond sophomore cohort. *Research in Higher Education, 31*(2), 161–176.

St. John, E. P. (1990b). Price response in persistence decisions: An analysis of the High School and Beyond senior cohort. *Research in Higher Education, 31*(4), 387–403.

St. John, E. P. (1991). What really influences minority attendance? Sequential analyses of the high school and beyond sophomore cohort. *Research in Higher Education, 32*(2), 141–158.

St. John, E. P. (1994a). Assessing tuition and student aid strategies: Using price-response measures to simulate pricing alternatives. *Research in Higher Education, 35*(3), 301–335.

St. John, E. P. (1994b). *Prices, productivity, and investment: Assessing financial strategies in higher education.* ASHE/ERIC Higher Education Report 3. Washington, DC: George Washington University, School of Education and Human Development.

St. John, E. P. (2003). *Refinancing the college dream: Access, equal opportunity, and justice for taxpayers.* Baltimore: Johns Hopkins University Press.

St. John, E. P. (Ed.). (2004). *Public policy and college access: Investigating the federal and state roles in equalizing postsecondary opportunity.* Readings on Equal Education 19. New York: AMS Press.

St. John, E. P. (2006). *Education and the public interest: School reform, public finance, and access to higher education.* Dordrecht, The Netherlands: Springer.

St. John, E. P. (Ed.) (2007). *Confronting educational inequality: Reframing, building under-standing, and making change.* Readings on Equal Education 22. New York: AMS Press.

St. John, E. P. (2009a). *Action, reflection, and social justice: Integrating moral reasoning into professional education.* Cresskill, NJ: Hampton Press.

St. John, E. P. (2009b) *College organization and professional development: Integrating moral reasoning and reflective practice.* New York: Routledge.

St. John, E. P. (2012). Academic capital formation: An emergent theory. In R. Winkle-Wagner, P. J. Bowman, & E. P. St. John (Eds.), *Expanding postsecondary opportunity for underrepresented students: Theory and practice of academic capital formation* (pp. 3–28). Readings on Equal Education 26. New York: AMS Press.

St. John, E. P. (2013). *Research, actionable knowledge, and social change: Reclaiming social responsibility through research partnerships.* Actionable Research for Social Justice in Education Series. Sterling, VA: Stylus.

St. John, E. P., & Bowman, P. J. (in press). Conclusion: Education, poverty, and public policy. In W. G. Tierney (Ed.), *Education and poverty.* Baltimore: Johns Hopkins University Press.

St. John, E. P., & Byce, C. (1982). The changing federal role in student financial aid. In M. Kramer (Ed.), *Meeting student aid needs in a period of retrenchment* (pp. 21–40). New Directions for Higher Education 40. San Francisco: Jossey-Bass.

St. John, E. P., & Chung, C. G. (2004). Merit and equity: Rethinking award criteria in the Michigan scholarship program. In E. P. St. John & M. D. Parsons (Eds.), *Public funding of higher education: Changing contexts and new rationales* (pp. 124–140). Baltimore: Johns Hopkins University Press

St. John, E. P., Daun-Barnett, N. J., & Moronski-Chapman, K. M. (2013). *Public policy and higher education.* New York: Routledge.

St. John, E. P., Fisher, A. S., Lee, M., Daun-Barnett, N., & Williams, K. (2008). *Educational opportunity in Indiana: Studies of the Twenty-First Century Scholars Program using state student unit record data systems*, www.umich.edu/~mpas/LuminaReport.pdf.

St. John, E. P., Hu, S., & Fisher, A. S. (2011). *Breaking through the access barrier: How academic capital formation can improve policy in higher education*. New York: Routledge.

St. John, E. P., Kim, J., & Yang, L. (2014). *Privatization and inequality: Comparative studies of college access, education policy, and public finance*. Issues in Globalization and Social Justice 1. New York: AMS Press.

St. John, E. P., Loescher, S. A., & Bardzell, J. S. (2003). *Improving reading and literacy in grades 1–5: A resource guide to research-based programs*. Thousand Oaks, CA: Corwin.

St. John, E. P., Massé, J. C., Fisher, A. S., Moronski-Chapman, K., & Lee, M. (2013). Beyond the bridge: Actionable research informing the development of a comprehensive intervention strategy. *American Behavioral Scientist, 58*(8), 1051–1070.

St. John, E. P., & Masten, C. L. (1990). Return on the federal investment in student financial aid: An assessment of the high school class of 1972. *Journal of Student Financial Aid, 20*(3), 4–23.

St. John, E. P., & Meyer, H.-D. (2013a). Reconciling efficiency with excellence and fairness: Proposals for policy and practice. In H.-D. Meyer, E. P. St. John, M. Chankseliani, & L. Uribe (Eds.), *Fairness in access to higher education in a global perspective: Reconciling excellence, efficiency, and justice* (pp. 289–308). Rotterdam, The Netherlands: Sense Publications.

St. John, E. P., & Meyer, H.-D. (2013b). Conclusion. In H.-D. Meyer, E. P. St. John, M. Chankseliani, & L. Uribe (Eds.), *Fairness in access to higher education in a global perspective: Reconciling excellence, efficiency, and justice* (pp. 277–288). Rotterdam, The Netherlands: Sense Publications.

St. John, E. P., & Mirón, L. F. (2003). A critical-empirical perspective on urban school reform. In L. F. Mirón & E. P. St. John (Eds.), *Reinterpreting urban school reform: Have urban schools failed, or has the reform movement failed urban schools?* (pp. 279–298). Albany: State University of New York Press.

St. John, E. P., & Musoba, G. D. (2010). *Pathways to academic success: Expanding opportunity for underrepresented students*. New York: Routledge.

St. John, E. P., Musoba, G. D., & Simmons, A. B. (2001). *Keeping the promise: The impact of Indiana's Twenty-First Century Scholars Program*. Policy Research Report 01-02. Bloomington, IN: Indiana Education Policy Center.

St. John, E. P., Musoba, G. D., & Simmons, A. B. (2003). Keeping the promise: The impact of Indiana's Twenty-First Century Scholars Program. *Review of Higher Education, 27*(1), 103–123.

St. John, E. P., & Ridenour, C. S. (2001). Market forces and strategic adaptation: The influence of private scholarships on planning in urban school systems. *Urban Review, 33*(4), 269–290.

St. John, E. P., & Ridenour, C. S. (2002). School leadership in a market setting: The influence of private scholarships on education leadership in urban schools. *Leadership and Policy in Schools, 1*(4), 317–344.

St. John, E. P., Simmons, A., & Musoba, G. D. (1999). *Merit-aware admissions in public universities: Increasing diversity without considering ethnicity*. Policy Bulletin No. PB-25. Bloomington: Indiana Education Policy Center, Indiana University.

St. John, E. P., Simmons, A. B., & Musoba, G. D. (2002). Merit-aware admissions in public universities. *Thought & Action, 17*(2), 35–46.

Schultze, C. L. (1968). *The politics and economics of public spending.* Washington, DC: Brookings Institution.

Sedlacek, W. E. (2004). *Beyond the big test: Noncognitive assessment in higher education.* San Francisco: Jossey-Bass.

Shen, C., & Tam, H. P. (2008). The paradoxical relationship between student achievement and self-perception: A cross-national analysis based on three waves of TIMSS data. *Educational Research and Evaluation, 14*(1), 87–100, doi:10.1080/13803610801896653.

Siddle Walker, V., & Snarey, J. R. (Eds.). (2004). *Race-ing moral formation: African American perspectives on care and justice.* New York: Teachers College Press.

Silver, E. A. (1994). On mathematical problem posing. *For the Learning of Mathematics, 14*(1), 19–28.

Silver, E. A., Ghousseini, H., Gosen, D., Charalambous, C., & Strawhun, B. T. F. (2005). Moving from rhetoric to praxis: Issues faced by teachers in having students consider multiple solutions for problems in the mathematics classroom. *Journal of Mathematical Behavior, 24*(3–4), 287–301.

Silver, E. A., Smith, M. S., & Nelson, B. S. (1995). The QUASAR project: Equity concerns meet mathematics education reform in the middle school. In W. G. Secada, E. Fennema, & L. Byrd Adajian (Eds.), *New directions in equity in mathematics education* (pp. 9–56). New York: Cambridge University Press.

Singha, K. W. (1997). Estimating first-time enrollment for the private, highly selective, national university: A market demography application of logistic regression-based price sensitivity analysis. PhD diss., Bowling Green State University.

Smart, J. C., Feldman, K. A., & Ethington, C. A. (2000). *Academic disciplines: Holland's theory and the study of college students and faculty.* Nashville: Vanderbilt University Press.

Snow, C. E., Burns, M. S., & Griffin, P. (Eds.). (1998). *Preventing reading difficulties in young children.* Washington, DC: National Academy Press.

Spokane, A. R. (1996). Holland's theory. In D. Brown and L. Brooks (Eds.), *Career choice and development* (3rd ed.), 33–74.

Spradlin, T. E., Kirk, R., Walcott, C., Kloosterman, P., Zaman, K., McNabb, S., Zapf, J., & associates. (2005). *Is the achievement gap in Indiana narrowing?* Bloomington, IN: Center for Evaluation and Education Policy.

Stage, F. K. (2007). Moving from probabilities to possibilities: Tasks for quantitative criticalists. *New Directions for Institutional Research, 2007*(133), 95–100.

Stein, M. K., Smith, M. S., Henningsen, M. A., & Silver, E. A. (2009). *Implementing standards-based mathematics instruction: A casebook for professional development* (2nd ed.). New York: Teachers College Press.

Stiglitz, J. E. (2012). *The price of inequality: How today's divided society endangers our future.* New York: W. W. Norton.

Strogatz, S. (2010). Fibbing with numbers: A science writer examines the many ways of fudging figures. *New York Times Review of Books,* September 19, 8.

Thelin, J. R. (2004). *A history of American higher education.* Baltimore: Johns Hopkins University Press.

Theobald, N. (2003). The need for issues-driven school funding reform in urban schools. In L. F. Mirón & E. P. St. John (Eds.), *Reinterpreting urban school reform: Have urban schools failed, or has the reform movement failed urban schools?* (pp. 33–52). Albany: State University of New York Press.

Tierney, W. G., Corwin, Z. B., & Colyar, J. E. (Eds.). (2005). *Preparing for college: Nine elements of effective outreach*. Albany: State University of New York Press.

Tierney, W. G., & Hagedorn, L. S. (Eds.). (2002). *Increasing access to college: Extending possibilities for all students*. Albany: State University of New York Press.

Tierney, W. G., & Venegas, K. (2007), The cultural ecology of financial aid decision making. In E. P. St. John (Ed.), *Confronting educational inequality: Reframing, building understanding, and making change* (pp. 1–36). Readings on Equal Education. 22. New York: AMS Press.

Tierney, W. G., Venegas, K. M., & De La Rosa, M. L. (Issue Eds.). (1995). Financial aid and access to college: The public policy challenges. Special issue, *American Behavioral Scientist, 49*(12).

Toch, T. (2003). *High schools on a human scale: How small schools can transform American education*. Boston: Beacon Press.

Trent, W. T., Gong, Y., & Owens-Nicholson, D. (2004). The relative contribution of high school origins to college access. In E. P. St. John (Ed.), *Improving access and college success for diverse students: Studies of the Gates Millennium Scholars Program* (pp. 45–70). Readings on Equal Education 20. New York: AMS Press.

Turnbull, B. J., Smith, M. S., & Ginsburg, A. L. (1981). Issues for a new administration: The federal role in education. *American Journal of Education, 89*(4), 396–427.

U.S. Census Bureau. (2012). Bachelor's degree attainment tops 30 percent for the first time, Census Bureau news release, February 23, www.census.gov/newsroom/releases/archives/education/cb12-33.html.

U.S. Department of Education. (1983). *A nation at risk: The imperative for educational reform*. Washington, DC: Author.

U.S. Department of Education. (2004). *Innovations in education: Successful charter schools*. Washington, DC: Office of Innovation and Improvement, www.ed.gov/admins/comm/choice/charter/.

U.S. Department of Education. (2006). *A test of leadership: Charting the future of U.S. higher education*. Washington, DC: author.

Vergari, S. (1999). Charter schools: A primer on the issues. *Education and Urban Society, 31*(4), 389–405.

Warren, E. (2014). *A fighting chance*. New York: Metropolitan Books.

Weathersby, G. B., & Balderston, F. E. (1972). PPBS in higher education planning and management: Part I, an overview. *Higher Education, 1*(2), 191–206.

Weissman, J. (2012). 53% of recent college grads are jobless or underemployed—how? *Atlantic*, April 23, www.theatlantic.com/business/archive/2012/04/53-of-recent-college-grads-are-jobless-or-underemployed-how/256237/.

Wildavsky, A. B. (1979). *Speaking truth to power: The art and craft of policy analysis*. Boston: Little, Brown.

Willie, C. V. (1976). Is school desegregation still a good idea? *School Review, 84*(3), 313–325.

Wilson, R. (1986). Overview of the minority/poverty enrollment problem. *Proceedings of the third annual NASSG/NCHELP Conference on Student Financial Aid Research, Chicago, Illinois, May 28–30, 1986*, vol. 1. Deerfield: Illinois State Scholarship Commission.

Winkle-Wagner, R. (2010). *Cultural capital: The promises and pitfalls in education research*. San Francisco: Jossey-Bass.

Winkle-Wagner, R. (2012). Academic capital formation: Can it help untangle confusion about social stratification in the study of college students? In R. Winkle-Wagner, P. J. Bowman, & E. P. St. John (Eds.), *Expanding postsecondary opportunity for underrepresented students: Theory and practice of academic capital formation* (pp. 293–306). Readings on Equal Education 26. New York: AMS Press.

Witte, J. F. (2000). *The market approach to education: An analysis of America's first voucher program.* Princeton, NJ: Princeton University Press.

Wong, K. K. (2003). Federal Title I as a reform strategy in urban schools. In L. F. Mirón & E. P. St. John (Eds.), *Reinterpreting urban school reform: Have urban schools failed, or has the reform movement failed urban schools?* (pp. 55–76). Albany: State University of New York Press.

college entrance exams, 71; and context, 20, 71, 99; and life experience, 71, 74; and math education, 90; and Sigma High School, 87, 97, 98, 99, 140; and social critical perspective, 145; and standards, 87

literacy education, 14, 71–99, 149; broad approaches vs. specialized areas in, 84; CCSS standards for, 76; challenges of, 20–21; in charter high schools, 20, 88, 90–98; and college entry requirements, 72; and college-level instruction, 93, 95, 96; and college preparation, 93–94, 95; and college readiness, 75–76, 83–84; collegiate vantage on, 77–80; and community colleges, 99; conflicting theories in, 145; across content areas, 72, 74, 75–76, 92, 93, 94; and critical frame, 82, 83; and cultural contexts, 20, 73, 77; direct vs. critical methods approach in, 75; early-reading outcomes in, 72; high school outcomes in, 72, 73–74; and interpretive frame, 82, 83; K–8, 74; and K–12 policy puzzle, 72–77; K–20, 80–87; and Kappa High School, 42, 90, 92; and liberal arts, 20, 76; and market, 72; and math education, 77–78, 88, 90; meaning in, 20, 74, 75; and nationally standardized tests and curriculum, 73; and numeracy, 80; in NYC school district, 20, 87–89; paradigms in, 72; policy rationales for, 72–87; remedial support for, 90, 92; school-wide strategies for, 94; sequence of instruction in, 93; at Sigma High School, 87, 93–98, 99, 130, 140, 141, 145; skills in, 74–75; and social frame, 82–83; standards for, 72, 87; and STEM fields, 20, 78; and teachers, 87, 92–93, 96, 97; and technical/scientific frame, 83; and test scores, 72

loans, 51, 133, 138, 141, 163n18; and college costs, 144; and college graduation, 68; and college knowledge, 100; earnings sufficient to pay off, 101; federal, 155n18; and lending industry, 11; from private lenders, 5; profits from, 6, 144; and Reagan administration, 26; repayment of, 6. *See also* debt

low-income families, 1; and CFES, 132; challenges facing, 150; and educational attainment, 22, 132, 133, 138; educational diversity of, 104; and employment, 132; and financial aid, 5–6; isolation of, 13; and tests, 38. *See also* poverty

low-income students, 39, 69, 72, 108, 125, 127; and academic capital, 136; and achievement-based admissions, 137; and Alpha High School, 120; and Beta High School, 129; in Catholic schools, 34; and college attendance, 53; and college completion, 106; and college enrollment, 54; and college knowledge, 100, 101, 136, 152; costs of college for, 106, 109; and debt, 144; and educational markets, 137; and finances and academic engagement, 136–37, 138; and Harlem Children's Zone, 23; and Kappa High School, 129; as left behind, 128–31; in NYC district schools, 130–31; at Onye Nkuzi High School, 37–38, 113–14; and penalties for low test scores, 33; and 21st Century Scholars Program, 103; and vouchers, 26, 30. *See also* financial aid

Lusher School, 28

Lutheran schools, 34

magnet schools, 27, 28, 31, 32, 157n7

market competition, 26–48, 140, 147; challenge of, 17–18; and Chubb and Moe, 33; and literacy education, 20, 71; policy rationales for, 26–35; and STEM curricula, 18–19; unequal, 24

market models and systems, 5, 12, 17, 22, 143, 146; and Chubb and Moe, 26; confirmatory evidence for, 33; and Reagan administration, 26; research to rationalize faulty, 35; and urban vs. suburban districts, 27

market niches, 13, 17, 21, 22, 29, 149; and Alpha High School, 39; approach of, 35; and Beta High School, 39; and charter schools, 14, 33–34; and college and career readiness, 34; and college majors, 48; development of, 35–47; and equity, 35; and Kappa High School, 39, 41–47; and literacy education, 71, 75; and math, 14, 68; in NYC schools, 36–39; and Onye Nkuzi High School, 37–38; in public charter schools, 39–47; and Remus High School, 38; and Sigma High School, 39; specialization in, 36; and STEM education, 48; and testing, 34; and urban vs. suburban districts, 27